contents

1: Place Value & Decimals

2: Calculations

3: Negative Numbers

7: Working with Measures

8: Shapes & Area

9: Fractions, Decimals & Percentages

Support Curriculum Book 1 Version 1.
First published 2021

Copyright Nicola Waddilove &
James Pearce 2021

Further support material, including
assessment, available at
www.mathspad.co.uk

chapter 1: place value & decimals

[Recommended Time: 13-17 hours]

Contents

reading & writing numbers up to 1 million

learn by heart

hundred thousands	ten thousands	thousands	hundreds	tens	units
100,000	10,000	1,000	100	10	1

Starting **from the right**, we place a comma after every 3 digits, so there is a comma between the hundreds and thousands column.

examples

Write the number twenty thousand, one hundred and four in digits.

= 20,104

Write a comma when you say the word 'thousand' and put zeros in the empty columns.

Write the number 439580 using commas

= 439, 580

We read this as 439 thousand, 580 Each set of three digits is read together as a group.

exercise 1a

1. Which of these numbers is four thousand and nine?

    a) 409   b) 4,009   c) 40,009   d) 4,900   e) 4,090

2. Write in digits:

    a) 2 hundred and 8

    b) 9 thousand and 4

    c) 6 thousand and 3

    d) 80 thousand, 5 hundred and 6

    e) 6 hundred and 4 thousand

    f) 3 hundred thousand and fifty

    g) Sixty two thousand, eight hundred and seven

    h) Four hundred and five thousand, two hundred and sixty

    i) Nine hundred thousand and thirty two

3. Which column is wrong?

millions	thousands	hundreds	tens	units

4. Which of these numbers is forty five thousand?

a) 450   b) 4,500   c) 45,000   d) 450,000   e) 4,005,000

5. Write the number 800,000 in words.

6. Re-write these numbers using commas correctly:

a) 5630   b) 305968   c) 50093   d) 475690

7. Which of these numbers is eighty seven thousand?

a) 87,000   b) 870,000   c) 8700   d) 87,000,000

8. Circle the number with 2 thousands, 7 hundreds and 4 units:

a) 2,407   b) 27,040   c) 200,704   d) 2,704

9. Write the number 906,000 in words.

10. Write in digits: eighty thousand and nine.

11. Which of these numbers is forty thousand, two hundred?

a) 4,200   b) 402,000   c) 42,000   d) 40,200

12. Which of these numbers has a 7 in the ten-thousands column?

a) 700   b) 7,000   c) 70,000   d) 700,000

13. True or False: 7 tens = Seventy

14. True or False: Seventy Thousand = 70,000

15. Find all the numbers that have a 3 in the thousands column:

A 4302	B 9,304	C 30045	D 304,204
E 306.9	F 30,405	G 3.005	H 453,104
I 3000	J 903	K 2,300	L 23895

16. Which number comes after 9,999?

17. Which number comes after 999,999?

exercise 1b

1. Re-write these numbers using commas:

    a) 8950   c) 10100   e) 40840

    b) 10940   d) 200000   f) 50000

2. Which of these numbers is four hundred and six thousand?

    a) 46,000   b) 406,00   c) 400,6000   d) 406,000

3. Write the number 902,000 in words.

4. Write the number **six hundred and two thousand and fifty three in digits**.

5. Which of these numbers are written incorrectly? Choose four answers.

    a) 3,005   c) 9,3400   e) 24,34   g) 600,000

    b) 430,00   d) 658,000   f) 98,400   h) 903,00

6. Write each of these numbers in digits:

    a) Eighty four thousand and nine   c) Twelve thousand and seventy two

    b) Twenty six thousand and fifty   d) Four hundred and sixty two
                                                thousand.

7. Which of these is eight hundred and two thousand?

    a) 2,800   b) 800,2000   c) 802,000   d) 800,200

8. Copy and complete the empty columns:

				tens	units

9. Which of these is one hundred thousand?

    a) 100   b) 1000   c) 100,000,000   d) 100,000

10. Ten thousand has _____ zeros.

Reading & Writing Integers Match

Match the numbers written in words at the top with their partners below.
Record your pairs in a table.

A	G
Four Thousand and Eighty Two	Eighty Two Thousand and Four

B	H
Four Hundred and Eight Thousand	Eight Hundred and Four Thousand

C	I
Forty Eight Thousand and Two	Forty Thousand, Eight Hundred

D	J
Fourteen Thousand, Eight Hundred and Twenty	Eight Thousand and Forty

E	K
Four Hundred Thousand and Eighty	Eighteen Thousand and Four

F	L
Forty Thousand and Eight	Eight Hundred and Forty Thousand, Eight Hundred

M	N	O	P	Q	R
48,002	408,000	8,040	400,080	40,800	4,082

S	T	U	V	W	X
840,800	40,008	804,000	82,004	14,820	18,004

A	B	C	D	E	F	G	H	I	J	K	L

reading & writing millions

learn by heart

1 million is the 7th column 1 million has 6 zeros 1 million = 1,000,000	10 million = 10,000,000 100 million = 100,000,000 1000 million = 1 billion (UK)

example

Write the number 3 million in figures
= 3,000,000

On the first comma (from the right), we say 'thousand'. On the second common we say 'million'

exercise 1c

1. Which of these numbers is eight million?

   a) 800,000   b) 8,000,000   c) 8,000,000,000   d) 80,000

2. Which of these numbers is eight hundred million?

   a) 800,000   b) 8,000,000   c) 800,000,000   d) 80,000

3. Write these numbers in digits, using commas:

   a) 6 million   f) 2 million and eight

   b) 18 million   g) 4 million and ten thousand

   c) 431 million   h) 18 million and 6 thousand

   d) 4 billion   i) 610 million and 18 thousand

4. Which of these numbers is eighteen million and forty five thousand?

   a) 18,450,000   b) 18,45,000   c) 18,045,000   d) 18,000,45000

5. Which of these numbers is written incorrectly? Circle all that apply.

   a) 4,203,000   b) 4,23,00   c) 2,3000,000   d) 18,456,000

6. Write in words: 19,002,165

6. Copy and complete the column names:

					tens	units

7. A million has _____ zeros

8. Ten million has _____ zeros

9. Which of these numbers is four hundred and six thousand?

   a) 46,000   b) 406,00   c) 400,6000   d) 406,000

10. Write the number 1,302,000 in words.

11. Write 3005000 correctly using commas.

12. Write down the whole number that is directly after 1 million.

13. Write down the whole number that is directly after 1 billion.

- -

matching activity

Match the numbers at the top to those at the bottom. Record your answers in a table.

1 Three million and sixty five	2 Three thousand and six	3 Three hundred and five thousand	4 Thirty six thousand, five hundred and thirty
5 Three hundred and fifty six thousand	6 Thirty five thousand, five hundred and six	7 Thirty six million, five hundred and fifty two	8 Three hundred and thirty thousand, six hundred
9 Thirty million, six hundred thousand	10 Three million, fifty six thousand		

1	2	3	4	5	6	7	8	9	10

- -

A. 3,006	B. 36,530	C. 356,000	D. 30,600,000	E. 36,000,552
F. 3,056,000	G. 3,000,065	H. 305,000	I. 330,600	J. 35,506

Millions Multiple Choice

In each row, choose the number that matches the question.

	A	B	C	D
1 1 Million	1,000	10,000	100,000	1,000,000
2 2 Million and Fifty	2,050	2,000,50	2,000,500	2,000,050
3 15 Million and Nine Thousand	15,9000	15,009,000	15,090,000	15,000,900
4 Two Hundred Million	200,000,000	200,0000	200,000	20,200,000
5 3 Million and Six Thousand	3,6000	3,600,000	3,006,000	003,060,000
6 Seventy Two Million and Fifteen	072,000,150	72,000,15	72,000,015	72,015
7 Four Hundred and Eight Million	400,800,000	400,008,000	8,000,400	408,000,000
8 Seventeen Million and Twenty Thousand	17,020,000	17,20,000	17,200,000	170,020,000
9 Five Hundred and Two Thousand	502,000,000	500,2000	500,2,000	502,000
10 Nine Hundred and Ninety Million and Nine	900,090,009	990,000,009	990,000,090	900,900,09

extension

1. What is the name for a thousand million?
2. How many zeros are there in a million million?
3. How many zeros does a googol have?

reading & writing integers review

exercise 1d

1. Which of these numbers is four hundred and nine million?

   a) 400,900,000   b) 409,000,000   c) 409,000   d) 490,000,000

2. Write 608,009 in words.

3. In the number 74,900, which column is the 4 in?

4. 4 million + 3 thousand + 6 = _____

5. 20 thousands + 7 hundreds = _____

6. Write seven million and ninety five in digits.

7. Write twenty six thousand in figures.

8. Re-write this number using commas: 3948500

9. Write forty two million and nine thousand in digits.

10. True or False:

    a) 3 million = 300000   d) 9 hundred million = 90000000

    b) 15 thousand = 150,000   e) 8 hundred thousand = 800,000

    c) 7 thousand and 2 = 7,002   f) 12 million and 12 = 12,000,12

11. Which of these numbers is written using commas correctly?

    a) 19,00   b) 183,0000   c) 4,095,000   d) 201,009,09

12. Which of these numbers is 1 billion?

    a) 1,000,000   b) 100,000,000   c) 1,000,000,000

13. How many zeros are at the end of a million?

14. True or False?

    a) The number 54009 has a 4 in the hundreds column.

    b) The number 652,109 has a 5 in the ten-thousands column.

    c) The number 852,356 has a 2 in the thousands column.

12. Write each of these numbers in words. Be careful - they are all different!

A Four thousand, two hundred 4, 200	**B** Forty thousand, two hundred	**C** Four hundred and two thousand	**D** Four hundred thousand and twenty
E Four thousand and twenty	**F** Forty thousand and twenty	**G** Four hundred thousand and two	**H** Four thousand and two
I Forty-two thousand	**J** Four hundred thousand, two hundred	**K** Forty thousand and two	**L** Four hundred and twenty thousand

13. Anna and Dan write the number "twelve thousand and nineteen" in digits.

   Anna writes: 12, 000, 19   Dan writes: 12, 019

   Who is right?

   What has the other person done wrong?

14. Write each of these numbers in words.

   a) 37,005   ....

   b) 9,006,030   ....

   c) 412,000   ....

15. Which of these numbers is four hundred million, thirty five thousand and nine?

   a) 400,035,009   b) 400,35,009   c) 4,035,009   d) 400,035,09

16. Which of the following numbers have the digit 8 in the ten thousands place value? Select all that apply.

   a) 809,400   b) 180,013   c) 8,432

   d) 8.0041   e) 5,080,190   f) 89,000

17. Which of the following numbers is equal to 6.2 million?

   a) 62,000,000   b) 6.2000000   c) 6.200000   d) 6,200,000

18. Which of these numbers is 1 billion?

   a) 1,000,000   b) 100,000,000   c) 1,000,000,000

ordering numbers

examples

True or false:
4098 is **more** than 5 thousand ?

False: 4,098 has only 4 thousands

Is 1049596 greater than 1 million?

1049596 = 1,049,596
which is more than 1 million

exercise 1e

1. Which of these numbers are **more** than 3 thousand? Choose all that apply.

   a) 504   b) 3000   c) 4098   d) 2819

2. Which of these numbers are **more** than Ten Thousand? Choose all that apply.

   a) 4,095   c) 857   e) 10495   g) 1009

   b) 1209   d) 1000   f) 9587   h) 92092

3. Put these numbers in order of size, from smallest to largest:

A	B	C	D
7,402	1 Thousand	983	1200

4. Which of these is smallest?

   a) 9 Hundred   b) Ninety Five   c) 923   d) 9039

5. Which of these numbers are bigger than five hundred thousand?

   a) 50,000   c) 600,000   e) 840800

   b) 90,200   d) 5,500   f) 40596

6. True or False?

   a) 7503 is more than 7 Thousand

   b) 25985 is more than Twenty Thousand

   c) 9048 is more than 10 Thousand

   d) 4899 is more than Forty Eight Thousand

7. Which of these is smallest?

   a) 109444   b) 10094   c) 10,940   d) 100,094

8. Which of these numbers are greater than 1 million?

a) 109,000   b) 130499   c) 100000   d) 1409488

9. In each row, select the largest number:

a)
| 543 | 5 Hundred | Fifty | 59 |

b)
| 40 Thousand | 3921 | 39,839 | 4,999 |

c)
| 600,000 | 75413 | 6126 | 60 Thousand |

d)
| 4 million | 41092 | 654,999 | 8657651 |

e)
| 70 Thousand | 17,000 | 160,000 | 16 Thousand |

f)
| 33 million | 6,958,000 | 43,858,000 | 999,000 |

10. Put these numbers in order of size, from smallest to largest:

A	B	C	D	E
5 million	550,000	55102	505102	54133

11. Which of these numbers is the smallest?

a) 217   b) 72.5   c) 207   d) 702

12. Which of these numbers are greater than 1 million? Circle all that apply.

a) 40009   c) 1093.33   e) 1000000

b) 20349   d) 847000   f) 10000000

13. Which number comes before 100,000?

14. Which number comes after 999,999?

15. Which number comes after 999,999,999?

inequality symbols

learn by heart

> : greater than

This side is greater [symbol] than this side

< : less than

This side is less [symbol] than this side

exercise 1f

1. Which of these means 5 is greater than 3?

   a) 5 > 3   b) 5 < 3   c) 5 = 3   d) 5 / 3

2. Decide whether these statements are true or false:

   a) 3 > 5   f) 4 < 2   k) 1,000 > 1 Thousand

   b) 6 > 4   g) 7 < 7   l) 3,849,000 > 1 million

   c) 2 > 2   h) 1,999 > 2000   m) 214,380 > 1 million

   d) 1 < 0   i) 20394 < 9039   n) 1,000,000 > 1 million

   e) 3 < 7   j) 1494 > 2 Thousand   o) 1,939,938 > 1 billion

3. Which of the following means A is less than B?

   a) A > B   b) A = B   c) B < A   d) A < B

4. Complete these statements using the symbols >, < or =

   a) 6 ____ 5   b) 200 ____ 300   c) 27 ____ 27.0   d) 95 ____ 100

5. What is the **biggest** whole number that makes each statement true?

   a) ____ < 100   b) ____ < 500   c) ____ < 1000   d) ____ < 1500

rounding to the nearest 10, 100, 1000

examples

Round 45 to the nearest 10	Round 573 to the nearest 100	Round 2,035 to the nearest 1,000
= 50	= 600	= 2000

exercise 1g

1. Round these numbers to the nearest 10:

   a) 64   c) 108   e) 15   g) 775

   b) 92   d) 203   f) 596   h) 1025

2. Round these numbers to the nearest 100:

   a) 556   c) 76   e) 3045   g) 14,250

   b) 289   d) 1450   f) 56,980   h) 7,500

3. True or false: 426 rounded to the nearest hundred is 500

4. True or false: 91 rounded to to the nearest hundred is 100

5. True or false: 19 rounded to the nearest 100 is 0

6. Round each number to the nearest 1000:

   a) 4892   c) 34,506   e) 14,006   g) 104,967

   b) 2084   d) 9,809   f) 94   h) 1,034,856

7. Arrange these cards to make a number that rounds to 9480, to the nearest ten:

   | 5 | 7 | 9 | 4 |

8. Arrange these cards to make a number that rounds to 2700, to the nearest hundred:

   | 4 | 7 | 2 | 9 |

9. Arrange these cards to make a number that rounds to 4000, to the nearest thousand:

   | 1 | 6 | 3 | 0 |

10. Anya thinks of a number. She rounds it to the nearest ten. The answer is 40.
    What is the smallest number Anya could have been thinking of?

11. Sarah thinks of a number. She rounds it to the nearest hundred. The answer is 300.
    What is the smallest number Sarah could have been thinking of?

12. Which of these numbers has been rounded to the nearest hundred?

    a) 30   b) 300   c) 320   d) 1450

13. Which of these numbers round to 300, to the nearest 100?

    a) 289   b) 3000   c) 242   d) 349.9   e) 250

rounds to 60

14. There are **8** numbers in the grid which round to 60, to the nearest 10.
    Can you find them?

A 45	B 58	C 67	D 32	E 64	F 59
G 54	H 51	I 72	J 60.5	K 56	L 68
M 55	N 53.5	O 40	P 60	Q 70	R 65.5
S 39	T 66	U 54.5	V 80	W 61	X 49

rounds to 500

15. There are **9** numbers in the grid which round to 500, to the nearest 100.
    Can you find them?

A 443	B 512	C 750	D 623	E 592	F 507
G 480	H 499	I 450	J 495	K 550	L 572
M 585	N 430	O 445	P 400	Q 520	R 500
S 399	T 1500	U 405	V 49.5	W 449.5	X 549

16. Eli thinks of a number. He rounds it to the nearest ten.
    Marcel thinks of a number. He rounds it to the nearest hundred.
    They both end up with the same answer!
    What numbers could they have been thinking of?

reading & writing tenths

learn by heart

Integer: *a whole number*

Decimal: a number including a decimal point, which separates the wholes from the parts.

tens	units	●	tenths
10	1		0.1
10	1		$\frac{1}{10}$

The decimal point: is *to the right of* the units column

Tenth: When one unit is split into ten equal parts, each part is called a tenth.
As a fraction this is written as $\frac{1}{10}$ and as a decimal it is 0.1
There are ten tenths in 1 unit.

Wholes and parts can be written together as a mixed number, e.g. $1\frac{3}{10}$ means $1 + \frac{3}{10}$

exercise 1h

1.   Write as a decimal:

   a) 3 tenths

   b) 7 tenths

   c) $\frac{5}{10}$

   d) $\frac{9}{10}$

   e) $\frac{10}{10}$

   f) $1\frac{4}{10}$

   g) $3\frac{5}{10}$

   h) $15 + \frac{2}{10}$

2.   Write as a fraction or mixed number:

   a) 0.8

   b) 0.4

   c) 0.1

   d) 1.1

   e) 1.8

   f) 3.9

   g) 12.6

   h) 18.9

3.   Which number does the arrow point to?

   a) 0.2

   b) 0.3

   c) 0.4

   d) 0.5

4.   Which number does the arrow point to?

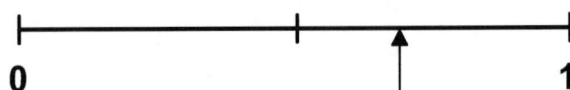

   a) 0.2

   b) 0.3

   c) 0.5

   d) 0.7

5. Which of these is 8 tenths?

   a) 80   b) $\frac{1}{8}$ c) 8.1   d) 0.8

6. Show the position of 0.3 on this number line:

   0 A B C D E F G H I 1

7. Show the position of 0.8 on this number line:

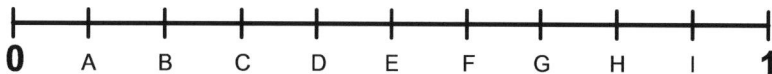

   0 A B C D E F G H I 1

8. Show the position of $\frac{9}{10}$ on this number line:

   0 A B C D E F G H I 1

9. Show the position of 1.6 on this number line:

   1 A B C D E F G H I 2

10. Show the position of $3\frac{4}{10}$ on this number line:

    3 A B C D E F G H I 4

11. '7 tenths' is written as a decimal like this _____ and as a fraction like this _____.

12. Which of these is the same as 'ten tenths'? Choose two answers.

    a) 10   b) $\frac{10}{10}$ c) 1   d) $\frac{1}{10}$

13. We write 9 tens as _____ and 9 tenths as _____

14. Write as a decimal:

    a) $9 + \frac{3}{10}$ b) $64\frac{1}{10}$ c) 6 + 0.6   d) $42 + \frac{9}{10}$

15. Which decimal number does the arrow point to?

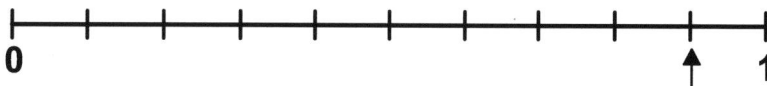

    0 ↑ 1

16. Which decimal number does the arrow point to?

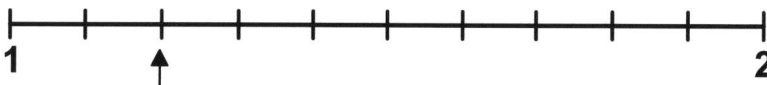

    1 ↑ 2

17. Which decimal number does the arrow point to?

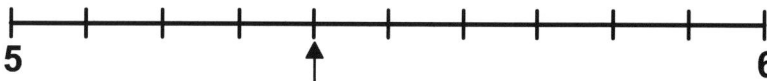

    5 ↑ 6

18. As a decimal, 7 tens + 7 tenths = _____ and as a mixed number it is _____

reading & writing decimal numbers 1

learn by heart

Hundredth: When 1 whole is split into 100 equal parts, each part is called a hundredth and this is written 0.01 as a decimal or $\frac{1}{100}$ as a fraction.
The hundredths column is to the right of the tenths.

tens	units		tenths	hundredths	thousandths	ten thousandths
10	1	●	0.1	0.01	0.001	0.0001
10	1		$\frac{1}{10}$	$\frac{1}{100}$	$\frac{1}{1000}$	$\frac{1}{10,000}$

examples

Write '3 tenths' as a decimal
= 0.3

Write $\frac{5}{100}$ as a decimal
= 0.05

In the number 46.803, what is the value of the digit 3?
= 3 thousandths

exercise 1i

1. Write as a decimal:

   a) 6 tenths

   b) 7 hundredths

   c) 5 thousandths

   d) 8 tens

   e) $\frac{7}{10}$

   f) $\frac{9}{100}$

   g) $\frac{3}{100}$

   h) $\frac{1}{1000}$

2. State the value of the digit 6 in each of these numbers. The first is done for you.

   a) 38.1**65**
      6 hundredths

   b) **6**.01

   c) 1.**6**924

   d) 309.85**6**

   e) 1.**6**93

   f) 0.000**6**

3. Which of these numbers have 8 tenths? Circle two answers.

   a) 8   b) 80   c) 800   d) 0.8   e) 0.80   f) 0.08

4. Which of these numbers has a 7 in the tenths column?

   a) 700   b) 70   c) 7.0   d) 0.7   e) 0.07

5. Write in digits: 9 hundredths = _____ and 9 hundreds = _____

18

6. Write as a fraction:

   a) 8 tenths

   b) 9 thousandths

   c) 0.009

   d) 0.06

   e) 0.2

   f) 0.04

7. Copy and complete the names of the columns. The first one is done for you.

	•	units			

8. Which of these are equal to 0.3 ? Circle 2 answers:

   a) $\frac{3}{10}$

   b) $\frac{3}{100}$

   c) 3 tenths

   d) $\frac{10}{3}$

9. Write in digits: 8 tens = _____ and 8 tenths = _____

10. Write as decimals:

    a) Zero point three seven

    b) One hundred point four nine zero

    c) Sixty seven point three

    d) Four thousand and eighty two point nine five

11. Which of these numbers has 9 tens and 9 tenths?

    a) 9.9   b) 9.90   c) 90.9   d) 90.09   e) 900.9

matching activity   Match each card on the left with one on the right:

A	B	C
0.6	0.5	0.003

D	E	F
3.0	60	6.6

G	H	I
0.06	5	600

J	K	L
0.005	6.0	50.5

M	N	O
$\frac{3}{1000}$	$\frac{6}{100}$	5 tenths

P	Q	R
3 units	6 units	6 tens

S	T	U
6 hundreds	6 tenths	$\frac{5}{1000}$

V	M	X
$6 + \frac{6}{10}$	5 tens + $\frac{5}{10}$	5 ones

A	B	C	D	E	F	G	H	I	J	K	L

19

reading & writing decimals 2 (mixed numbers)

learn by heart

Mixed Number: *an integer + a fraction, e.g.* $3\frac{1}{10}$ *means 3 wholes +* $\frac{1}{10}$

example

Write as a decimal the number with:

a) Two tens, three units and four hundredths   *23.04*

b) Five units, $\frac{3}{10}$ and $\frac{7}{100}$ *5.37*

c) $42\frac{1}{100}$ *42.01*

Use a zero to show an empty column.

exercise 1j

1. Write these as decimals:

   a) $\frac{1}{10}$ c) $\frac{3}{10}$ e) $1\frac{4}{10}$ g) $2\frac{1}{1000}$

   b) $\frac{9}{100}$ d) $\frac{7}{1000}$ f) $5\frac{8}{100}$ h) $\frac{7}{10,000}$

2. Write these decimals as fractions or mixed numbers:

   a) 0.6   c) 1.2   e) 0.007

   b) 0.09   d) 3.04   f) 5.9

3. Which of these is 4 tens + 4 tenths?

   a) 4.4   b) 40.4   c) 40.04   d) 400.4

4. Which of these is 3.07?

   a) 37   b) $3\frac{7}{10}$ c) 307   d) $3\frac{7}{100}$

5. Write the following as decimals:

   a) 4 tens + 2 tenths   d) 7 tens + 3 thousandths

   b) 3 hundreds + 5 tenths   e) 9 tens + 5 tenths

   c) 6 tenths + 4 hundredths   f) 6 thousands + 3 tenths

6. Write down the decimal number with exactly 4 tens, 3 tenths and 2 thousandths.

7. True or False: 60.8 means 6 tens + 8 tenths

8. In each number, write down the value of the digit in bold.

    a) 38.**65**   e) **1**.06

    b) 1.9**3**   f) 3.00**5**

    c) **4**5.9   g) 2,**6**49.6

    d) 309.8**7**   h) 23.6**78**

9. Write $\frac{1}{10} + \frac{2}{100} + \frac{3}{1000}$ as a decimal

10. Decide whether each statement is true:

    a) $\frac{6}{100} = 0.06$ h) 3 tens + 4 tenths = 40.3

    b) $\frac{3}{10} = 0.03$ i) $\frac{3}{100} = 0.03$

    c) $\frac{3}{10} + \frac{4}{100} = 0.34$ j) $\frac{3}{10} + \frac{2}{100} + \frac{4}{1000} = 0.324$

    d) $\frac{6}{1000} = 0.0006$ k) $\frac{1}{8} = 0.8$

    e) 7 hundreds = 0.07   l) $\frac{8}{10} = 0.8$

    f) $1 + \frac{3}{100} = 1.03$ m) $\frac{1}{10}$ is more than $\frac{1}{100}$

    g) $2 + \frac{4}{10} = 240$ n) $\frac{1}{4} = 0.4$

11. Complete these sentences:

    a) 7.89 = _____ units + _____ tenths + _____ hundredths

    b) 20.64 = 2 _____ + 6 _____ + _____ hundredths

    c) 3.045 = _____ units + 4 _____ + 5 _____

reading and writing decimal numbers 3

examples

| Decimal numbers are equivalent to fractions with denominators of 10, 100, 1000, ... 0.427 $= \frac{4}{10} + \frac{2}{100} + \frac{7}{1000}$ | Tenths $\frac{3}{10} = 0.3$ $3\frac{4}{10} = 3.4$ $\frac{14}{10} = 1.4$ | Hundredths $\frac{3}{100} = 0.03$ $\frac{24}{100} = 0.24$ $\frac{206}{100} = 2.06$ | Thousandths $\frac{3}{1000} = 0.003$ $\frac{37}{1000} = 0.037$ $\frac{409}{1000} = 0.409$ |

We can read 0.23 as '23 hundredths' because it ends in the hundredths column. This helps us remember it is the same as $\frac{23}{100}$

exercise 1k

1. Write as a decimal:

   a) $\frac{12}{100}$

   b) $\frac{346}{1000}$

   c) $\frac{470}{1000}$

   d) $\frac{28}{1000}$

   e) $\frac{208}{1000}$

   f) $\frac{81}{1000}$

   g) $\frac{5}{1000}$

   h) $1\frac{34}{100}$

   i) $2\frac{109}{1000}$

2. Write as a fraction:

   a) 0.49

   b) 0.07

   c) 0.301

   d) 0.047

   e) 0.009

   f) 0.148

3. $\frac{23}{1000}$ is the same as:

   a) 0.23   b) 0.203   c) 0.023   d) 2.3

4. True or False?

   a) $0.64 = \frac{64}{100}$

   b) $\frac{91}{1000} = 0.91$

   c) $1.08 = 1\frac{8}{100}$

   d) $0.7 = \frac{7}{10}$

   e) $\frac{1}{10,000} = 0.001$

   f) $\frac{4}{100} = 0.4$

5. Write as a decimal:

   a) $\dfrac{27}{100}$ c) $\dfrac{19}{100}$ e) $\dfrac{3}{10} + \dfrac{1}{1000}$

   b) $\dfrac{172}{1000}$ d) $2\dfrac{5}{10}$ f) $4 + \dfrac{26}{100}$

6. The numbers 54.829 and $\dfrac{28}{1000}$ have the same digit in which column?

   a) units   b) tenths   c) hundredths   d) thousandths

7. Write as a fraction or mixed number:

   a) 0.7   b) 0.92   c) 3.04   d) 0.609

8. Write down the decimal number that has exactly 7 hundreds, 3 tenths and 2 hundredths.

9. Write down the value of the digit '1' in each number:

   a) 0.31   b) 2.1   c) 5.441   d) 0.6001

10. 6 hundreds and 6 tenths make:

    a) 600.6   b) 0.66   c) 60.6   d) 600.06

11. Ten tenths make:

    a) 10   b) 1   c) 0.1   d) 0.01

12. Write as a decimal

    a) $\dfrac{4}{10} + \dfrac{3}{100}$ b) $6 + \dfrac{1}{1000}$ c) $300 + \dfrac{3}{10} + \dfrac{3}{1000}$

13. Write 0.0409 as a fraction.

14. The numbers 4.128 and $4\dfrac{1}{1000}$ have the same digit in which column?

    a) units   b) tenths   c) hundredths   d) thousandths

15. 8 tens and 8 hundredths make:

    a) 80.08   b) 80.8   c) 8.8   d) 8.08   e) 0.88

16. Fill in the blanks with fractions or integers:

    a) 0.402 = _____ + _____   c) 20.64 = _____ + _____ + _____

    b) 3.99 = ___ + ___ + ___   d) 305.106 = ___ + ___ + _____ + _____

16. Write as a decimal the number with:

    a) 3 tens + 4 tenths   b) Twenty five hundredths

17. Write as a fraction or mixed number:

    a) 0.1   b) 0.02   c) 1.005   d) 1.3

18. The numbers 1.49263 and $\frac{296}{1000}$ have the same digit in which column?

19. True or False? All decimal numbers are less than 1 whole.

20. True or False? The largest decimal number is 0.99.

21. How many different decimal numbers are there between 0 and 1?

- -

Writing Decimals Match

Match these cards to their decimal equivalents at the bottom.

1	
2	
3	
4	
5	
6	
7	
8	
9	
10	
11	
12	
13	
14	
15	
16	
17	
18	

1 2 hundreds

2 2 hundredths

3 2 tens + 6 units

4 2 thousands + 2 units

5 6 tens + 6 tenths

6 6 tens

7 6 thousandths

8 6 thousands

9 10 tenths

10 2 tenths

11 6 tenths + 2 hundredths

12 2 tenths + 6 hundredths

13 6 tenths

14 2 tenths + 6 thousandths

15 2 tens + 6 tenths

16 6 tenths + 6 hundredths

17 6 hundreds

18 2 tens + 2 tenths

20.2	200	20.6	0.26	1	60	26	0.006	0.02
2002	6000	0.2	0.62	0.66	0.206	600	0.6	60.6

comparing decimals

learn by heart

Decimal Places: the number of digits after the decimal point, e.g. 0.405 has 3 decimal places.

Adding zeros to the end of a decimal does not effect its size, so 0.1 = 0.10 = 0.10000000

examples

Which is larger 0.4 or 0.34?

0.4 = 0.40,
so 0.4 is larger.

By adding a zero to 0.4, both numbers have two decimal places and we can easily see that '40 hundredths' is bigger than '34 hundredths'

exercise 1

1. 0.6 is the same as:

    a) 0.600   b) 6.0   c) 0.06   d) 0.66

2. In each pair, select the **bigger** number. Or write = if they are equal.

    a) 0.6 or 0.07   e) 0.9 or 0.9000   i) 0.12 or 0.4

    b) 0.1 or 0.02   f) 0.04 or 0.4   j) 0.004 or 0.05

    c) 0.3 or 0.30   g) 0.6 or 0.42   k) 0.501 or 0.51

    d) 0.2 or 0.03   h) 0.23 or 0.3   l) 0.34 or 0.335

3. Decide whether these statements are true or false:

    a) 0.4 > 0.3   d) 0.23 < 0.230   g) 0.43 = 0.430

    b) 0.2 < 0.1   e) 0.61 > 0.62   h) 2.8 > 2.79

    c) 0.01 < 0.2   f) 1 = 1.00   i) 3.5 = 3.500

4. Which of these numbers is the **largest**?

    a) 0.92   b) 0.149   c) 0.840   d) 0.09999

5. Which of these numbers is the **smallest**?

    a) 0.02   b) 0.4   c) 0.009   d) 0.013

6. Which is bigger, 1.6 or 2? Explain your answer.

7. In each row, decide which is the smallest number:

a) | 0.3 | | 0.29 | | 0.301 | | 0.4 | | 0.06 |

b) | 0.07 | | 0.03 | | 0.10 | | 0.009 | | 0.2 |

c) | 0.009 | | 0.08 | | 0.21 | | 0.24 | | 0.098 |

d) | 0.41 | | 0.401 | | 0.4 | | 0.041 | | 0.004 |

e) | 0.082 | | 0.208 | | 0.028 | | 0.28 | | 0.008 |

8. Which is bigger 0.8cm or 0.75cm?

9. Which is more, 0.205kg or 0.3kg?

10. Which of these numbers get bigger when you add a zero on the end?
Choose all that apply.

a) 45   b) 230   c) 4.65   d) 8.9   e) 3.0

11. Which of these numbers stays the same size when you remove the final 0?
Choose all that apply.

a) 450   b) 5.30   c) 2900   d) 4,750

- -

Guess My Number

Use the clues to work out which number in the grid is being described.

My number is less than 0.7

My number is more than 0.2

My number has an 8 in the thousandths column

My number is less than 0.42

My number contains the digit 2

The digit in the hundredths column is odd

0.144	0.8	0.248
0.288	0.25	0.825
0.418	0.141	0.118
0.88	0.44	0.114
0.458	0.258	0.552

examples

Which is bigger, $\frac{1}{10}$ or 0.7?

0.7 because it equals $\frac{7}{10}$

Which is bigger, 0.42 or $\frac{5}{10}$?

$\frac{5}{10}$ because it equals 0.5

exercise 1m

1. Decide which number is bigger in each pair, or say if they are equal.

   a) 0.3 or $\frac{4}{10}$

   b) 0.9 or $\frac{8}{10}$

   c) 0.6 or $\frac{8}{100}$

   e) $\frac{6}{10}$ or 0.60

   f) 0.04 or $\frac{4}{10}$

   g) 1.5 or $1\frac{3}{10}$

   h) 1.06 or $1\frac{6}{10}$

   i) 0.23 or $\frac{3}{10}$

   k) 0.7 or $\frac{7}{100}$

   l) 0.66 or $\frac{6}{10}$

   m) 2.35 or $2\frac{4}{10}$

   n) 1.6 or $1\frac{6}{10}$

   o) 0.008 or $\frac{9}{1000}$

   q) $\frac{6}{100}$ or 0.51

   r) $\frac{23}{100}$ or 0.1

2. Which of these numbers are bigger than 0.6? Circle all that apply.

   a) 0.304   b) $\frac{6}{10}$ c) 1.0   d) $\frac{3}{10}$ e) $1\frac{4}{10}$

3. Which of the following are equal to 3 tenths?

   a) 0.30   b) 0.03   c) $\frac{3}{100}$ d) 30   e) $\frac{3}{10}$

4. Put these in order of size, from smallest to largest: 0.07, 7.07, $\frac{7}{10}$, 7.1

5. Decide whether these statements are true or false:

   a) 0.3 > $\frac{1}{10}$

   b) 0.01 < 0.010

   c) $\frac{1}{10}$ < $\frac{1}{100}$

   d) $\frac{4}{10}$ = 0.4

   e) $\frac{3}{100}$ = 0.3

   f) $1\frac{1}{10}$ = 1.10

   g) 0.4 = 0.40

   h) $\frac{61}{100}$ = 0.061

   i) $8\frac{3}{10}$ = 83.1

   j) 0.3 = $\frac{3}{10}$

   k) $5\frac{4}{1000}$ = 0.504

   l) $\frac{1}{1000}$ = 0.001

6. Complete these statements using one of these symbols: $<$ $>$ $=$ ⭐ extra challenge

a) 0.4 ◯ $\frac{7}{100}$

b) 0.06 ◯ $\frac{6}{100}$

c) 0.72 ◯ $\frac{7}{10}$

d) 0.019 ◯ $\frac{9}{100}$

e) 3.28 ◯ $3\frac{8}{100}$

f) 1.007 ◯ $1\frac{7}{10}$

7. Which of these numbers are **smaller** than 0.05? Choose all that apply.

a) one tenth

b) one hundredth

c) one thousandth

d) six hundredths

e) four tenths

f) nine thousandths

8. Which of these are the same as 0.4? Circle three answers.

a) 0.40   b) 0.04   c) $\frac{4}{10}$ d) 0.400   e) $\frac{4}{100}$

9. First change each set of numbers to decimals.
   Then write each set in order, from smallest to largest:

i)
A	B	C	D
$\frac{1}{10}$	0.8	$\frac{2}{100}$	0.6

ii)
A	B	C	D
0.6	0.66	$\frac{6}{100}$	0.61

iii)
A	B	C	D
$\frac{7}{1000}$	0.05	0.25	$\frac{4}{10}$

iv)
A	B	C	D
2.45	2.427	2.4	2.47

v)
A	B	C	D
$\frac{8}{100}$	$\frac{8}{1000}$	$\frac{8}{10}$	0.85

vi)
A	B	C	D
7	7.1	$7\frac{3}{100}$	$\frac{7}{100}$

10. In each pair, select the larger number, or write = if they are the same.

a) 0.7 or $\frac{6}{10}$

b) 0.51 or $\frac{5}{100}$

c) 1.6 or $1\frac{6}{10}$

d) 0.19 or $\frac{8}{10}$

e) 1.07 or $1\frac{6}{100}$

f) 0.26 or $\frac{3}{100}$

half way between ⭐ extra challenge

example

Write down the number half way between 0.3 and 0.31

0.3 = 0.300 and 0.31 = 0.310
so half way between is 0.305

exercise 1n

1. Which of these numbers are between 3.4 and 3.7 ? Choose all that apply.

   a) 3.05   b) 3.65   c) 3.518   d) 3.72

2. Which of these numbers are **between** 0.3 and 0.4? Choose 2 answers.

   a) 0.32   b) 3.3   c) 0.034   d) 0.40   e) 0.356

3. Which of these numbers are **between** 1.5 and 1.6? Choose all that apply.

   a) 1.45   b) 1.59   c) 1.62   d) 1.7   e) 1.501

4. Write down a number that is between 4.2 and 4.3

5. Write down the number that is half way between 0.4 and 0.5

6. Write down the number that is half way between:

   a) 0.7 and 0.8   d) 1.7 and 1.8   g) 2 and 3

   b) 0.3 and 0.4   e) 5 and 6   h) 10 and 11

   c) 0.6 and 0.7   f) 1.7 and 1.8   i) 0.9 and 1

7. Copy the number line and estimate the position of 4.6

   ```
   |———————————————+———————————————|
   4                                5
   ```

8. Write down the number that is half way between 0.8 and $\frac{9}{10}$

9. Which of these numbers are greater then $\frac{8}{10}$ and less than $\frac{9}{10}$? Choose 2 answers.

   a) 0.085   b) 0.82   c) 0.10   d) 0.9   e) 0.802

10. Which of these numbers is greater then $\frac{4}{10}$ and less than 0.41?

    a) 0.408   b) 0.45   c) 0.40   d) 0.7   e) 0.39

11. How many decimals are there between 1 and 2?

Sort It Out! ⭐ extra challenge

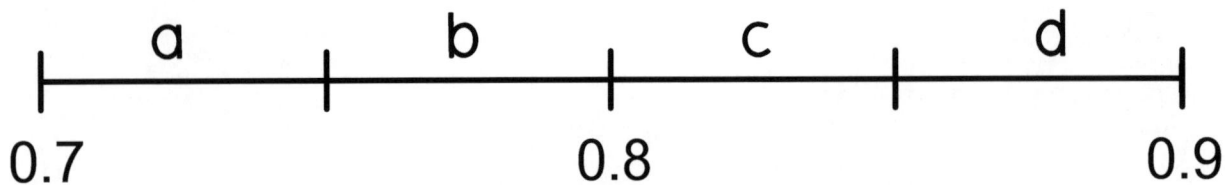

a   b   c   d

0.7   0.8   0.9

0.801   Decide which section of the number line above each of these numbers would go in   0.78   0.74

0.852

0.72   0.7501

0.799

0.887

0.76   0.709

0.845   0.840   0.89   0.7499   0.820

a   b   c   d

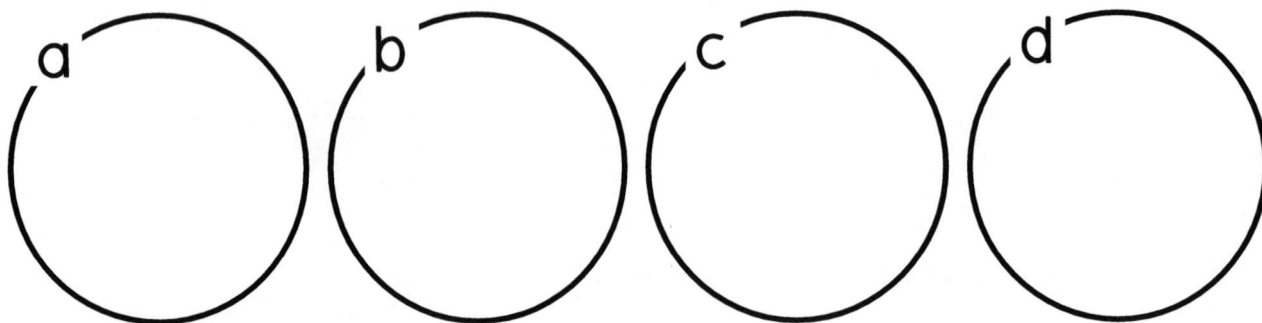

Guess My Number

Each statement describes a number in the grid.
Can you work out which number?

301	1.03	0.01
0.3	1.3	3.03
0.301	0.103	0.13

A. This is the smallest number

B. This number equals $\frac{3}{10}$

C. This number is greater than $\frac{3}{100}$ but less than 1

D. This number is greater than $\frac{1}{10}$ but less than 0.12

E. This number equals $\frac{1}{10} + \frac{3}{100}$

F. This is the largest number

G. This number is greater than 1 but less than $1\frac{3}{10}$

H. This number equals $\frac{13}{10}$

I. This number equals $3 + \frac{3}{100}$

rounding (nearest whole)

learn by heart

Sometimes we do not want to write all the digits of a decimal down and we can shorten it by rounding.

example

Round 6.83 to the nearest whole (integer)
= 7

An integer is a whole number. 6.83 has 6 wholes + some extra, so it is between 6 and 7 wholes.
Half way between 6 and 7 would be 6.5, and 6.83 is more than this, so it is closer to 7.

exercise 1o

1. Which of these numbers are **integers?** Choose all that apply.

   a) 45.8   b) 36   c) 2.83   d) 1.5   e) 2

2. Round each number to the nearest whole:

   a) 3.6   c) 2.3   e) 6.5

   b) 4.7   d) 14.9   f) 201.3

3. Round each number to the nearest integer:

   a) 2.68   c) 3.15   e) 14.782

   b) 4.79   d) 0.86   f) 156.345

4. Copy and complete the table:

Number	Nearest 10	Nearest 100	Nearest 1000	Nearest Whole Number
426.24				
690.104				

5. Find all the numbers that round to 17, to the nearest integer:

A 17.5	B 16.5	C 16.2	D 15.1	E 17.5	F 17.23
G 17.1	H 16.9	I 17.8	J 16.4	K 16.45	L 17.51

6. Arrange the cards to make a number that rounds to 21, to the nearest integer:

   | 0 | . | 4 | 2 |

rounding to 1 decimal place (d.p.)

learn by heart

A number with 1 decimal place has 1 digit after the decimal point, e.g. 3.4

When rounding to 1 d.p, we look at the digit in the 2nd decimal place.
If it is 5 or more, we round UP, meaning we increase the value of the digit in
the 1st decimal place by 1.

examples

Round:

a) 4.327 to 1 decimal place	4.3|27	4.3
b) 2.759 to 1 decimal place	2.7|59	2.8
c) 3.9997 to 1 decimal place	3.9|997	4.0
d) 1.996 to the nearest 0.1	1.9|96	2.0

→ This means 1 decimal place

exercise 1p

1. Which of these numbers have 1 decimal place? Choose all that apply.

   a) 43   b) 4.5   c) 2.75   d) 62.0   e) 200.30

2. Round each number to 1 decimal place:

   a) 3.62   d) 2.45   g) 4.319   j) 105.1098

   b) 1.84   e) 13.19   h) 26.453   k) 459.821

   c) 2.01   f) 4.55   i) 19.65   l) 8.98

3. Find all the numbers that round to **3.5** to 1 decimal place:

A 3.48	B 3.41	C 3.45	D 3.34	E 3.41
F 3.51	G 3.62	H 3.55	I 3.56	J 3.509
K 3.63	L 3.81	M 3.67	N 3.39	O 3.409

4. Round 4.87 to the nearest 0.1

rounding (decimal places)

example

Round 0.46889 to
2 decimal places
$= 0.47$

For 2 decimal places, the answer
can either stay as 0.46, or
increase to 0.47.
What is in the middle of these? 0.465
Is the number bigger or smaller than this? If it is
bigger, round up to 0.47

exercise 1q

1. Which of these has 2 decimal places?

    a) 4.09   b) 5.203   c) 6.2   d) 2.0

2. Round each number to 2 decimal places:

    a) 4.085   b) 23.1279   c) 604.30567

3. Round each number to 3 decimal places:

    a) 4.0858   b) 23.127   c) 604.30567

4. Copy and complete the table by rounding each number to 1, 2 and 3 decimal places.

	Number	to 1 d.p.	to 2 d.p.	to 3 d.p.
a)	3.7281			
b)	52.5917			
c)	0.1853			
d)	9.6458			
e)	4.0028			

5. Which of these numbers is 24.976 correctly rounded to one decimal place?

    a) 24.9   b) 24.10   c) 25   d) 24.98   e) 25.0

6. Which of these numbers are closer to 3 than 4?

    a) 3.2   b) 3.5   c) 3.8   d) 3.09

7. Show how these cards can be arranged
    to make a number that rounds to 27.5 to
    one decimal place.

    7 4 2 8 •

Rounding Decimals
Code Breaker

Round each number as shown.
Find your answer in the code box and
write down the letter. The letters
should spell a secret message!

0.3 = K	0.69 = Q	0.8 = I	1.2 = M
0.4 = X	0.7 = G	0.81 = R	1.21 = F
0.48 = ?	0.71 = V	0.9 = S	1.22 = U
0.5 = E	0.74 = C	0.91 = D	1.23 = A
0.51 = H	0.75 = B	1 = J	1.24 = T
0.6 = O	0.78 = L	1.01 = Z	1.3 = Y
0.65 = U	0.79 = N	1.1 = P	1.31 = K

a)   0.34 to 1 d.p. = _____ =   **K**

b)   0.483 o 1 d.p. = _____ =

c)   0.51 to 1 d.p. = _____ =

d)   1.05 to 1 d.p. = _____ =

e)   0.94 to 1 d.p. = _____ =

f)   1.22 to 1 d.p. = _____ =

g)   0.784 to 1 d.p. = _____ =

h)   0.784 to **2 d.p.** = _____ =

i)   0.809 to 1 d.p. = _____ =

j)   0.789 to **2 d.p.** = _____ =

k)   0.749 to 1 d.p. = _____ =

l)   1.234 to **2 d.p.** = _____ =

m) 0.781 to **2 d.p.** = _____ =

n)   0.779 to **2 d.p.** = _____ =

o)   0.911 to **2 d.p.** = _____ =

p)   1.225 to **2 d.p.** = _____ =

q)   1.27 to 1 d.p. = _____ =

r)   0.777 to **2 d.p.** = _____ =

s)   0.58 to 1 d.p. = _____ =

t)   0.792 to **2 d.p.** = _____ =

u)   0.699 to 1 d.p. = _____ =

chapter review

exercise 1r

1. Match the numbers on the left with the ones on the right:

A. Five million and eight	B. Fifty eight
C. Five hundred and eight thousand	D. Eight hundred and fifty thousand
E. Fifty thousand and eighty	F. Eight hundred and five
G. Eight million, five hundred and five	H. Eight thousand and fifty
I. Eighty five	J. Five million and eighty five

K. 58	L. 8,050
M. 5,000,085	N. 8,000,505
O. 850,000	P. 5,000,008
Q. 50,080	R. 508,000
S. 85	T. 805

A	B	C	D	E	F	G	H	I	J

2. Copy and complete the blanks:

a) 4095 is made of ___ thousands, ___ hundreds, ___ tens and ___ units

b) 21908 is made of ____ thousands, ___ hundreds, ___ tens and ___ units

c) 10,602 is made of ___ thousands, ___ hundreds, ___ tens and ___ units

d) 90002 is made of ___ thousands, ___ hundreds, ___ tens and ___ units

e) 10,094,060 is made of ____ millions, ____ thousands, ___ hundreds, ___ tens and __ units

f) 9094500 is made of ___ millions, ____ thousands, ___ hundreds, ___ tens and __ units

g) 906405023 is made of _____ millions, ____ thousands, ___ hundreds, ___ tens and __ units

3. Write these as fractions or mixed numbers:

   a) 4 tenths   b) 0.005   c) 0.9   d) 0.06

   e) 1.4   f) 0.4   g) 0.3   h) 0.002

4. Write these as decimals

   a) $\frac{3}{10}$ b) $1\frac{3}{10}$ c) $1\frac{6}{100}$ d) $\frac{9}{1000}$

   e) $\frac{1}{10}$ f) $\frac{2}{100}$ g) $\frac{9}{100}$ h) $61\frac{9}{10}$

5. Put these numbers in order of size from smallest to largest:

A $\frac{8}{10}$	B 4 hundredths	C 4 tens	D 0.4	E 5 tenths

6. '8 tenths' as a decimal is _____ and as a fraction it is _____

7. Which is bigger, 0.304 or 0.4?

8. Write in digits: 7 tenths = _____ and 7 tens = _____

9. Complete the blanks with >, < or =

   a) 0.7 _____ $\frac{7}{10}$ b) 0.24 _____ 0.204   c) 1.4 _____ $1\frac{4}{10}$

10. True or false?

   a) $6 + \frac{3}{10} = 6.3$ c) $20 + \frac{2}{100} = 20.2$

   b) $100 + \frac{1}{100} = 200$ d) $\frac{1}{9} = 0.9$

11. Round 4.83 to the nearest whole number

12. Round 14.806 to 1 decimal place.

13. Write as a decimal:

   a) $\frac{29}{100}$ b) $\frac{3}{100}$ c) $\frac{42}{1000}$ d) $2\frac{4}{100}$

   e) $\frac{9}{10}$ f) $2\frac{3}{100}$ g) $\frac{15}{1000}$ h) $12\frac{9}{100}$

   i) $14\frac{1}{100}$ j) $\frac{604}{1000}$ k) $8\frac{5}{1000}$ l) $\frac{3}{10} + \frac{4}{100} + \frac{5}{1000}$

12. In each of these numbers, write down
    the value of the digit in bold.

Hint
Try putting a comma after the
thousands to help read them

a) **4**05   f) 6**7**489

b) 10**2**34   g) **3**02914

c) 3**9**500   h) 8728**9**3

d) 103**94**   i) 91**2**034

13. Which of these numbers is one hundred thousand and eighty?

   a) 1,080   b) 100,000,80   c) 100,800   d) 100,080

14. Write the number two hundred and seven thousand and ninety three in digits.

15. Which number is 1 less than 100,000?

16. Which number is 1 less than 1 million?

matching activity

17. Match the numbers to their descriptions. Record your answers in a table.

A. 4,039	B. 15,349	C. 6,245	D. 21,043	E. 54,061
F. 90,201	G. 4,372	H. 96,411	I. 87,124	J. 97,932

1 The digit 5 means 5 units	2 The digit 7 means 70	3 The digit 1 stands for Ten Thousand	4 The digit 5 stands for 50,000
5 The digit 6 means 6 Thousand	6 The digit 8 stands for 80 Thousand	7 This is the largest number	8 This is the smallest number
9 The digit 4 stands for Forty	10 There is a 0 in the thousands column		

1	2	3	4	5	6	7	8	9	10

Place Value Puzzles

In each of these puzzles, work out which number from the grid is being described:

Puzzle 1

My number is not an integer.

My number has a 1 in the units column

My number is greater than thirty

My number is not 31.3

My number has 1 in the hundredths column

1.01	301	31.1
3.1	3.101	31.3
30.1	31.01	1.03

Puzzle 2

My number is less than eighteen thousand

My number is not 180

My number is > 18

My number has 8 in both the tens and tenths columns

180	18.01	1.81
0.18	1800	188
180.8	18180	18.8

Puzzle 3

My number is ≤ 0.2

My number is not 0.15

My number is greater than one tenth

My number has no hundredths

0.24	0.2	0.12
0.02	0.01	0.5
0.15	2.02	0.1

Puzzle 4

My number is < 44,000

My number is more than five thousand four hundred and fifty

My number is not 5454

My number has 5 hundreds

My number is greater than fifteen thousand

14,500	15,501	45000
5401	5444	5454
14,534	4544	10,500

Puzzle 5

What is the largest number that can be made by rearranging these cards?

| 1 | 2 | 4 | . | 8 |

Puzzle 6

What is the **smallest** number that can be made by rearranging these cards?

| 5 | 3 | 2 | . | 6 |

Puzzle 7

Put these numbers in order of size, from smallest to largest

0.04,   0.4,   4.4,   1.4,   0.104

Puzzle 8

Complete these statements using the symbols

=, >, <

0.40	0.400
0.35	0.300
0.2	0.25
1.5	1.05
1.8	1.80
0.01	0.1
0.99	0.999

chapter 2: calculations

[Recommended Time: 13 - 15 hours]

Contents

adding decimals mentally (tenths)

learn by heart

1 tenth = 0.1 = $\frac{1}{10}$	Ten tenths make 1 whole

examples

Calculate 0.4 + 0.6 $= 1$	Calculate 0.8 + 0.4 $= 1.2$

this will be more than 1 whole

exercise 2a

1. Complete the sentences:

    a) As a decimal, one tenth is written _____.

    b) As a fraction, one tenth is written _____.

    c) One whole contains _____ tenths.

2. Continue these decimal sequences:

    a) | 0.7 | 0.8 | 0.9 | | |

    b) | 1.8 | 1.9 | | | |

    c) | 1.2 | 1.1 | | | |

3. Calculate:

    a) 0.7 + 0.3   b) 0.4 + 0.5   c) 0.1 + 0.9

4. Complete these sums:

    a) 0.8 + _____ = 1   e) 1.6 - _____ = 1

    b) 0.3 + _____ = 1   f) 1.9 + _____ = 2

    c) 0.1 + _____ = 1   g) 1 - _____ = 0.7

    d) 1.4 - _____ = 1   h) 2.3 - _____ = 2

5. True or False: 0.9 + 0.1 = 0.10. Explain your answer.

6. Calculate:

a) 0.2 + 0.6   d) 0.5 + 0.5   g) 0.8 + 1.2

b) 0.9 + 0.1   e) 0.7 + 0.9   h) 0.4 + 1.3

c) 0.4 + 0.9   f) 1.5 + 2.3   i) 1.3 + 3.9

7. Calculate 0.4 + 0.6 + 0.3 + 0.7

8. From the list below, choose three numbers that add up to 1 whole:

a) 0.2   b) 0.3   c) 0.4   d) 0.5   e) 0.6

9. Calculate 4.5 + 0.5 + _____ = 6

10. Calculate 6 + 0.5 + _____ = 7

11. Work out the next numbers in each of these sequences:

a) | 0.2 | 0.5 | 0.8 | | | |

b) | 0.4 | 0.7 | 1 | | | |

c) | 0.1 | 0.5 | 0.9 | | | |

d) | 1.4 | 1.6 | 1.8 | | | |

e) | 2.7 | 2.4 | 2.1 | | | |

f) | 0 | 0.3 | 0.6 | | | |

g) | 1.1 | 0.9 | 0.7 | | | |

h) | 3.7 | 3.3 | 2.9 | | | |

i) | 4.6 | 4.2 | 3.8 | | | |

12. Write down a sequence of numbers that starts with 0.4 and increases by 0.2 each time.

Decimal Number Lines

Work out which number each arrow points to:

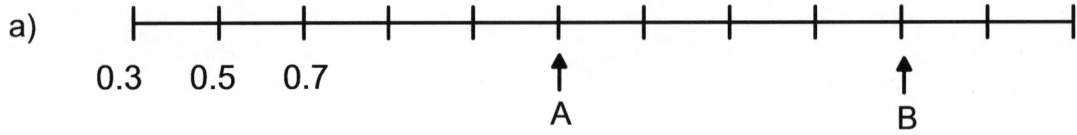

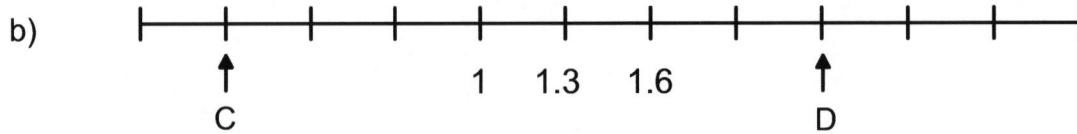

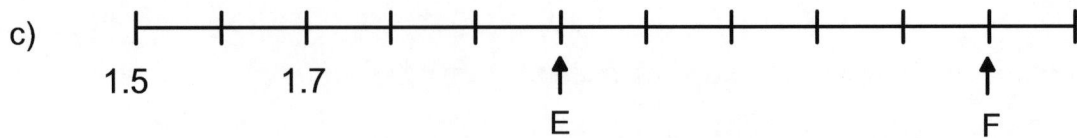

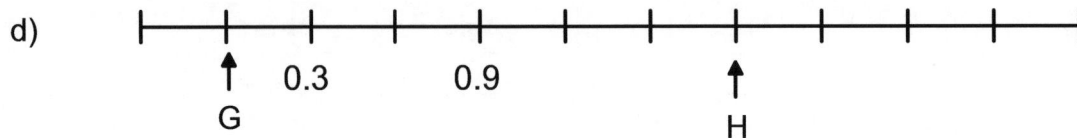

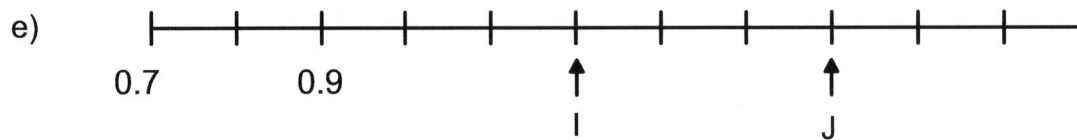

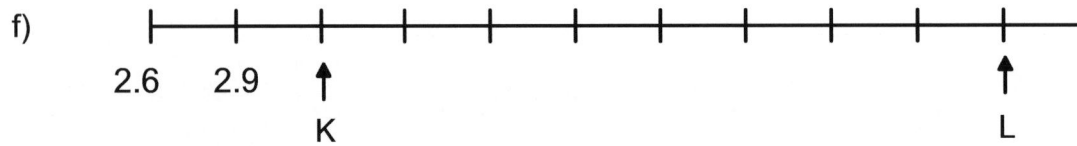

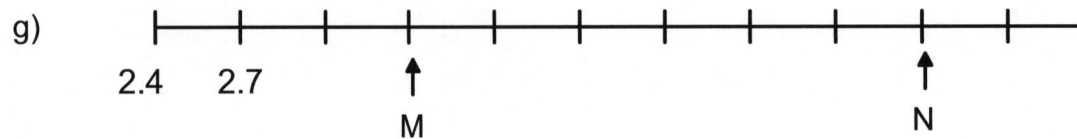

a)

0.3   0.5   0.7   A   B

b)

C   1   1.3   1.6   D

c)

1.5   1.7   E   F

d)

G   0.3   0.9   H

e)

0.7   0.9   I   J

f)

2.6   2.9   K   L

g)

2.4   2.7   M   N

adding & subtracting tenths (written as fractions or decimals)

examples

Work out $\frac{5}{10}$ + 0.3

$= 0.8$ or $\frac{8}{10}$

Work out $0.7 - \frac{3}{10}$

$= \frac{4}{10}$ or 0.4

Work out $1 - \frac{3}{10}$

$= 0.7$ or $\frac{7}{10}$

exercise 2b

1. Calculate the following. Give your answer as a decimal:

a) $\frac{3}{10} + \frac{7}{10}$

b) $1 - \frac{4}{10}$

c) $\frac{6}{10} - \frac{4}{10}$

d) $1 - \frac{3}{10}$

e) $\frac{5}{10} + \frac{3}{10}$

f) $\frac{6}{10} + \frac{6}{10}$

g) $\frac{4}{10} + \frac{9}{10}$

h) $2 + \frac{3}{10}$

i) $2 - \frac{3}{10}$

j) $4\frac{3}{10} + 1\frac{2}{10}$

k) $0.3 + 0.5$

l) $\frac{3}{10} + 0.4$

m) $\frac{5}{10} + 0.5$

n) $1 - 0.6$

o) $0.7 + 0.3$

p) $1 + 0.4$

q) $\frac{2}{10} + 1$

r) $\frac{8}{10} + 0.2$

s) $\frac{4}{10} + \frac{10}{10}$

t) $0.2 + \frac{5}{10} + 0.8$

u) $0.7 - \frac{7}{10}$

2. Complete the missing blanks with a decimal number:

a) $\frac{1}{10}$ + _____ = 1

b) $\frac{4}{10}$ + _____ = 1

c) 0.3 + _____ = 1

d) 0.9 + _____ = 1

e) $1\frac{8}{10}$ - _____ = 1

f) 1.3 - _____ = 1

g) 0.2 + _____ = 1

h) 1.7 - _____ = 1

i) $1\frac{3}{10}$ - _____ = 1

3. Calculate 2 + 0.3

4. Calculate 1.3 + 0.6 + $\frac{2}{10}$

Tenths Matching Activity

Match the calculations at the top to their answers at the bottom:

A	B	C	D
$1 + 0.1$	$1 - \frac{4}{10}$	$0.7 + 0.3$	$1 + 1.9$

E	F	G	H
$1 - \frac{9}{10}$	$\frac{3}{10} + \frac{4}{10}$	$1 + \frac{3}{10}$	$1 - 0.2$

I	J	K	L
$0.6 + 0.6$	$\frac{2}{10} + \frac{3}{10}$	$2 + \frac{2}{10}$	$1 + 1 + 0.1$

M	N	O	P
$1.4 + 0.6$	$\frac{2}{10} + 0.7$	$\frac{3}{10} + 1.1$	$1 - \frac{8}{10}$

Q	R	S	T
$1 + \frac{5}{10}$	$2.4 - 0.1$	$0.2 + \frac{1}{10}$	$1\frac{1}{10} + 0.5$

U	V	W	X
$1 + \frac{7}{10} + 0.7$	$1\frac{3}{10} + 1.9$	$2 + 0.3 + 0.7$	$1\frac{9}{10} + 2\frac{1}{10}$

Y	Z
$0.10 - \frac{1}{10}$	$3 - 0.2$

Jumbled Answers

0.1 1.5 1.2 1.1 1.6

2.8 0.5 0.7 3 0.9

1 0 0.6 2 2.9

1.3 4 0.8 2.3 2.2

0.2 1.4 2.4 2.1 0.3 3.2

A		N	
B		O	
C		P	
D		Q	
E		R	
F		S	
G		T	
H		U	
I		V	
J		W	
K		X	
L		Y	
M		Z	

written methods: addition & subtraction

examples

```
50 Thousand + 8,654
  = 50 000
     8 654  +
    58 654
```

```
3421 - 304
  = 3421
     304  -
    3117
```

Write the larger number on top
Line up the columns from the right
Borrow from the left if the digit
on top is smaller

exercise 2c

1. Which of the following is the correct working out for 5,720 + 186?

   a)
   ```
     5 7 2 0
     1 8 6  +
     6 5 9 0
   ```

   b)
   ```
     5 7 2 0
       1 8 6  +
     5 8 0 6
   ```

   c)
   ```
     5 7 2 0
       1 8 6  +
     5 9 0 6
   ```

   d)
   ```
     5 7 2 0
       1 8 6  +
     7 5 8 0
   ```

2. Calculate:

   a) 1,065 + 21,009

   b) 4,378 + 5,880,949

3. Calculate the following, using a written or mental method as necessary:

   a) 2 Thousand + 49,500

   d) 5 million + 8006

   b) 850 Thousand + 651,000

   e) 894,005 + 5 Hundred Thousand

   c) 9 million + 800,000

   f) 5 million + 870,000

4. Which of the following is the correct calculation of 3847 - 554?

   a)
   ```
     3 8 4 7
     5 5 4  -
     2 3 0 7
   ```

   b)
   ```
     3 8 4 7
       5 5 4  -
     3 3 1 3
   ```

   c)
   ```
     3 8 4 7
       5 5 4  -
     -2 3 0 7
   ```

   d)
   ```
     3 8 4 7
       5 5 4  -
     3 2 9 3
   ```

5. Calculate:

   a) 721 - 55

   d) 63,006 - 48,903

   b) 8,643 - 298

   e) 1 million - 452,806

   c) 5,002 - 32

   f) 90 million - 5,879,000

written methods: addition & subtraction of decimals

example

342.8 + 65.26

$$\begin{array}{r} 342.8 \\ 65.26 + \\ \hline 408.06 \\ \hline \end{array}$$

821.5 - 3.098

$$\begin{array}{r} 821.500 \\ 3.098 - \\ \hline 818.402 \\ \hline \end{array}$$

Line up your decimals before calculating

exercise 2d

1. Which of the these shows the correct way of working out 3.1 + 2.57?

$$\begin{array}{r} 3.1 \\ 2.57 + \\ \hline 5.67 \\ \hline \end{array}$$

$$\begin{array}{r} 3.1 \\ 2.5\,7 + \\ \hline 2.8\,8 \\ \hline \end{array}$$

2. Calculate:

   a) 3.05 + 24.8

   b) 423.89 + 19

   c) 6.008 + 0.5090

   d) 7653.986 + 27.06

3. True or False: 5.8 + 1.2 = 6.10

4. True or False: 3.2 + 1.04 = 1.36

5. Which of the following is the correct way to calculate 4.07 - 3.4?

$$\begin{array}{r} 4.07 \\ 3.4 - \\ \hline 1.47 \\ \hline \end{array}$$

$$\begin{array}{r} 4.07 \\ 3.4 - \\ \hline 0.67 \\ \hline \end{array}$$

$$\begin{array}{r} 4.0\,7 \\ 3.4 - \\ \hline 3.7\,3 \\ \hline \end{array}$$

6. Calculate:

   a) 5.09 - 3.8

   b) 90.08 - 6.145

7. Calculate using a written or mental method:

   a) 2.3 + 2.8

   b) 4 + 0.2

   c) 2.01 + 3

   d) 4.05 + 3.6

   e) 2.85 + 0.9

   f) 3.6 + 0.03

8. Calculate 2.89 + 1.5 + 3.098

9. Fill in the blanks:

   a)   3.8 + _____ = 3.85

   b) 2.07 + _____ = 3.17

Arrange the Digits

In each box, arrange the digits to make the calculation true.

A

| 2 | 6 |
| 7 | 7 |

$$\begin{array}{r} \square\ \square \\ \square\ \square + \\ \hline 9\ 4 \end{array}$$

B

| 4 | 5 |
| 8 | 9 |

$$\begin{array}{r} \square\ \square \\ \square\ \square + \\ \hline 1\ 5\ 2 \end{array}$$

C

0	1
2	4
8	

$$\begin{array}{r} \square\ \square \\ \square\ \square\ \square + \\ \hline 2\ 0\ 4 \end{array}$$

D

1	2
3	7
9	

$$\begin{array}{r} \square\ \square \\ \square\ \square\ \square + \\ \hline 2\ 6\ 5 \end{array}$$

E

2	2
3	3
7	7

$$\begin{array}{r} \square\ \square\ \square \\ \square\ \square\ \square + \\ \hline 5\ 4\ 6 \end{array}$$

F

1	2
7	8
9	9

$$\begin{array}{r} \square\ \square\ \square \\ \square\ \square\ \square + \\ \hline 4\ 6\ 8 \end{array}$$

G

1	1
2	3
5	5

$$\begin{array}{r} \square \\ \square\ \square \\ \square\ \square\ \square + \\ \hline 2\ 5\ 1 \end{array}$$

H

1	2
2	3
4	4

$$\begin{array}{r} \square\ \square \\ \square\ \ 9 \\ \square\ \square\ \square + \\ \hline 4\ 0\ 3 \end{array}$$

47

ten times larger: multiplying by 10, 100, 1000...

learn by heart

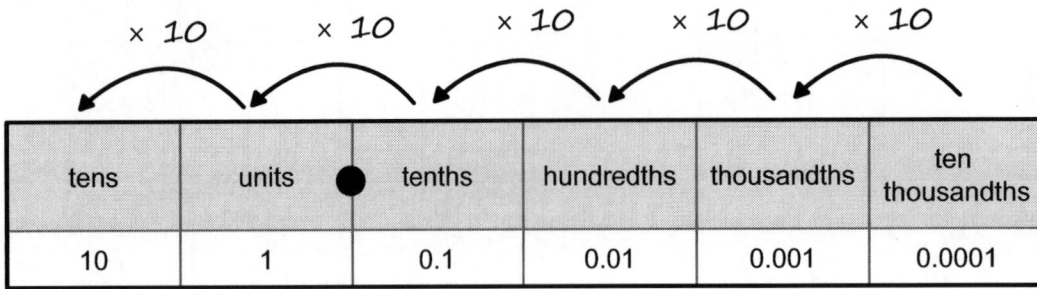

$\times 10$ $\times 10$ $\times 10$ $\times 10$ $\times 10$

tens	units	tenths	hundredths	thousandths	ten thousandths
10	1	0.1	0.01	0.001	0.0001

examples

$34 \times 100 = 3400$ $10 \times 5.902 = 59.02$ $0.84 \times 1000 = 840$

exercise 2e

1. True or False: $3.5 \times 10 = 3.50$

2. Calculate:

   a) 64×100 e) 2.6×10 i) 0.054×10

   b) 358×1000 f) 0.35×10 j) 123.89×1000

   c) 49×10 g) 3.5×100 k) 0.8×1000

   d) 500×1000 h) 0.89×1000 l) $0.904 \times 10,000$

3. Fill in the missing boxes:

   a) $3.8 \times \boxed{} = 380$ e) $0.21 \times \boxed{} = 2.1$

   b) $0.4 \times \boxed{} = 400$ f) $0.5 \times \boxed{} = 500$

   c) $9.3 \times \boxed{} = 930$ g) $0.07 \times \boxed{} = 70$

   d) $0.65 \times \boxed{} = 65$ h) $18.9 \times \boxed{} = 18,900$

4. If you add a zero to the end of _____ it doesn't get any bigger:

   a) 3   b) 42   c) 0.9   d) 10

5. If you remove the decimal point _____ gets 100 times bigger:

   a) 43.1   b) 1.92   c) 0.4   d) 5.904

ten times smaller: dividing by 10, 100, 1000...

examples

| $1700 \div 10 = 170$ | $439 \div 100 = 4.39$ | $0.7 \div 1000 = 0.0007$ |

exercise 2f

1. Calculate:

   a) $64 \div 100$ e) $2.6 \div 10$ i) $54 \div 10$

   b) $358 \div 100$ f) $4,600 \div 10$ j) $123.89 \div 1000$

   c) $49 \div 10$ g) $350 \div 100$ k) $8000 \div 1000$

   d) $500 \div 1000$ h) $89 \div 1000$ l) $9,004 \div 10,000$

2. Complete the missing boxes:

   a) $380 \div \boxed{} = 3.8$ e) $210 \div \boxed{} = 2.1$

   b) $0.4 \div \boxed{} = 0.04$ f) $50 \div \boxed{} = 0.05$

   c) $93 \div \boxed{} = 0.93$ g) $7 \div \boxed{} = 0.7$

   d) $65 \div \boxed{} = 0.65$ h) $1890 \div \boxed{} = 1.89$

3. If you remove the decimal point from the number 26.35, it gets _____ times bigger

4. Work out these mixed up multiplication and divisions:

   a) $21 \div 100$ d) $2.1 \div 1000$ g) $0.074 \div 10$

   b) 35.2×100 e) 52×10 h) $324.99 \div 1000$

   c) $4.9 \div 10$ f) 5.89×100 i) 0.9×100

5. Work out the missing numbers:

   a) $0.43 \times \underline{} = 430$ b) $50.7 \div \underline{} = 5.07$

   c) $\underline{} \div 100 = 83.2$ d) $\underline{} \times 10 = 5.2$

   e) $\underline{} \div 1000 = 2.3$ f) $100 \times \underline{} = 40$

matching activity

Match these calculations to their answers:

A 0.45 × 10	B 20.6 ÷ 100	C 4.5 × 100	4500	0.045
			450	45
D 450 ÷ 1000	E 0.45 × 100	F 4.5 ÷ 100	4.5	0.45
G 4.5 × 1000	H 2.6 × 100	I 260 ÷ 1000	26	2.06
			0.206	260
J 206 ÷ 100	K 2.06 × 100	L 0.026 × 1000	0.26	206

Record your answers in a table:

A	B	C	D	E	F	G	H	I	J	K	L

challenge

For each question, work out the missing numbers in the circles.

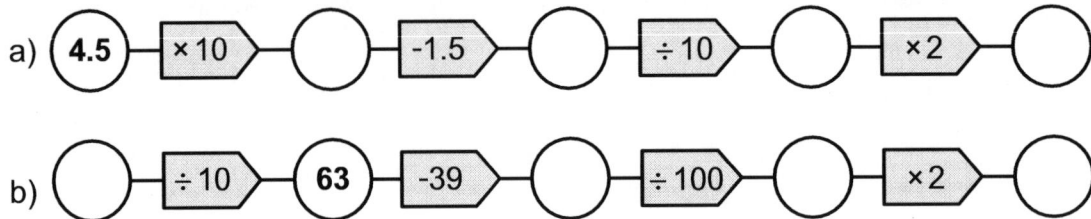

a) $\boxed{4.5}$ — ×10 — ◯ — −1.5 — ◯ — ÷10 — ◯ — ×2 — ◯

b) ◯ — ÷10 — $\boxed{63}$ — −39 — ◯ — ÷100 — ◯ — ×2 — ◯

multiple choice

For each question, choose the correct answer:

1. Calculate 6.5 × 100

   a) 65   b) 6.500

   c) 650   d) 0.065

2. Calculate 0.3 ÷ 1000

   a) 300   b) 30

   c) 0.003   d) 0.0003

3. Calculate 8.02 × 1000

   a) 802   b) 8020

   c) 8200   d) 8002

4. Calculate 2.1 ÷ 100

   a) 0.021   b) 0.201

   c) 2.001   d) 0.210

multiplying integers (related calculations)

example

Given that 34 × 7 = 238, calculate 340 × 70

= 23,800

Each number became 10 times larger, so the answer became 100 times larger

exercise 2g

1. Calculate:

a)
| 6 × 4 = 24 |
| 6 × 400 = _____ |
| 60 × 4 = _____ |
| 60 × 40 = _____ |

b)
| 9 × 2 = 18 |
| 9000 × 2 = _____ |
| 9 × 200 = _____ |
| 90 × 20 = _____ |

c)
| 5 × 3 = _____ |
| 50 × 3 = _____ |
| 5 × 3000 = _____ |
| 5000 × 3 = _____ |

2. Calculate:

a) 2 × 60

b) 3 × 400

c) 90 × 2

d) 90 × 4

e) 7 × 30

f) 20 × 6

g) 900 × 3

h) 7000 × 4

i) 800 × 3

j) 60 × 4

k) 40 × 7

l) 500 × 5

3. Copy and complete these multiplication grids:

a)
×	6	8	10
3			
4			
20			

b)
×	3	20	
2			60
5			
40			

c)
×	5		25
2		60	
20			
			2500

d)
×		50	100
4	8		
		350	
	180		

51

4. Calculate:

a) 20 × 30

b) 20 × 80

c) 400 × 20

d) 80 × 30

e) 90 × 20

f) 4000 × 60

g) 900 × 20

h) 500 × 300

i) 9000 × 300

5. Work out the missing numbers:

a) 2 × ☐ = 220

b) 5 × ☐ = 1500

c) 3 × ☐ = 210

d) 40 × ☐ = 2800

e) 9 × ☐ = 270

f) 12 × ☐ = 360

g) 7 × ☐ = 2800

h) 600 × ☐ = 1800

i) 50 × ☐ = 2500

6. Given that 4 × 3 = 12, work out:

a) 40 × 30

b) 400 × 3

c) 4 × 3,000

d) 400 × 300

e) 40 × 300

f) 4 × 3,000,000

7. Given that **19 × 25 = 475**, complete these related calculations:

a) 19 × 2500 = ☐

b) 190 × 2500 = ☐

c) 19 × ☐ = 4750

d) 1900 × 250 = ☐

e) ☐ × 25 = 47500

f) ☐ × 2500 = 475,000

g) ☐ × 25 = 4750

h) 1,900 × 2,500 = ☐

i) 1,900 × ☐ = 4,750,000

j) 19 × ☐ = 47,500

- -

Countdown Target : 506

Using each number only once, how close can you get to 506?
You can add, subtract, multiply or divide the numbers.

| 3 | 4 | 6 | 8 | 9 | 10 | 100 |

multiplying integers (written methods)

example

Calculate 45 × 232

= 10,440

```
   232
    45 ×
  1160  ←——— 5 × 232
  9280  ←——— 40 × 232
 10440
```

exercise 2h

1. Use a written method to calculate:

   a) 18 × 42

   b) 63 × 39

   c) 453 × 6

   d) 21 × 953

   e) 16 × 84

   f) 1245 × 37

2. A decade is 10 years.
   How many days are there in 10 years?

3. How many hours are there in 1 week?

4. How many minutes are there in 1 day?

5. How many hours are there in 1 year?

6. How many hours are there in a decade?

7. How many minutes are there in 1 year?

8. How many minutes are there in 1 decade?

9. Which is longer, 1 million days or 1000 years?

- -

Countdown Target : 801

Using each number only once, how close can you get to 801?
You can add, subtract, multiply or divide the numbers.

| 1 | 2 | 5 | 7 | 8 | 9 | 10 |

multiplying decimals

example

each number is 10 times smaller...

...so the answer is 100 times smaller

Given that 6 × 7 = 42,   calculate 0.6 × 0.7 = 0.42

exercise 2i

1. Complete each table of related calculations:

a)

3 × 4 = __12__
3 × 0.4 = _____
3 × 0.04 = _____
0.3 × 4 = _____

b)

5 × 3 = _____
0.5 × 3 = _____
0.5 × 0.3 = _____
5 × 0.03 = _____

c)

12 × 2 = _____
1.2 × 2 = _____
0.12 × 2 = _____
1.2 × 0.2 = _____

d)

6 × 3 = _____
0.06 × 3 = _____
0.6 × 0.3 = _____
60 × 3 = _____

e)

12 × 6 = __72__
120 × 6 = _____
1.2 × 6 = _____
1.2 × 0.6 = _____

f)

14 × 1 = _____
1.4 × 1 = _____
14 × 0.1 = _____
14 × 0.01 = _____

2. Given that **17 × 24 = 408**, work out the value of:

a) 1.7 × 24   b) 17 × 0.24

c) 1.7 × 2.4   d) 0.17 × 2.4

3. Compared with the answer to 12 × 146, the answer to 12 × 0.146 would be:

a) 10 times smaller   b) 100 times smaller   c) 1000 times smaller

4. Compared with the answer to 64 × 18, the answer to 6.4 × 1.8 would be:

a) 10 times smaller   b) 100 times smaller   c) 1000 times smaller

example

Calculate 3 × 0.4   *think 3 × 4 = 12*
so 3 × 0.4 = 1.2

- -

5. Calculate:

a) 0.2 × 6   d) 1.2 × 3   g) 1.5 × 3

b) 0.5 × 3   e) 0.9 × 2   h) 10 × 0.1

c) 0.3 × 8   f) 1.4 × 2   i) 9 × 0.3

6. Which of the following is 0.6 × 3?

a) 0.18   b) 1.8   c) 18.0   d) 180

7. Fill in the missing blanks:

a) 0.2 × _____ = 1.6   d) 6 × _____ = 1.2

b) 7 × _____ = 2.1   e) 5 × _____ = 2.5

c) 3 × _____ = 0.9   f) 10 × _____ = 35

8. Calculate:

a) 5 × 0.03   c) 0.02 × 6

b) 8 × 0.04   d) 0.03 × 6

9. Decide whether these statements are true or false:

a) 0.6 × 100 = 6   b) 0.2 × 0.4 = 0.8

c) 0.3 × 4 = 0.12   d) 0.05 × 0.3 = 0.015

e) 0.6 × 6 = 3.6   f) 0.5 × 0.5 = 2.5

10. Work out:

a) 0.7 × 0.2   b) 0.9 × 0.3   c) 0.4 × 0.6

d) 0.04 × 3   e) 60 × 0.3   f) 0.07 × 40

g) 15 × 0.03   h) 120 × 0.4   i) 11 × 0.3

Multiplication Arithmagons

Complete the arithmagons so that the numbers in the circles multiply together to make the number in the rectangle in between them.

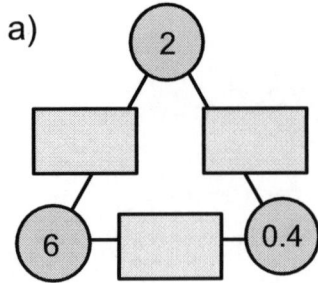

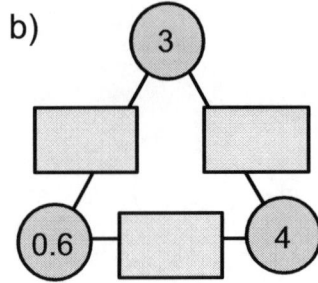

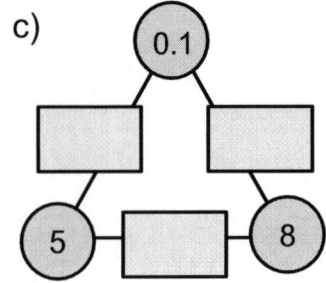

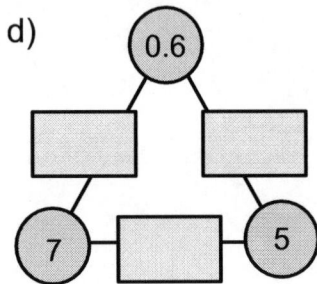

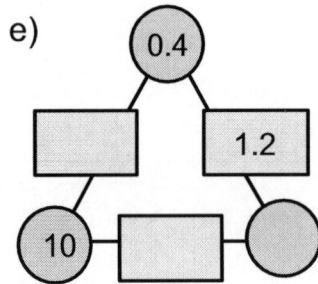

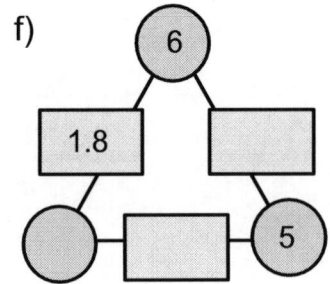

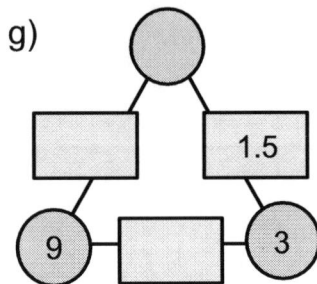

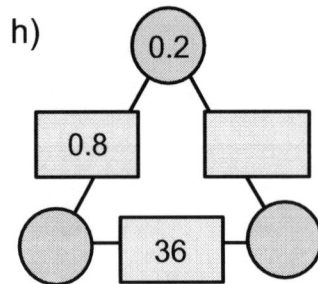

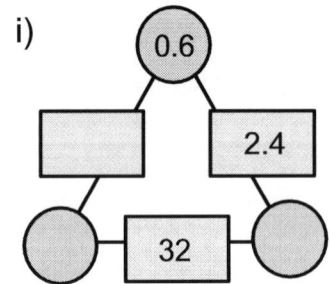

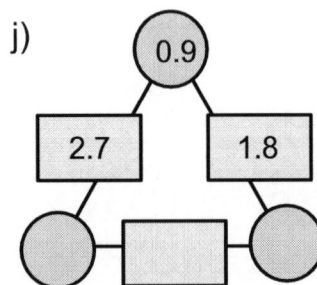

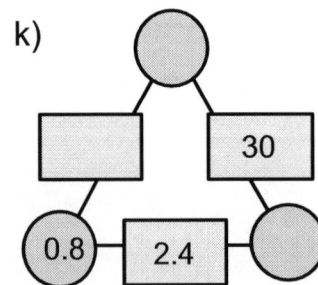

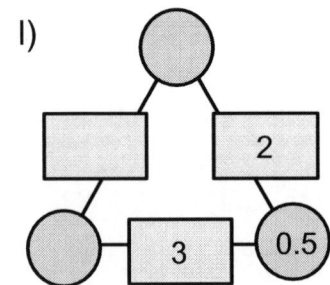

a)

2 · 6 · 0.4

b)

3 · 0.6 · 4

c)

0.1 · 5 · 8

d)

0.6 · 7 · 5

e)

0.4 · 10 · 1.2

f)

6 · 1.8 · 5

g)

9 · 1.5 · 3

h)

0.2 · 0.8 · 36

i)

0.6 · 2.4 · 32

j)

0.9 · 2.7 · 1.8

k)

30 · 0.8 · 2.4

l)

2 · 3 · 0.5

mixed practice

exercise 2j

1. Calculate:

   a) 0.3 × 4

   b) 0.26 × 10

   c) 40 × 30

   d) 4 × 0.1

   e) 5.4 × 10

   f) 180 ÷ 100

   g) 2.8 × 100

   h) 4 × 0.2

   i) 0.8 × 5

   j) 0.6 × 3

   k) 0.35 × 100

   l) 1.2 × 10

2. Fill in the missing blanks:

   a) 6 × ____ = 60

   b) 0.5 × ____ = 50

   c) 0.42 × ____ = 4.2

   d) 3 × ____ = 0.3

   e) 4 × _____ = 1.2

   f) 2 × ____ = 5

   g) 8 × ____ = 2.4

   h) ____ × 100 = 420

   i) ____ × 10 = 3.8

   j) ____ × 10 = 64

   k) ____ × 100 = 3800

   l) 0.06 × _____ = 6

3. True or false: 0.4 × 10 = 0.40

4. True or false: 0.4 + 0.6 = 0.10

5. True or false: *Multiplication always makes a number larger*

matching activity

Work out each calculation and find your answers at the bottom.

A 3 × 0.5	B 5 × 0.7	C 0.3 × 10
D 27 ÷ 10	E 6 × 0.2	F 0.07 × 10
G 5.5 × 100	H 0.12 × 100	I 3.4 × 1000
J 77 ÷ 10	K 0.4 × 5	L 0.1 × 8

| 3400 | 1.2 | 12 | 2.7 | 0.7 | 7.7 | 550 | 0.8 | 3.5 | 2 | 1.5 | 3 |

Calculations Spiral

Start in the middle and work your way around the spiral,
finding your answers at the bottom as you go.

×3   ÷10   +0.6   ×1.2   **2**

×100

×0.1   ×0.3   ×10   +$\frac{2}{10}$

-0.3   **start**   +$\frac{4}{10}$ ×3

0.2   +0.1

-5.5   -1   -0.4

0.8   -$\frac{4}{10}$ ×2   +$\frac{2}{10}$

-$\frac{4}{10}$

+0.9   ×0.7   -$\frac{5}{10}$ ×2

- -

jumbled answers

| 1 | 0.3 | 0.3 | 0.7 | 3 |

4.6   0.8   2.8   1.8   1.8   2.3   90

7   4   2.4   3.5   0.6   9   0.4

0.9   2.1   3.1

short division

example

Calculate $42 \div 8$

$$8 \overline{) 4\,^4 2\,.\,^2 0\,^4 0\,0} = 5\,.\,2\,5$$

Start by asking, how many 8's in 4? None.
Carry the 4 - how many 8's in 42? 5. Remainder 2.
Carry the remainder - how many 8's in 20? 2. Remainder 4.
Carry the remainder - how many 8's in 40? 5.

exercise 2k

1. Calculate the following. The answers are all integers:

   a) $448 \div 8$

   b) $2766 \div 6$

   c) $468 \div 9$

   d) $665 \div 5$

   e) $639 \div 9$

   f) $20{,}095 \div 5$

2. Calculate the following. The answers are all decimals:

   a) $100 \div 8$

   b) $122 \div 8$

   c) $211 \div 5$

   d) $313 \div 4$

   e) $941 \div 5$

   f) $2558 \div 5$

3. Calculate

   a) $44.5 \div 5$

   b) $89.8 \div 8$

   c) $112.5 \div 9$

4. Calculate the following. The answers are all less than 1:

   a) $1 \div 4$

   b) $1 \div 8$

   c) $1 \div 5$

   d) $2 \div 5$

   e) $3 \div 5$

   f) $4 \div 5$

- -

Countdown Target : 53.4

Using each number only once, how close can you get to 53.4?
You can add, subtract, multiply or divide the numbers.

| 0.1 | 0.5 | 2 | 3 | 4 | 5 | 10 |

writing recurring decimals using dot notation

learn by heart

A Recurring Decimal: *continues forever, following a pattern, e.g. 5.7373....*

A Terminating Decimal: *a decimal whose digits do not go on forever, e.g. 0.25*

examples

Recurring decimals continue forever with a repeating pattern.
They can be written using dot notation.

a) $0.44444444... = 0.\dot{4}$ b) $1.37777777... = 1.3\dot{7}$

c) $4.12525252... = 4.1\dot{2}\dot{5}$ d) $0.12341234... = 0.\dot{1}23\dot{4}$

exercise 2

1. Which of the following equals 0.676767...?

   a) $0.6\dot{7}$ b) $\dot{0}.6\dot{7}$ c) $0.\dot{6}7$ d) $0.\ddot{6}\ddot{7}$

2. Which of the following equals 1.588888...?

   a) $1.5\dot{8}$ b) $\dot{1}.5\dot{8}$ c) $1.\dot{5}8$ d) $1.\ddot{5}\ddot{8}$

3. Which of the following equals 4.219219...?

   a) $4.21\dot{9}$ b) $4.2\dot{1}\dot{9}$ c) $4.\dot{2}1\dot{9}$ d) $4.\ddot{2}1\ddot{9}$

4. Write each of these recurring decimals using dot notation:

   a) 0.7222222... b) 4.3232323...

   c) 1.421421421... d) 5.5555555...

   e) 6.728282828... f) 3.4151515....

5. Which of the following equals $0.\dot{0}9\dot{7}$?

   a) 0.0979797... b) 0.9797979... c) 0.0977777... d) 0.0970970...

6. True or false? $0.\dot{3} = 0.3\dot{3}$

7. Explain why $0.1\ddot{2}5$ is an impossible number.

Short division 2 (recurring decimals)

example

Calculate 22 ÷ 6

$$6\overline{)2^22.{}^40{}^40{}^40}$$

3.666... $= 3.\dot{6}$

You can see that the remainder is always 4... this means the decimal will continue forever

exercise 2m

1. Calculate the following. The answers are all recurring decimals:

   a) 52 ÷ 3   d) 70 ÷ 6   g) 74 ÷ 9

   b) 80 ÷ 3   e) 80 ÷ 6   h) 125 ÷ 3

   c) 40 ÷ 3   f) 92 ÷ 9   i) 58 ÷ 9

2. Calculate the following. The answers are all less than 1:

   a) 1 ÷ 6   c) 2 ÷ 3   e) 3 ÷ 9

   b) 4 ÷ 6   d) 5 ÷ 6   f) 5 ÷ 9

3. True or false: 1 ÷ 3 = 0.33

In Pairs: 3 in a Row

Choose any two numbers below and divide them. Find your answer in the grid on the right. Claim this square with a counter. Take it in turns with your partner. You can use the numbers more than once. The first person to get 3 squares in a row, wins!

1	2	3	4
5	6	9	10

4.5	2	0.25	0.5	0.6	1.5
0.75	10	0.8	2.5	$0.\dot{6}$	5
$0.\dot{5}$	2.25	$1.\dot{1}$	$0.\dot{1}$	0.2	6
$1.\dot{6}$	$0.\dot{3}$	1.2	0.3	3	1.8
$0.\dot{2}$	0.1	0.4	$1.\dot{3}$	$0.8\dot{3}$	$3.\dot{3}$
$0.\dot{4}$	4	1.25	$0.1\dot{6}$	9	0.9

fractions to decimals

examples

Convert $\frac{34}{100}$ to a decimal	Convert $\frac{1}{8}$ to a decimal
0.34	0.125 $1 \div 8 = 8\overline{)1.000}$

If the denominator is 10,100, 1000 etc, we can write it as a decimal straight away using our knowledge of place value

If not... we can use short division.

exercise 2n

1. Change each of these fractions into decimals.
   Write recurring decimals using dot notation

$\frac{1}{3} =$	$\frac{2}{3} =$	$\frac{3}{3} =$	$\frac{4}{3} =$

$\frac{1}{4} =$	$\frac{2}{4} =$	$\frac{3}{4} =$	$\frac{4}{4} =$	$\frac{5}{4} =$

$\frac{1}{5} =$	$\frac{2}{5} =$	$\frac{3}{5} =$	$\frac{4}{5} =$	$\frac{5}{5} =$	$\frac{6}{5} =$

$\frac{1}{6} =$	$\frac{2}{6} =$	$\frac{3}{6} =$	$\frac{4}{6} =$	$\frac{5}{6} =$	$\frac{6}{6} =$	$\frac{7}{6} =$

2. Convert these fractions to decimals. What do you notice?

   a) $\frac{1}{9}$ c) $\frac{3}{9}$ e) $\frac{5}{9}$ g) $\frac{7}{9}$

   b) $\frac{2}{9}$ d) $\frac{4}{9}$ f) $\frac{6}{9}$

3. Looking at the pattern above, can you predict what $\frac{8}{9}$ will be as a decimal?

4. Convert these fractions to decimals:

   a) $\frac{3}{10}$ c) $\frac{8}{10}$ e) $\frac{6}{1000}$ g) $\frac{9}{10}$

   b) $\frac{5}{100}$ d) $\frac{94}{100}$ f) $\frac{42}{100}$ h) $\frac{442}{1000}$

5. Find all of the statements that are true:

A $\frac{1}{3} = 0.3333...$	B $\frac{2}{3} > 1$	C $\frac{1}{10} > 0.5$	D $\frac{2}{5} = 2.5$	E $\frac{9}{10} > 1$
F $\frac{3}{8} = 0.5$	G $\frac{8}{100} = 0.8$	H $0.6 > \frac{6}{10}$	I $\frac{1}{8} = 0.8$	J $\frac{5}{10} = 0.5$
K $\frac{4}{5} = 0.8$	L $\frac{1}{50} = 0.02$	M $\frac{1}{6} = 0.16$	N $\frac{3}{10} = 0.03$	O $\frac{1}{9} = 0.\dot{1}$

6. Which of these is 0.6?

   a) $\frac{1}{6}$ b) $\frac{6}{10}$ c) $\frac{6}{1}$ d) $\frac{6}{100}$

Matching Decimals and Fractions

Match these fractions and decimals into pairs.
Record your answers in a table

A $\frac{1}{4}$	B $\frac{4}{9}$	0.4	0.$\dot{3}$
C $\frac{1}{8}$	D $\frac{3}{10}$	0.25	0.125
E $\frac{1}{10}$	F $\frac{2}{3}$	0.2	0.3
G $\frac{2}{9}$	H $\frac{1}{5}$	0.$\dot{6}$	0.6
I $\frac{2}{5}$	J $\frac{1}{2}$	0.$\dot{2}$	0.1
K $\frac{1}{3}$	L $\frac{3}{5}$	0.5	
M $\frac{1}{9}$		0.$\dot{1}$	0.$\dot{4}$

Fraction	Decimal
A	
B	
C	
D	
E	
F	
G	
H	
I	
J	
K	
L	
M	

mental maths: quick doubling

learn by heart

1	2	3	4	5	6	7	8	9
2	4	6	8	10	12	14	16	18

) double

examples

Double 64	Double 87
$= 60 \times 2 + 4 \times 2$ $= 128$	$= 80 \times 2 + 7 \times 2$ $= 160 + 14 = 174$

exercise 20

1. Work out:

    a) 14 × 2   e) 63 × 2   i) 16 × 2

    b) 28 × 2   f) 29 × 2   j) 39 × 2

    c) 36 × 2   g) 88 × 2   k) 58 × 2

    d) 48 × 2   h) 47 × 2   l) 98 × 2

2. Try some larger numbers:

    a) 134 × 2   e) 613 × 2   i) 1062 × 2

    b) 258 × 2   f) 239 × 2   j) 3412 × 2

    c) 786 × 2   g) 888 × 2   k) 5668 × 2

    d) 468 × 2   h) 457 × 2   l) 9098 × 2

3. Think about doubles to work out these sums:

    a) 45 + 46   e) 35 + 37   i) 49 + 50

    b) 25 + 26   f) 30 + 31   j) 25 + 27

    c) 15 + 16   g) 39 + 40   k) 40 + 41

4. True or False: When you double a number, the answer is always even.

5. Complete these number sequences by doubling:

a) | 4 | 8 | 16 | | | |

b) | 5 | 10 | 20 | | | |

c) | 6 | 12 | 24 | | | |

d) | 7 | 14 | 28 | | | |

e) | 8 | 16 | 32 | | | |

f) | 9 | 18 | 36 | | | |

g) | 10 | 20 | | | | |

h) | 12 | 24 | | | | |

7. Sara doubles the number 126.
She says the answer is 2412.
What mistake did she make?
What is the correct answer?

what's left?

Match each number to its double. Which number is left on its own?

42   16   25   17   84

50   56   88   37   32   30

28   34   74   15   62   44

mental maths: halving

learn by heart

1	2	3	4	5	6	7	8	9	10
0.5	1	1.5	2	2.5	3	3.5	4	4.5	5

⟩ half

examples

78 ÷ 2

Half of 70 = 35
Half of 8 = 4
Half of 78 = 39

75 ÷ 2

Half of 70 = 35
Half of 5 = 2.5
Half of 75 = 37.5

exercise 2p

1. Calculate:

   a) 26 ÷ 2

   b) 48 ÷ 2

   c) 60 ÷ 2

   d) 68 ÷ 2

   e) 84 ÷ 2

   f) 100 ÷ 2

   g) 76 ÷ 2

   h) 38 ÷ 2

   i) 94 ÷ 2

   j) 122 ÷ 2

   k) 130 ÷ 2

   l) 142 ÷ 2

   m) 150 ÷ 2

   n) 148 ÷ 2

   o) 190 ÷ 2

2. Calculate:

   a) 3 ÷ 2

   b) 5 ÷ 2

   c) 7 ÷ 2

   d) 9 ÷ 2

   e) 13 ÷ 2

   f) 17 ÷ 2

   g) 21 ÷ 2

   h) 25 ÷ 2

   i) 29 ÷ 2

   j) 31 ÷ 2

   k) 41 ÷ 2

   l) 51 ÷ 2

   m) 57 ÷ 2

   n) 59 ÷ 2

   o) 77 ÷ 2

mental maths: half way between

examples

Find the number half way between 10 and 16

10 + 16 = 26
Half of 26 = 13

Find the number half way between 24 and 27

24 + 27 = 51
Half of 51 = 25.5

exercise 2q

1. Find the number half way between:

   a) 3 and 7

   b) 2 and 6

   c) 9 and 15

   d) 8 and 12

   e) 14 and 20

   f) 15 and 20

   g) 27 and 32

   h) 17 and 21

   i) 1 and 8

   j) 3 and 7

   k) 30 and 31

   l) 12 and 18

   m) 14 and 19

   n) 47 and 63

   o) 18 and 33

2. Calculate:

   a) 17×2

   b) $9 \div 2$

   c) $27 \div 2$

   d) 16×2

   e) $21 \div 2$

   f) 25×2

   g) $29 \div 2$

   h) 32×2

   i) 38×2

   j) $14 \div 2$

   k) $18 \div 2$

   l) $28 \div 2$

   m) 57×2

   n) 37×2

   o) $103 \div 2$

3. Work out half of 9999.

4. What is half of 1 million?

5. What is half way between 500,000 and 1 million?

the effect of dividing by 0.5, 0.1, 0.01 and 0

learn by heart

Dividing by 0.5 is like doubling
Dividing by 0.1 is like multiplying by 10
Dividing by 0 is undefined

examples

Calculate
$12 \div 0.5$

$= 24$

Calculate
$12 \div 0.1$

$= 120$

Calculate
$12 \div 0.01$

$= 1200$

exercise 2r

1. Calculate, if possible:

   a) $8 \div 0.5$

   b) $12 \div 0.1$

   c) $4 \div 0.01$

   d) $0.23 \div 0.1$

   e) $\dfrac{9}{0.5}$

   f) $\dfrac{7}{0.1}$

   g) $\dfrac{9}{0.01}$

   h) $6.1 \div 0.5$

   i) $15 \div 0$

   j) $0 \div 15$

   k) $0.2 \div 0.5$

   l) $0.1 \div 0.1$

2. True or false?

   a) $18 \div 0.5 = 9$

   b) $6 \div 0.1 = 0.6$

   c) $4 \div 0.5 = 8$

   d) $84 \div 0.01 = 840$

3. Which of these cannot be calculated?

   a) $8 \div 0.3$ b) $8 \div 0.01$ c) $8 \div 900$ d) $8 \div 0$

4. Calculate

   a) $18 \div 0.01$

   b) $1.3 \div 0.01$

   c) $0.5 \div 0.5$

   d) $0.3 \div 0.1$

   e) $\dfrac{8.6}{0.01}$

   f) $\dfrac{0.039}{0.01}$

5. True or false? *Division always makes things smaller.*

6. Which of these give an answer of 190? Circle all that apply.

   a) $\dfrac{19}{100}$ b) $\dfrac{19}{10}$ c) $\dfrac{19}{1}$ d) $\dfrac{19}{1.0}$ e) $\dfrac{19}{0.1}$

7. Dividing by 0.1 is the same as multiplying by _____.

8. Dividing by 0.01 is the same as multiplying by _____.

9. Dividing by _____ is the same as doubling.

10. Complete the sentence: Dividing 32 by 0.1 has the same effect as...

    a) multiplying by 10   c) adding 10

    b) dividing by 10   d) subtracting 10.

11. Calculate:

    a) $3 \div 0.01$ c) $0.5 \div 0.5$ e) $0 \div 0.1$

    b) $12 \div 0.5$ d) $0.1 \div 0$ f) $0.2 \div 0.5$

12. Dividing 25 by _____ will give an answer bigger than 25. Choose from below:

    a) 100   b) 25   c) 1   d) 0.5   e) 0.1

13. To work out $6 \div 0.1$, we could calculate:

    a) 6×0.1 b) $6 \div 1$ c) $6 \div 10$ d) 6×10

14. Calculate:

    a) $\frac{9}{10} \div 0.1$ b) $\frac{14}{100} \div 0.1$ c) $1\frac{3}{10} \div 0.1$

    d) $\frac{4}{10} \div 0.5$ e) $\frac{8}{100} \div 0.01$ f) $2\frac{1}{10} \div 0.5$

matching activity

Match these calculations to their answers:

A	B	C
$6 \div 0.5$	6×0.5	$6 \div 10$

D	E	F
$3 \div 0.01$	0.6×0.3	$18 \div 0.1$

G	H	I
$6 \div 0.01$	$12 \div 0.01$	3×0.5

J	K	L
$3 \div 0.5$	3×0.1	$3 \div 0.1$

300	3
0.3	180
600	6
12	30
1200	0.6
0.18	1.5

A	B	C	D	E	F	G	H	I	J	K	L

Dividing by a Decimal
Code Breaker ⭐ extra challenge

Calculate the following and find your
answer in the code box.
Write down each word
to reveal an inspirational message!

code box

0 = change	20 = to	50 = are	300 = world
2 = the	22 = last	70 = past	320 = door
2.5 = do	25 = river	100 = crazy	450 = game
8 = on	30 = the	120 = people	600 = believe
10 = they	40 = who	200 = fairy	640 = between
11 = every	45 = time	250 = can	700 = who
12 = enough	48 = ones	270 = snow	1000 = partner

a) $\dfrac{15}{0.5}$ = _30_ = **The**

b) $\dfrac{12}{0.1}$ = _____ =

c) $\dfrac{4}{0.1}$ = _____ =

d) $\dfrac{25}{0.5}$ = _____ =

e) $\dfrac{10}{0.1}$ = _____ =

f) $\dfrac{6}{0.5}$ = _____ =

g) $\dfrac{2}{0.1}$ = _____ =

h) $\dfrac{6}{0.01}$ = _____ =

i) $\dfrac{1}{0.1}$ = _____ =

j) $\dfrac{25}{0.1}$ = _____ =

k) $\dfrac{0}{3}$ = _____ =

l) $\dfrac{15}{0.5}$ = _____ =

m) $\dfrac{3}{0.01}$ = _____ =

n) $\dfrac{0.5}{0.01}$ = _____ =

o) $\dfrac{1}{0.5}$ = _____ =

p) $\dfrac{24}{0.5}$ = _____ =

q) $\dfrac{7}{0.01}$ = _____ =

r) $\dfrac{0.25}{0.1}$ = _____ =

– Quote by Steve Jobs

chapter review

exercise 2S

1. Calculate:

   a) 4 × 100

   b) 0.4 × 100

   c) 0.1 + 0.9

   d) 0.1 × 100

   e) 2.67 × 10

   f) 0.35 × 100

   g) 15 ÷ 10

   h) 0.3 × 4

   i) 28 ÷ 10

   j) 28 ÷ 100

   k) 4.2 + 3.5

   l) 0.4 + $\frac{4}{10}$

2. Which numbers are the arrows pointing to?

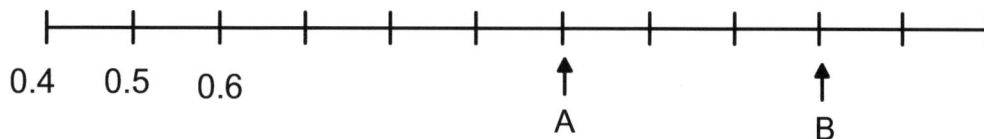

3. Which of these is the answer to 46 × 100?

   a) 46.00   b) 0.46   c) 460   d) 4600

4. Work out 64 ÷ 4

5. Convert these fractions to decimals

   a) $\frac{1}{4}$

   b) $\frac{3}{8}$

   c) $\frac{1}{2}$

   d) $\frac{3}{4}$

   e) $\frac{5}{8}$

   f) $\frac{1}{6}$

   g) $\frac{1}{10}$

   h) $\frac{5}{6}$

6. Calculate:

   a) 56 ÷ 10

   b) 84 ÷ 4

   c) 9.3 ÷ 10

   d) 552 ÷ 2

   e) 90 ÷ 4

   f) 57 ÷ 3

   g) 0.1 × 6

   h) 800 ÷ 4

   i) 86 ÷ 9

   j) 0.4 ÷ 10

   k) 56 ÷ 5

   l) 48 ÷ 5

7. Calculate:

a) 42 × 10

b) 0.8 × 3

c) 41 ÷ 10

d) 520 ÷ 100

e) 92 × 2

f) 0.07 × 10

g) 3.4 + 0.6

h) 0.1 × 65

i) 9 ÷ 2

j) 0.09 × 1000

k) 6324 ÷ 10

l) 1.23 + 0.8

8. Which number gets 100 times bigger if you remove the decimal point?

a) 4.7

b) 2.35

c) 0.1

d) 95.6

9. Fill in the gaps:

a) 6 × ☐ = 6000

b) 5.2 ÷ ☐ = 0.52

c) 950 ÷ ☐ = 0.95

d) 0.04 × ☐ = 40

e) 526 ÷ ☐ = 52.6

f) 9.9 × ☐ = 990

g) 65 ÷ ☐ = 0.065

h) 0.1 × ☐ = 100

10. Calculate:

a) 0.4 + 0.6

b) 1 - 0.3

c) 2.4 × 10

d) 12 ÷ 10

e) 2.5 + 2.5

f) 3.1 - 0.1

g) 4 + 0.6

h) 0.4 × 100

i) 84 ÷ 100

j) 1 - 0.7

k) $\frac{4}{10}$ + 2.4

l) $\frac{3}{10}$ - 0.3

11. Work out 7 × 10 × 8 × 10

12. Complete these sentences. The first one is done for you.

a) 65 is __10__ times __larger__ than 6.5

b) 900 is _____ times _____ than 9

c) 1.2 is _____ times _____ than 120

cumulative review (chapters 1 & 2)

exercise 24

1. Write these decimals as fractions or mixed numbers:

   a) 0.9   d) 0.05   g) 0.99   j) 0.33

   b) 0.24   e) 0.2   h) 4.2   k) 2.8

   c) 0.1   f) 0.101   i) 0.004   l) 23.05

2. Calculate:

   a) 1.5 + 1.5   d) 426 - 399   g) 1 - 0.6   j) $1 + \frac{4}{10}$

   b) 40 × 30   e) 94 ÷ 2   h) 4 × 0.3   k) 3.7 × 2

   c) 2.6 × 10   f) 12 × 3.0   i) 80 × 100   l) 1023 ÷ 2

3. Write the number **eight hundred and ten thousand** in digits.

4. Three tens and three tenths make:

   a) 3.3   b) 30.3   c) 30.03   d) 33

5. Round these numbers to 1 decimal place:

   a) 5.89   b) 22.344   c) 104.05

6. Write **1 million** in figures.

7. Fill in the blanks with >, < or =

   a) 24 _____ 30   c) $\frac{3}{10}$ _____ 0.3   e) 0.8 _____ 0.79

   b) 0.2 _____ 0.20   d) 0.24 _____ 0.25   f) 1,000,000 _____ 1 million

8. Given that 18 × 45 = 810, work out 180 × 4,500

9. Write each of these as decimals:

   a) 3 tenths   b) $\frac{7}{100}$ c) $\frac{9}{1000}$ d) $1\frac{7}{10}$

10. Round 2,480 to the nearest hundred.

11. Round 18.5 to the nearest integer.

12. Which of these numbers is smallest?

    a) 0.6   b) $\frac{6}{10}$ c) 0.61   d) 0.555

13. Given that 42 × 36 = 1,512, work out

    a) 4.2 × 36   b) 42 × 3.6

14. Put these in order of size, starting with the smallest:

A	B	C	D
0.6	$\frac{8}{10}$	0.602	0.45

15. Find the number half way between 45 and 70

16. Calculate:

    a) 24 ÷ 2   c) 0.4 × 0.3   e) 24 ÷ 10

    b) 0.308 × 10   d) 3 ÷ 8   f) 12 × 100

17. Which of these does **NOT** equal seven tenths?

    a) 0.7   b) 0.70   c) $\frac{7}{10}$ d) 70

- -

Countdown Target :   31.3

Using each number only once, how close can you get to 31.3?
You can add, subtract, multiply or divide the numbers.

0.1	0.2	0.5	2	5	10	20

chapter 3: negative numbers

[Recommended Time: 9 - 12 hours]

Contents

ordering negative numbers

learn by heart

Numbers get smaller as we go down the number line

example

Which is bigger, -6 or -2?
> -2 because it is higher on the number line

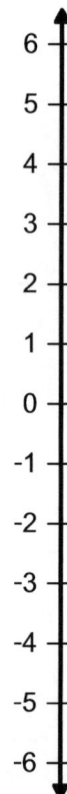

exercise 3a

1. From this list, circle the negative numbers: 6   -2.1   0   -4

2. Which of these numbers is the largest?

   -4   -3   -6   -2

3. What is the largest negative whole number?

4. Write each set of numbers in order, starting with the smallest:

   a) -4, 2, 0, -3 _____ _____ _____ _____

   b) 5, -5, -2, -7 _____ _____ _____ _____

   c) -9, 0, 3, -5 _____ _____ _____ _____

4. On the number line, which number is directly **below**:

   a) -3   b) -9   c) -24   d) -61

5. In each pair, which number is larger?

   a) -6 or -5   d) -2 or 0   g) -94 or -98

   b) -2 or 2   e) -6 or -4   h) -62 or -100

   c) -3 or -8   f) 2 or -3   i) -46 or 37

6. On the number line, which number is directly **above**:

   a) -6   b) -10   c) -15   d) -94

7. State the number that each arrow is pointing to on the number line.

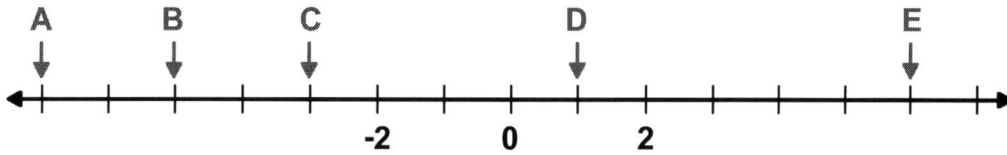

8. On the number line:

a) Which number is 3 places **above** -2?

b) Which number is 2 places **below** -5?

c) Which number is 4 places **below** 0?

d) Which number is 10 places **above** -3?

9. Each of these number sequences goes **down in equal steps**. Work out the missing numbers.

a) | 3 | 2 | | | | | | |

b) | 5 | 3 | | | | | | |

c) | 20 | 15 | | | | | | |

d) | 25 | 15 | | | | | | |

10. Complete these statements using the symbols >, < or =:

a) 5 _____ 0   d) -5 _____ -10   g) -100 _____ -50

b) -2 _____ 0   e) 6 _____ -3   h) 7 _____ -20

c) 0 _____ -4   f) -8 _____ -1   i) 0 _____ -8

11. Which of these numbers is closest to 0?

| -3 | | 4 | | -2 | | -8 | | 5 |

12. Put these numbers in order, from smallest to largest:

| -99 | | 82 | | 51 | | -82 | | -101 |

13. Write down all the negative whole numbers that are above -5.

14. Write down all the negative whole numbers that are between -8 and -2.

negative number journeys (addition)

learn by heart

When **adding a positive number**, move **up** the the number line.

examples

-8 + 3 = -5	-2 + 5 = 3	-12 + ___ = 5 = 17

exercise 3b

1. Write down the number that is 2 places above:

    a) 7   c) -2   e) -10   g) -40

    b) -7   d) -8   f) -1   h) -61

2. Calculate

    a) -4 + 4   b) -10 + 10   c) -3 + 3   d) -21 + 21

3. Calculate:

    a) -8 + 2   e) -1 + 2   i) 5 + 9

    b) -5 + 3   f) -4 + 5   j) -100 + 5

    c) -2 + 2   g) -7 + 10   k) -30 + 2

    d) -6 + 5   h) -20 + 5   l) -7 + 1

4. Complete the missing number: -16 + _____ = 0

5. Which of these calculations will have a negative answer?

A	B	C	D	E
-2 + 5	-3 + 4	-1 + 4	-7 + 9	-8 + 7

F	G	H	I	J
-6 + 1	-3 + 3	-4 + 6	-20 + 19	-12 + 21

6. Fill in the missing number: _____ + 34 = 0

7. True or False:

    a) -9 + 9 = 0   b) -6 + 10 = -4

8. Decide whether the answer will be positive, negative or zero:

   a) -4 + 5

   b) -10 + 8

   c) -3 + 6

   d) -8 + 8

   e) -200 + 45

   f) -1000 + 854

9. Calculate:

   a) -492 + 1

   b) -500 + 1

   c) -1000 + 1

10. Calculate:

   a) -10 + 6

   b) -8 + 12

   c) -15 + 10

   d) -6 + 10

   e) -20 + 30

   f) -30 + 20

   g) -5 + 18

   h) -3 + 16

   i) -29 + 27

11. True or False: -5 + 10 = 10 - 5

12. True or False: -4 + 15 = 15 - 4.

13. Complete the flow charts:

   a)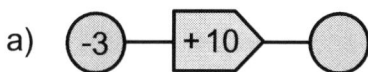

   b)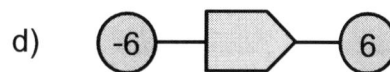

   c)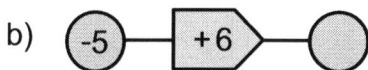

   d)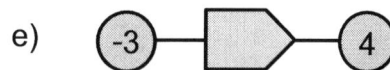

   e)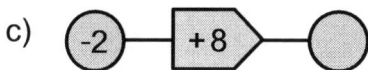

   f)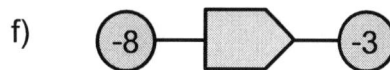

14. Fill in the blanks:

   a) -4 + ____ = 0

   b) -4 + ____ = 2

   c) -4 + ____ = 10

   d) -10 + ____ = -3

   e) -10 + ____ = -1

   f) -10 + ____ = 1

   g) -6 + ____ = -4

   h) -6 + ____ = 5

   i) -6 + ____ = 12

15. Complete these statements with the symbols: >, < or =:

   a) -3 + 4 ___ 0

   b) -6 + 6 ___ 0

   c) -60 + 75 ___ 0

   d) -45 + 20 ___ 0

   e) -12 + 36 ___ 0

   f) -82 + 103 ___ 0

negative number journeys (subtraction 1)

learn by heart

When **subtracting a positive number**, move **down** the number line.

Any number subtract itself = zero

examples

| 8 - 10 = -2 | 0 - 5 = -5 | 8 - ____ = -10 = 18 | 12 - 15 = - 3 |

You could find the difference between the numbers (3) then decide if it will be positive or negative

exercise 3c

1. Which number is 5 places below:

   a) 0   b) 2   c) -2   d) -5

2. Complete the missing number: 84 - _____ = 0

3. Calculate:

   a) 8 - 5   e) 9 - 2   i) 10 - 6

   b) 5 - 8   f) 2 - 9   j) 6 - 10

   c) 6 - 4   g) 8 - 4   k) 8 - 7

   d) 4 - 6   h) 4 - 8   l) 7 - 8

4. Which of these will have a negative answer?

   | A 5 - 8 | B 3 - 1 | C 4 - 8 | D 8 - 7 | E 43 - 30 |
   | F 8 - 5 | G 3 - 3 | H 6 - 13 | I 99 - 100 | J 30 - 43 |

5. Fill in the blanks:

   a) 12 - ____ = 0   d) 6 - ____ = 0   g) 8 - _____ = -1

   b) 12 - ____ = -1   e) 6 - ____ = -1   h) 8 - ____ = -3

   c) 12 - ____ = -5   f) 6 - ____ = -3   i) 8 - ____ = 5

6. Fill in the blank 777 - _____ = 0

7.   Which of these will have a negative answer? Circle two answers.

   a) 5 - 4   b) 5 - 5   c) 5 - 6   d) 5 - 7

8.   Fill in the missing number: _____ - 145 = -1

9.   Decide whether these statements are true or false:

   a) 8 - 5 = 5 - 8   b) 6 - 4 = -2   c) 9 - 9 = 0

10. Decide whether the answer will be positive or negative:

   a) 16 - 45   c) 5000 - 3857   e) 4356 - 599

   b) 324 - 165   d) 189 - 285   f) 710 - 985

11. Calculate:

   a) 20 - 8   d) 6 - 10   g) 7 - 10

   b) 8 - 20   e) 15 - 30   h) 20 - 6

   c) 8 - 12   f) 20 - 25   i) 4 - 20

12. True or false: *the answer to 22 – 23 is less than 0.*

13. True or False: 16 - 30 = 30 - 16

14. Calculate 4 - 4 - 4

15. Fill in the blanks:

   a) 3 - _____ = 0   c) 62 - _____ = -1   e) 174 - _____ = 0

   b) 4 - _____ = -1   d) 15 - _____ = -2   f) 45 - _____ = -2

challenging

16. Complete these statements with the symbols: >, < or =

   a) 27 - 27 _____ 0   b) 94 - 100 _____ 0   c) 101 - 100 _____ 0

17. Calculate 400 - 1000

18. Calculate 945 - 1000

19. If **a** and **b** are two different numbers, is it possible that: **a** - **b** = 0?

negative number journeys (subtraction 2)

example

-5 - 4

= -9

In total you will travel 9 places down the number line

exercise 3d

1. Write down the number that is 2 places below:

   a) -3   c) 0   e) -10

   b) -8   d) 1   f) -15

2. Calculate:

   a) -3 - 7   d) -7 - 7   g) -4 - 10

   b) -6 - 2   e) -5 - 5 - 5   h) 4 - 10

   c) -4 - 6   f) 8 - 10   i) 3 - 5

3. Fill in the blanks:

   a) 7 - ☐ = 0   d) 8 - ☐ = 5   g) 4 - ☐ = -1

   b) -4 - ☐ = -10   e) 10 - ☐ = -10   h) 7 - ☐ = -1

   c) -3 - ☐ = -6   f) -6 - ☐ = -9   i) 9 - ☐ = -1

4. Calculate -100 - 100 - 100

5. Ashraf says that to calculate -42 - 20, we can add together 42 and 20 and then make the answer negative. Will this work?

6. Calculate:

   a) 12 - 12   d) -5 - 3   g) -9 - 2

   b) 2 - 5   e) 5 - 3   h) 2 - 9

   c) -2 - 5   f) 5 - 6   i) 12 - 9

7. Calculate 5 - 5 - 5

8. Calculate -700 - 230

negative number journeys mixed problems

exercise 3e

1. Calculate:

   a) 6 - 8

   b) -2 + 9

   c) -3 + 3

   d) 4 - 9

   e) -1 - 2

   f) 10 - 4

   g) -5 + 3

   h) -7 + 9

   i) 10 + 4

   j) -10 - 7

   k) 2 - 4

   l) -11 + 11

   m) -8 - 8

   n) -3 - 5

   o) -1 + 8

2. Which of these calculations equal zero?

A -4 + 4	B 8 - 18	C -3 + 5	D -2 + 2	E -5 - 5	F 4 - 4
G -83 + 83	H 7 + 7	I -51 + 15	J -9 + 9	K -3 + 7	L 9 - 8

3. Work out the missing numbers to make the calculations correct.

   a) -1 + ☐ = 3

   b) -7 + ☐ = -2

   c) -2 - ☐ = -10

   d) 4 - ☐ = -6

   e) -9 + ☐ = -3

   f) -6 - ☐ = -12

4. Calculate:

   a) 25 - 26

   b) 34 - 35

   c) 45 - 46

5. Calculate 2 - 2 - 2

6. Which two calculations below have the same answer?

   a) -7 + 1

   b) 1 - 7

   c) -7 - 1

   d) 7 - 1

7. Complete the statements:

   a) -4 + _____ = 1

   b) -2 + _____ = 1

   c) -6 + _____ = 1

8. Complete the flow charts:

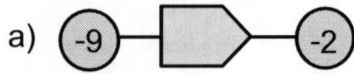

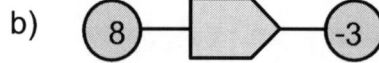

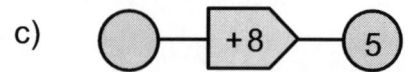

a) (-9)—[ ]—(-2)   b) (8)—[ ]—(-3)   c) ( )—[+8]—(5)

9. Fill in the missing numbers:

a) -6 + [ ] = 0

b) 3 - [ ] = -2

c) -4 - [ ] = -8

d) -3 + [ ] = 10

e) 6 - [ ] = -4

f) -2 + [ ] = 5

g) 8 - [ ] = -2

h) -2 - [ ] = -10

i) -7 + [ ] = -3

j) 4 - [ ] = 0

10. Use the numbers in the box on the right to make these sums true:

[5] + [ ] = [ ]

[ ] - [6] = [ ]

[ ] - [ ] = [-3]

-2	0
5	7
4	4

11. Which of the following have **negative** answers?

A 96 - 132   B -67 + 59   C -34 - 97   D -48 + 56   E -85 + 89

12. Calculate:

a) -25 + 15

b) -20 + 8

c) -35 + 10

f) -9 + 20

g) -40 + 12

h) -16 + 20

k) -20 + 15

l) -30 + 45

m) -16 + 8

13. Work out:

a) 4 - 5 - 6

d) -2 - 2 - 2

b) -2 + 1 + 2

e) -3 - 3 - 3 - 3

c) -3 - 4 - 5

f) -6 + 6 + 6

Negative Journeys Match

Complete these calculations and find your answer at the bottom. Record your answers in a table.

A	B	C	D
-4 + 8	-6 - 3	-12 + 2	4 - 10

E	F	G	H
-6 - 2	8 + 3	-4 + 2	-12 - 3

I	J	K	L
-1 - 4	-8 - 8	6 - 9	14 - 14

M	N	O	P
0 - 7	6 - 10	-2 + 5	-20 - 10

Q	R	S	T
12 - 13	-13 + 14	-9 + 11	-50 - 50

U	V	W	X
-5 + 10	-2 - 18	1 - 19	1 - 1.5

- -

jumbled answers

5   11   -100

0

2   -20   4   -30

-8   -4

-5   -2   -6   1   -1

-7   -10

-0.5   -15   3

-3   -18   -16   -9

A	
B	
C	
D	
E	
F	
G	
H	
I	
J	
K	
L	
M	
N	
O	
P	
Q	
R	
S	
T	
U	
V	
W	
X	

Number Line Journeys ⭐ extra challenge

Fill in the empty boxes with numbers or operations to complete these number line journeys.

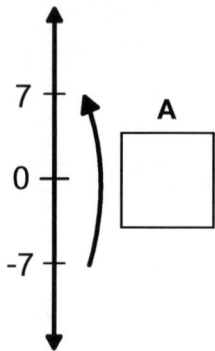

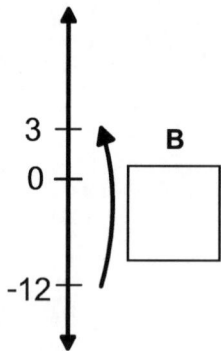

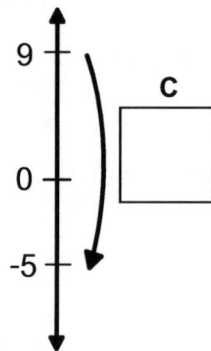

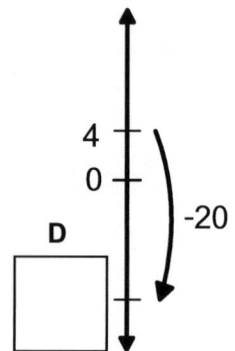

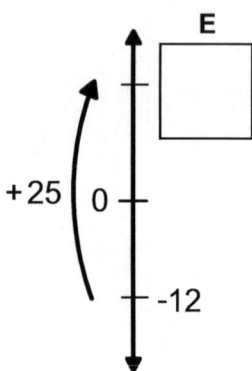

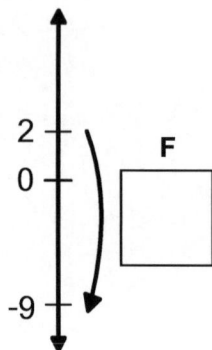

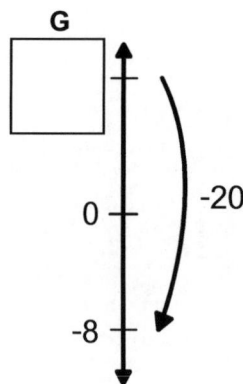

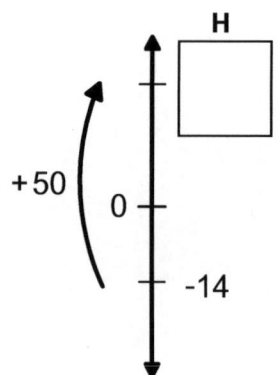

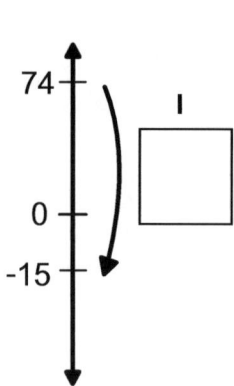

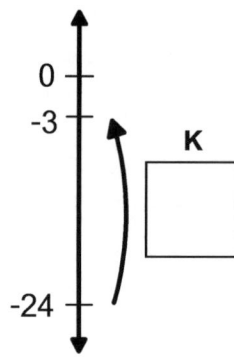

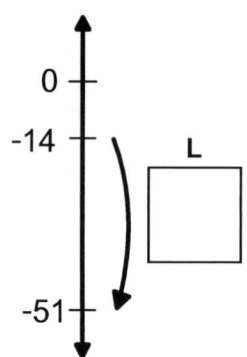

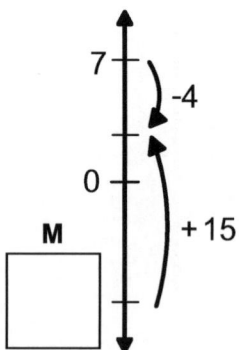

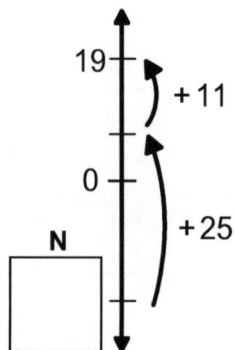

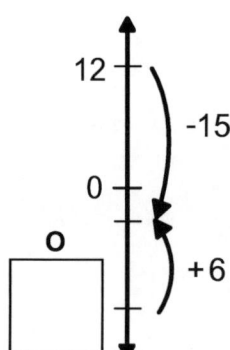

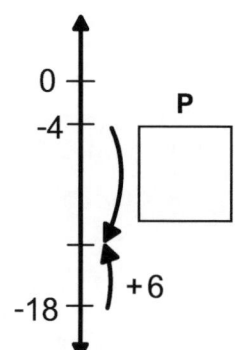

A
7
0
-7

B
3
0
-12

C
9
0
-5

D
4
0
-20

E
+25
0
-12

F
2
0
-9

G
0
-20
-8

H
+50
0
-14

I
74
0
-15

J
+70
0
-34

K
0
-3
-24

L
0
-14
-51

M
7
-4
0
+15

N
19
+11
0
+25

O
12
-15
0
+6

P
0
-4
-18
+6

adding a negative

When **adding a negative number**, move **down** the number line.

examples

5 + -2
$= 5 - 2$
$= 3$

-5 + -2
$= -5 - 2$
$= -7$

exercise 3f

1. Calculate:

   a) 10 + -3   f) -6 + -6   k) -5 + -3

   b) 5 + -5   g) -3 + -2   l) -2 + -7

   c) 6 + -3   h) -9 + -3   m) -6 + -4

   d) 4 + -4   i) 7 + -3   n) 0 + -9

   e) 10 + -7   j) 8 + -5   o) -10 + -2

2. Which of the following is the same as: 7 + -3?

   a) 7 + 3   b) 7 - 3   c) 3 - 7   d) 3 + 7

3. Complete the statement: 5 + _____ = 0

4. True or False: Two negative numbers can add up to make a positive number.

5. Which of the following is the same as 4 + -6?

   a) -4 - 6   b) -4 + 6   c) 6 - 4   d) 4 - 6

6. Complete the missing numbers:

   a) -7 + _____ = 0   d) -3 + _____ = -4   g) -9 + _____ = -10

   b) 20 + _____ = 0   e) 8 + _____ = 2   h) -2 + _____ = -5

   c) 5 + _____ = 2   f) -4 + _____ = 0   i) 20 + _____ = 15

7. Calculate

   a) -3 + -3 + -3   b) -4 + -4 + -4

Pyramid Puzzles

Copy and complete the pyramids by adding two numbers to make the box directly above.

a)
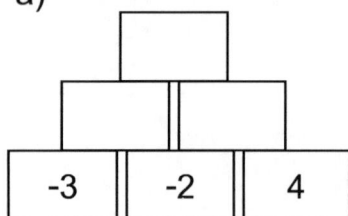

-3 | -2 | 4

b)

-4 | -5 | -1

c)
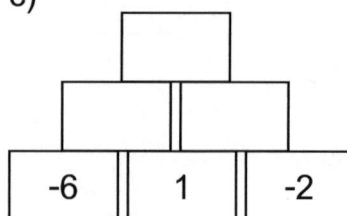

-6 | 1 | -2

d)
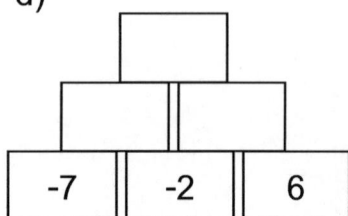

-7 | -2 | 6

e)
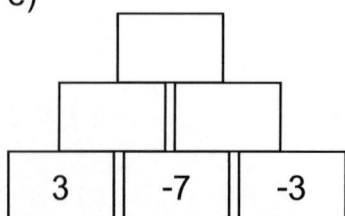

3 | -7 | -3

f)
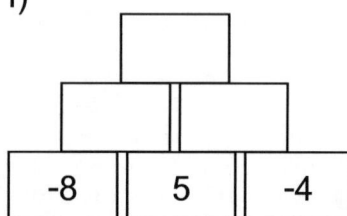

-8 | 5 | -4

g)
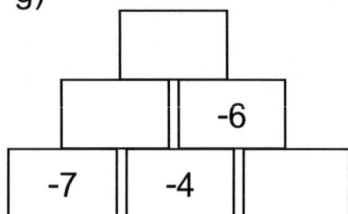

-6

-7 | -4

h)
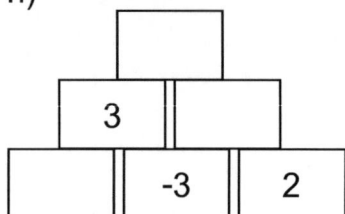

3

-3 | 2

i)
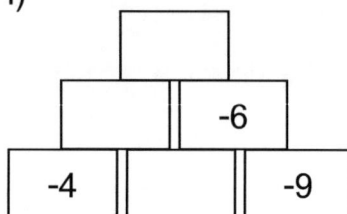

-6

-4 | -9

j)
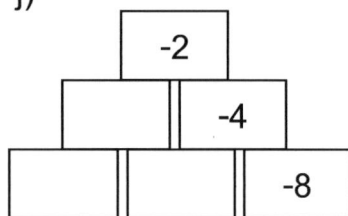

-2

-4

-8

k)
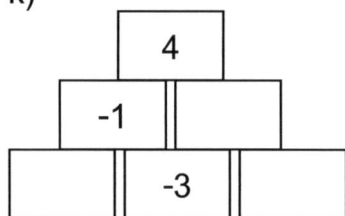

4

-1

-3

l)
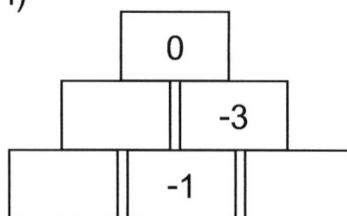

0

-3

-1

m)
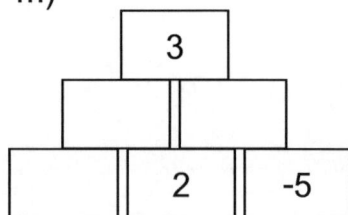

3

2 | -5

n)
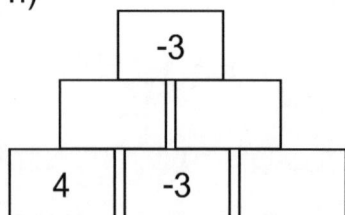

-3

4 | -3

o)
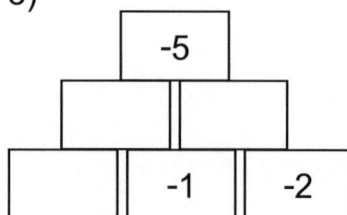

-5

-1 | -2

subtracting a negative

learn by heart

When **subtracting a negative number**, move **up** the number line.

examples

$5 - -2$
$= 5 + 2$
$= 7$

$-5 - -2$
$= -5 + 2$
$= -3$

exercise 3g

1. Calculate:

   a) 3 - -5

   b) -2 - - 4

   c) 7 - - 10

   d) 8 - - 4

   e) -4 - - 4

   f) -6 - -6

   g) -3 - -2

   h) 9 - -3

   i) 7 - -3

   j) 8 - -5

   k) -5 - -3

   l) -2 - -7

   m) -6 - -4

   n) 3 - - 4

   o) 2 - - 8

2. Which of these is the same as 5 - - 10?

   a) 5 - 10   b) 10 - 5   c) -5 + 10   d) 5 + 10

3. Which of the following will have a negative answer?

   a) 8 - 10   b) 8 - - 10   c) -8 + 10   d) 10 - 8

4. Complete the missing number: 6 - _____ = 10

5. True or False: Subtraction always makes things smaller.

6. Complete the missing numbers:

   a) 8 - _____ = 0

   b) 10 - _____ = 15

   c) 6 - _____ = 12

   d) -2 - _____ = 0

   e) -3 - _____ = 0

   f) 14 - _____ = 20

   g) 16 - _____ = 10

   h) 4 - _____ = 8

   i) -1 - _____ = 5

7. Which of the following has the same answer as 42 - -36?

   a) 42 - 36   b) 42 + 36   c) 36 - 42   d) -42 - 36

8. Calculate:

a) 8 - 8   f) 4 - 6   k) 8 - 5

b) -3 - 5   g) 4 - - 6   l) 5 - 8

c) 2 - 8   h) -2 - - 5   m) 7 - - 3

d) -5 - 3   i) -3 - 4   n) -4 - - 5

e) 10 - 15   j) -8 - 10   o) -6 - - 6

9. Which of these calculations have a negative answer?

A	B	C	D	E
-4 - - 2	-4 - - 6	2 - - 9	-3 - - 6	-5 - - 3

F	G	H	I	J
-2 - - 9	4 - - 2	-1 - - 1	-8 - - 6	-1 - - 2

K	L	M	N	O
-7 - - 12	-11 - - 8	-9 - - 16	-12 - - 18	-7 - - 8

10. Work out the missing numbers to make the calculations correct.

a) [6] - [ ] = [7]   b) [-3] - [ ] = [3]

c) [-3] - [ ] = [-8]   d) [0] - [ ] = [5]

e) [ ] - [-7] = [-1]   f) [ ] - [-10] = [13]

multiple choice

Choose the correct answer for each question:

1. Calculate -6 - 4

   a) 10   b) -10

   c) 2   d) -2

2. Calculate -3 - - 6

   a) 9   b) -9

   c) 3   d) -3

3. Calculate -7 - - 5

   a) -12   b) 2

   c) -2   d) 12

4. Calculate 3 - - 2

   a) 1   b) -1

   c) 5   d) -5

adding & subtracting negatives mixed practice

exercise 3h

1. Calculate:

    a) -4 + 8   f) -5 + 8   k) -8 + 3

    b) 3 - 7   g) 4 - -1   l) 7 + -4

    c) -2 + 2   h) -1 + -5   m) -2 - -6

    d) -7 - -3   i) -6 - 5   n) -9 + 6

    e) -4 + -5   j) 4 - 9   o) -3 - -7

2. Work out the missing numbers to make the calculations correct.

    a) [-5] + [ ] = [1]   b) [2] - [ ] = [6]

    c) [-1] - [ ] = [-7]   d) [1] + [ ] = [-9]

    e) [ ] + [-4] = [-3]   f) [ ] - [4] = [-7]

matching activity

3. Match the questions to their answers.

A -9 - 1	F 3 - 10	K -1 - -11
B -8 + -3	G -3 - 3	L 2 - -4
C -4 - -5	H -7 - -7	M 3 + -7
D -12 + 3	I -3 + 8	N 2 + -4
E -4 + -1	J -2 - -4	O -4 - -3

-6

10   -5

2   -2

-7   -10

-11   1

-1   0

-4   -9

5   6

A	B	C	D	E	F	G	H	I	J	K	L	M	N	O

4. Which number is directly below:

   a) -4   b) -10   c) -15   d) -50

5. Calculate:

   a) 2 + -3   b) -3 + -1   c) -4 + 3

   d) -1 - -4   e) -1 - 4   f) 3 - -7

   g) -4 + -2   h) 1 + -1   i) -6 - 3

6. Use the symbols >, < and = to make these statements true:

   a) -10 + 6 ( ) 0   f) -7 + 8 ( ) 0

   b) -5 - - 5 ( ) 0   g) 1 - - 4 ( ) 0

   c) 8 - - 10 ( ) 0   h) -3 - - 4 ( ) 0

7. Work out the missing numbers to make the calculations correct.

   a) [4] + [ ] = [1]   b) [-3] + [ ] = [-1]

   c) [-5] + [ ] = [4]   d) [-1] + [ ] = [-11]

   e) [ ] + [-2] = [-8]   f) [ ] + [-9] = [7]

sorting activity

Will these calculations give a positive, negative or zero answer?
Sort them into the correct categories.

| A -3 + 6 | F 2 + -2 | K -5 - -2 |

| B -2 + -7 | G 7 - 7 | L -7 - -9 |

| C 3 - -4 | H -3 - -4 | M -13 + -8 |

| D -10 + 8 | I -1 + -1 | N -12 + 12 |

| E 4 + -3 | J -5 - 12 | O -9 - -15 |

Positive Answers

Negative Answers

Answer Equals Zero

Negative Numbers Mystery Activity

Use the clues to complete the grid.

the number in the top left is 3 less than -4

the number in the top right is 3 - 8

the number below -5 is 10 - 16

the number below -7 is 2 less than 0

the top row adds up to 0

the number in the bottom left is -4 + 8

the number next to 4 is -3 - 6

the numbers in the right hand column add up to -15

	0	

Missing Numbers Puzzle

Use the numbers below to make the calculations on the right correct.

11	1	-1
-2	-3	-4
-5	-6	-7
-8		

A   [ ] + -3 = -6

B   -5 + -2 = [ ]

C   6 + [ ] = 5

D   [ ] - [ ] = -5

E   6 - [ ] = [ ]

F   [ ] - [ ] = [ ]

93

multiplying negative numbers

learn by heart

Negative × Negative = Positive   Negative × Positive = Negative

Product = the result of multiplying

The order here doesn't matter, positive × negative = negative

examples

Calculate -3 × -5
= 15

Calculate -3 × 5
= -15

Calculate 3 × -5
= -15

Calculate -2 × -3 × -4
= -24

exercise 3i

1. Calculate

   a) -2 × 3

   b) -2 × -3

   c) 4 × -2

   d) -4 × 1

   e) -4 × 0

   f) -4 × -1

   g) 7 × -1

   h) -5 × -5

   i) -5 × 5

2. Fill in the gaps:

   a) -2 × ____ = 20

   b) -2 × ____ = -20

   c) -5 × ____ = 20

   d) 10 × ____ = 100

   e) 3 × ____ = -30

   f) -10 × ____ = -100

   g) -6 × ____ = 36

   h) 6 × ____ = -36

   i) -2 × ____ = -12

3. The product of -2 and 5 is _____

4. The product of -6 and -4 is _____

5. The product of -2 and _____ is 0

6. Gemma says that -427 × -23 = -9821
   Without calculating, explain how you know she is definitely wrong.

7. True or false?

   a) -4 × -4 = -16

   b) -4 × 2 = -8

   c) 5 × -2 = 10

8. Given that 19 × 24 = 456, work out:

   a) -19 × 24

   b) -19 × -24

   c) 19 × -24

9. Fill in the blanks:

a) -3 × _____ = 24

b) 3 × _____ = -18

c) _____ × 4 = -16

d) _____ × -2 = 22

e) -6 × _____ = 36

f) _____ × -3 = 0

g) -17 × _____ = 17

h) -1 × _____ = 200

more challenging

10. Calculate:

a) -2 × 3 × 4

b) -2 × -3 × 4

c) -2 × -3 × -4

11. What is the product of -3, -5 and -2?

12. Calculate

a) -3 × -3 × -3

b) -1 × -2 × -2

c) -1 × -3 × -3

d) -2 × -3 × -3

e) -1 × -2 × -3 × -4

f) -1 × -2 × -2 × -3

g) -1 × -1 × -1 × -1 × -1

h) -1 × -1 × -1 × -1 × -1 × -1

i) -3 × -2 × -1 × -1

j) -4 × -3 × -2 × -1

mixed multiplications, additions & subtractions

13. Calculate:

a) -4 + 6

b) -4 × 6

c) -4 + -6

d) 7 × -3

e) -3 × -7

f) -3 + -7

g) -8 - 2

h) -8 × 2

i) 8 + -2

j) 5 × -5

k) 5 + -5

l) -5 × -5

dividing negative numbers

<u>learn by heart</u>

It is also true that
Positive ÷ Negative =
Negative

Negative ÷ Negative = Positive	Negative ÷ Positive = Negative

<u>examples</u>

$15 \div -3 = -5$	$-15 \div -3 = 5$	$-15 \div 3 = -5$	$\dfrac{-15}{3} = -5$	$\dfrac{-20}{-5} = 4$

<u>exercise 3j</u>

1. Calculate:

   a) $-20 \div 5$

   b) $-20 \div -5$

   c) $20 \div -5$

   d) $-20 \div 1$

   e) $-20 \div 2$

   f) $\dfrac{-15}{-5}$

   g) $\dfrac{12}{-3}$

   h) $0 \div -5$

   i) $\dfrac{10}{-10}$

2. Calculate:

   a) $\dfrac{-40}{8}$

   b) $\dfrac{-22}{-11}$

   c) $\dfrac{14}{-7}$

   d) $\dfrac{-100}{2}$

   e) $\dfrac{-25}{-5}$

   f) $\dfrac{0}{-3}$

   g) $\dfrac{14}{-1}$

   h) $\dfrac{-240}{-10}$

3. Fill in the blanks:

   a) $-30 \div \rule{2cm}{0.15mm} = -3$

   b) $15 \div \rule{2cm}{0.15mm} = -5$

   e) $-7 \div \rule{2cm}{0.15mm} = 1$

   f) $\rule{2cm}{0.15mm} \div -5 = 0$

4. Complete these statements to make them true:

   a) $-5 \times \boxed{} = 25$

   b) $40 \div \boxed{} = 8$

   c) $-3 \times \boxed{} = -27$

   d) $-5 \times \boxed{} = -20$

   e) $30 \div \boxed{} = 6$

   f) $24 \div \boxed{} = -4$

   g) $-60 \div \boxed{} = 20$

   h) $-4 \times \boxed{} = -32$

   i) $-7 \times \boxed{} = 28$

   j) $44 \div \boxed{} = -4$

multiplying & dividing negative numbers

exercise 3k

1. Calculate:

   a) -3 × 5

   b) -6 ÷ -2

   c) -8 × -3

   d) 8 ÷ -2

   e) -3 × -10

   f) -40 ÷ 10

   g) -20 ÷ 5

   h) -6 × 10

   i) -2 × -12

   j) -7 × -3

   k) -4 × -4

   l) -30 ÷ -6

   m) -15 ÷ 5

   n) -2 × -5

   o) 50 ÷ -2

2. Calculate:

   a) $\frac{-18}{2}$

   b) $\frac{-12}{-6}$

   c) $\frac{-27}{3}$

   d) $\frac{9}{-3}$

3. Work out:

   a) double -4

   b) half of -12

   c) half of -3

4. Can you find a pair of numbers that add up to -4 and multiply to make -12?

5. Given that **26 × 17 = 442**, work out the value of:

   a) 26 × -17

   b) -26 × -17

6. Arrange the number to make each set of calculations correct:

   a)

   ☐ × ☐ = 12

   ☐ × ☐ = -12

   ☐ × ☐ = 5

   [-1] [-2] [-3] [-4] [-5] [6]

   b)

   ☐ ÷ ☐ = -2

   ☐ × ☐ = 18

   ☐ × ☐ = -24

   [-12] [-8] [-6] [-3] [2] [4]

   c)

   ☐ ÷ ☐ = 4

   ☐ ÷ ☐ = -3

   ☐ ÷ ☐ = 2

   [-24] [-18] [-12] [-9] [-3] [8]

   d)

   ☐ ÷ ☐ = -2

   ☐ × ☐ = -24

   ☐ ÷ ☐ = 2

   [-6] [-6] [-4] [-3] [4] [8]

four operations with negative numbers

learn by heart

The rules for adding and subtracting negative numbers are different from the rules for multiplying and dividing

examples

$-3 \times -4 = 12$ $-3 + -4 = -7$

exercise 31

1. Calculate:

   a) -5 + 3   d) 7 - 10   g) 2 - 4   j) -5 - 3

   b) -2 - 3   e) 4 - 5   h) 6 - 3   k) -2 + 2

   c) - 6 - 10   f) -3 + 3   i) 8 + -3   l) -4 + 6

2. True or false: A *negative* **add** *a negative is a positive*

3. True or false: A *negative* **times** *a negative is a positive*

4. Calculate:

   a) -4 + 8   e) -7 × -3   i) 100 ÷ -2

   b) -2 × -4   f) -4 + 1   j) 3 - -5

   c) - 5 - 2   g) -20 ÷ 5   k) -7 + 2

   d) -10 ÷ 2   h) -6 - 3   l) -4 × 6

four operations puzzle

5. Use 8 of the numbers below to make the sums on the right true:

-3	3	10
4	-2	-9
7	-4	-12

☐ - ☐ = -3

☐ + ☐ = 0

☐ × ☐ = -27

☐ ÷ ☐ = 4

6. Complete these addition and subtraction chains:

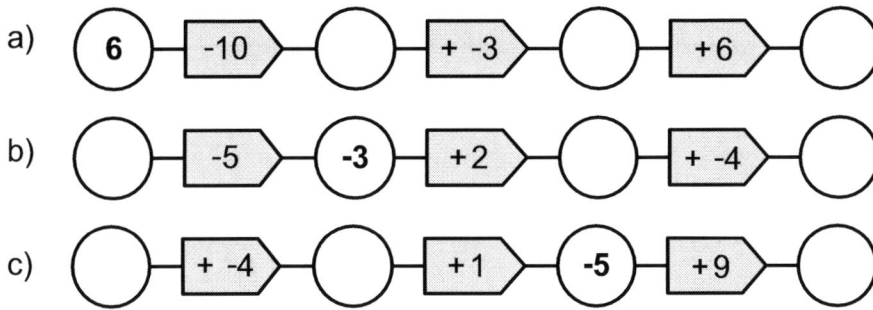

a) (6) —[-10]— ( ) —[+ -3]— ( ) —[+6]— ( )

b) ( ) —[-5]— (-3) —[+2]— ( ) —[+ -4]— ( )

c) ( ) —[+ -4]— ( ) —[+1]— (-5) —[+9]— ( )

7. Calculate:

a) 2 + -3

b) -3 + -1

c) -4 + 3

d) -1 - -4

e) -1 - 4

f) 3 - -7

g) -4 + -2

h) 1 + -1

i) -6 - 3

8. Work out:

a) $\frac{15}{-3}$

b) $\frac{-21}{-7}$

c) $\frac{-20}{5}$

d) $\frac{16}{-8}$

9. Complete these number pyramids.
   Add side by side numbers to make the box above.

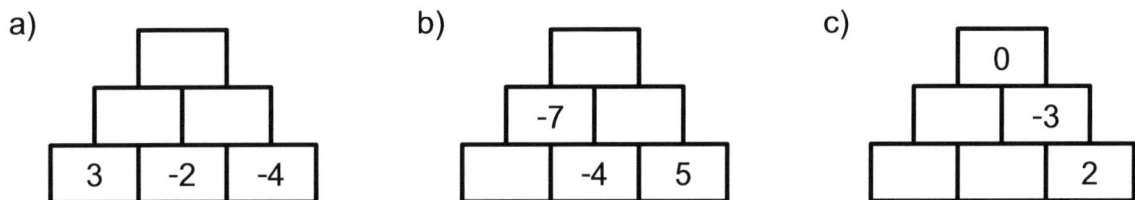

a)

3	-2	-4

b)

-7		
	-4	5

c)

	0	
		-3
		2

10. Calculate:

a) -12 ÷ 3

c) -12 - 3

e) -12 ÷ -3

g) 12 + -3

b) -12 + 3

d) -12 × -3

f) 12 - - 3

h) -12 + -3

11. Work out the missing number in each calculation:

a) -6 × _____ = -24

b) -40 ÷ _____ = -5

c) -3 × _____ = 18

d) -5 × _____ = 25

e) -8 ÷ _____ = 8

f) _____ × -7 = 63

g) _____ ÷ -4 = 12

h) _____ ÷ -6 = 12

12. True or false? If two negative numbers are added, the result can be a positive number.

Negative Numbers Countdown ⭐ extra challenge

In each section, use the four numbers on the left to make the target number on the right. You do not need to use all the numbers and you can only use each number once. You can add, subtract, multiply or divide in any order.

A | -5 | | -1 | | 2 | | 3 |

target
-14

B | -4 | | -3 | | -2 | | -1 |

target
-10

C | -4 | | -3 | | -2 | | -1 |

target
9

D | -5 | | -2 | | 3 | | 4 |

target
-11

E | -9 | | -6 | | -3 | | 2 |

target
0

F | -10 | | -4 | | 1 | | 7 |

target
39

exercise 3m

1. Calculate:

   a) -4 - 2

   b) -3 + 1

   c) -5 × -2

   d) -1 + 3

   e) -6 - 2

   f) 10 ÷ -2

   g) -15 ÷ -3

   h) 2 × -4

   i) 8 - - 2

   j) 5 + -3

   k) -2 + -3

   l) -1 + 8

   m) 9 - 10

   n) -4 - 3

   o) -2 - - 3

   p) 24 - 25

   q) 22 + -22

   r) -16 - 4

2. Which of these have a negative answer?

   a) 6 - - 8

   b) -6 × -8

   c) -12 + 10

   d) -9 - -10

3. **Multiplication Arithmagons:** *The numbers in the circles multiply to make the numbers in the squares between them.*

   a)

   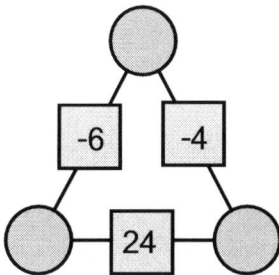

   b)

   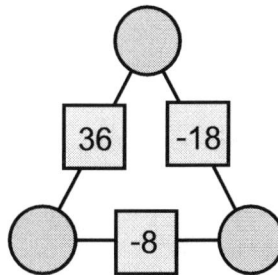

   c)

   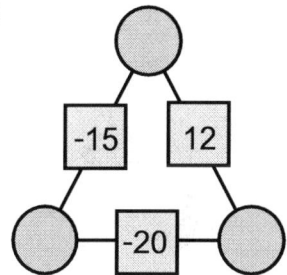

four operations puzzle

4. Use 8 of the numbers below to make the sums on the right true:

-15	-11	-2
3	-1	11
10	6	-3

   $\square$ - $\square$ = -8

   $\square$ + $\square$ = 0

   $\square$ × $\square$ = 30

   $\square$ ÷ $\square$ = 5

Negative Numbers
Code Breaker

Calculate the following and find your
answer in the code box.
Write the words you find down
to reveal an inspirational message!

code box

-24 = just	-9 = The	-3 = to	5 = way
-21 = wonder	-8 = weakness	-2 = front	7 = up.
-17 = good	-7.5 = find	-1.5 = more	6 = time.
-16 = try	-7 = one	-1 = path	9 = giving
-14 = Our	-6 = certain	0 = phone	11 = is
-11 = wait	-5 = greatest	2 = call	12 = always
-10 = in	-4 = succeed	4 = most	16 = lies

a) -7 × 2 = _____ =   **Our**

b) -7 + 2 = _____ =

c) -5 - 3 = _____ =

d) -4 × -4 = _____ =

e) -20 ÷ 2 = _____ =

f) 6 - -3 = _____ =

g) 2 + -9 = _____ =

h) -4 - 5 = _____ =

i) 6 + -2 = _____ =

j) -7 - - 1 = _____ =

k) 8 + -3 = _____ =

l) 15 ÷ -5 = _____ =

m) -4 × 1 = _____ =

n) 14 + -3 = _____ =

o) -3 × -4 = _____ =

p) -24 ÷ 8 = _____ =

q) -8 - 8 = _____ =

r) -12 + -12 = _____ =

s) 8 - 15 = _____ =

t) -15 ÷ 10 = _____ =

u) -1 × -2 × 3 = _____ =

–Quote by Thomas Edison

cumulative review (chapters 1-3)

exercise 3n

1. Write in digits:

   a) Three hundred and fifty two

   b) Five thousand and eight

   c) Twenty six thousand and fourteen

   d) Nine hundred thousand

   e) Four hundred and six thousand

   f) 1 million and five

2. Which of these is 8 tenths?

   a) 0.08   b) 0.8   c) 8.0   d) 80

3. Round 483 to the nearest hundred

4. Work out half of each of these numbers:

   a) 9   b) 42   c) 90   d) 81

5. Round each of these numbers to the nearest whole number:

   a) 4.8   b) 2.67   c) 3.5   d) 27.405

6. Write each of these as decimals:

   a) 7 tenths

   b) 8 hundredths

   c) 4 tens + 4 tenths

   d) $\frac{3}{100}$

   e) $\frac{4}{1000}$

   f) $6\frac{1}{10}$

   g) $3\frac{5}{100}$

   h) 5 hundreds + $\frac{5}{100}$

   i) $90 + 4 + \frac{1}{10} + \frac{3}{100}$

7. Which number is 5 places above -3 on the number line?

8. Write these numbers in order, from smallest to largest: -3,   0,   2,   -8,   -1.5

9. What goes in the gap?   -145 + _____ = 1

10. Calculate:

   a) 0.2 + 0.8

   b) 3 × 100

   c) 42 ÷ 10

   d) 1 - 0.3

   e) 0.4 × 6

   f) 0.5 × 10

   g) 2.1 + 0.8

   h) 520 ÷ 10

   i) 0.3 × 100

   j) 0.5 × 0.3

   k) 0.6 + 1.4

   l) 1 - 0.1

11. Put these in order of size, starting with the smallest:

   A 0.7   B 0.07

   C 0.71   D 0.701   _____ _____ _____ _____

12. Which of these statements are TRUE?

   A -6 < 0   B 5 > 0   C -3 > 0   D -6 < -1   E 0 > -1

   F -2 = 2   G -2 > 0   H -5 < -2   I 4 > -4   J 4 < 8

13. Use short division or place value to write each fraction as a decimal:

   a) $\frac{4}{9}$

   b) $\frac{8}{10}$

   c) $\frac{1}{5}$

   d) $\frac{3}{100}$

   e) $\frac{1}{4}$

   f) $\frac{18}{100}$

Countdown Target : -84

Using each number only once, how close can you get to -84?
You can add, subtract, multiply or divide the numbers.

| -2 | -1 | 1 | 2 | 4 | 8 | 10 |

Decimal Magic Squares

In each magic square, the rows, columns and diagonals all add up to the same number. Fill in the missing numbers.

A

0.3		0.1
0.2		0.6
		0.5

B

0.4	0.9	0.2
	0.5	
0.8		

C

0.6		1
1.3		
0.8	0.7	

D

0.7		0.5
	0.4	
		0.1

E

0.9		
1.4	0.7	1.2

F

		0.7
	0.6	
0.5		0.9

G

	1.3	
	1.1	
	0.9	1.4

H

		0.8
0.5	0.7	
0.6		

I

1.7	2.2	1.5
	1.4	

Countdown Target : 4.2

Using each number only once, how close can you get to 4.2?
You can add, subtract, multiply or divide the numbers.

0.01	0.1	0.3	1	2	5	10

chapter 4: fractions

[Recommended Time : 12 - 14 hours]

Contents

fraction notation

learn by heart

> Fraction: a number of **equal parts**

> Numerator: the top number in a fraction - it tells us the number of parts selected

> Denominator: the bottom number in a fraction - it tells us how many **equal parts** to split each whole into.

$$\frac{2}{5}$$

> When all of the parts are selected, it equals 1 whole, so $\frac{5}{5}$ = 1 whole, or $\frac{8}{8}$ = 1 whole.

> 1 of 2 equal parts = $\frac{1}{2}$ = one half

> 1 of 3 equal parts = $\frac{1}{3}$ = one third

> 1 of 4 equal parts = $\frac{1}{4}$ = one quarter

> 1 of 5 equal parts = $\frac{1}{5}$ = one fifth

exercise 4a

1. Write in fraction notation:

   a) Two Thirds
   b) One Fifth

   c) Six Sevenths
   d) Eight Tenths

   e) Three Quarters
   f) Four Ninths

2. Six children share a cake equally. What fraction does each child get?

3. Nine children share a bottle of lemonade equally.
   What fraction does each child get?

4. In which diagram is $\frac{1}{3}$ shaded blue? Explain your answer.

   a)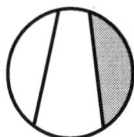
   b)
   c)
   d)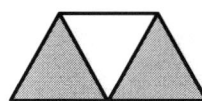

5. Copy the diagram and:

   a) shade $\frac{1}{5}$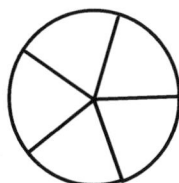
   b) Shade $\frac{2}{5}$
   c) Shade $\frac{5}{5}$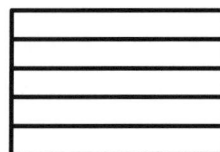

6. What fraction is shaded in each diagram?

a) 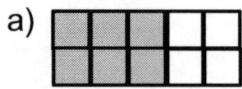 b) 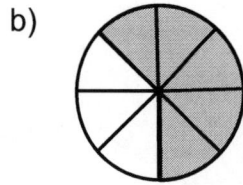 c) 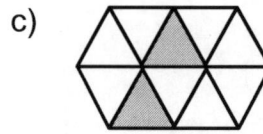 d)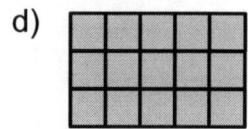

7. Which number does each arrow point to?

a)
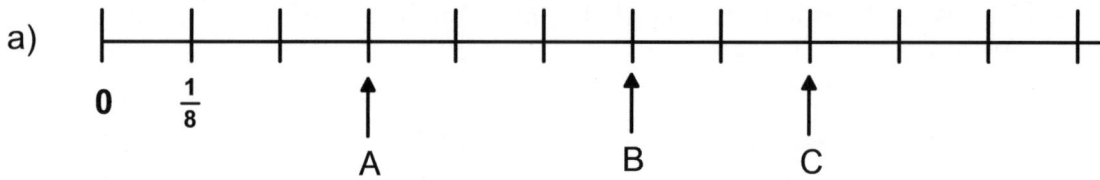

0   $\frac{1}{8}$ A   B   C

b)
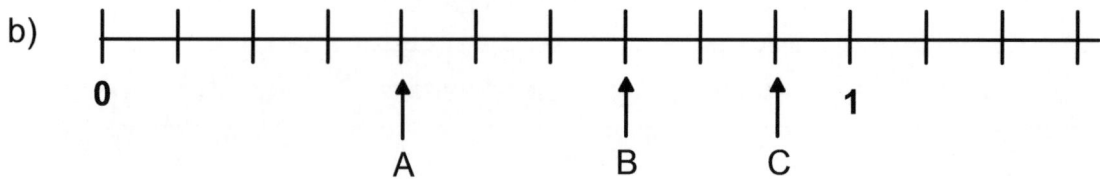

0   A   B   C   1

c)
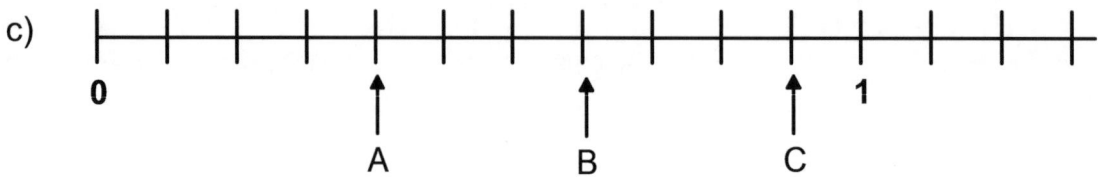

0   A   B   C   1

d)
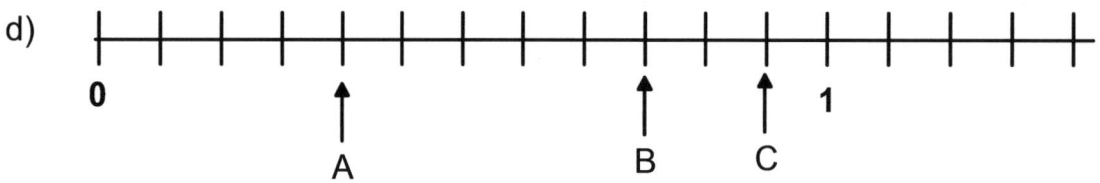

0   A   B   C   1

e)
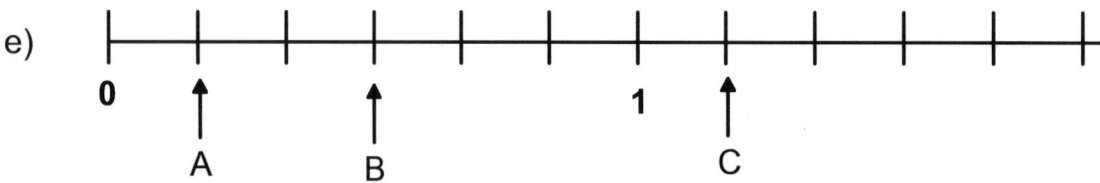

0   A   B   1   C

f)
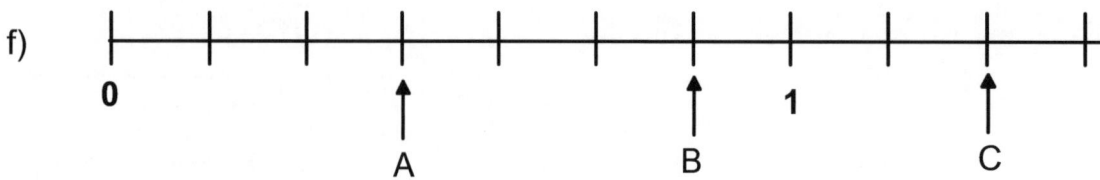

0   A   B   1   C

learn by heart

Like Fractions: fractions with the same denominators, e.g. $\frac{1}{5}$ and $\frac{3}{5}$

they can be added or subtracted directly, e.g. $\frac{1}{5} + \frac{3}{5} = \frac{4}{5}$

A whole unit: 1, or the sum of all the parts, e.g. $\frac{7}{7}$ or $\frac{9}{9}$

exercise 4b

1. Calculate:

   a) $\frac{1}{5} + \frac{2}{5}$

   b) $\frac{3}{7} + \frac{4}{7}$

   c) $\frac{9}{10} - \frac{3}{10}$

   d) $\frac{2}{7} + \frac{1}{7} + \frac{3}{7}$

   e) $\frac{5}{7} - \frac{1}{7}$

   f) $\frac{5}{8} - \frac{5}{8}$

   g) $\frac{3}{7} - \frac{1}{7} + \frac{7}{7}$

   h) One fifth + $\frac{2}{5}$

   i) $\frac{6}{6} - \frac{4}{6}$

2. Calculate:

   a) $\frac{4}{5} + \frac{1}{5}$

   b) $\frac{2}{10} + \frac{8}{10}$

   c) $\frac{12}{13} + \frac{1}{13}$

3. Circle the fractions that **equal** 1 whole:

   a) $\frac{4}{5}$
   b) $\frac{6}{6}$
   c) $\frac{9}{3}$
   d) $\frac{2}{2}$
   e) $\frac{1}{7}$

4. Complete the sentences:

   a) 1 whole is _____ tenths

   b) 1 whole is _____ fifths

   c) 1 whole is _____ ninths

   d) 1 whole is 6 _____

   e) 1 whole is 3 _____

   f) 1 whole is _____ lots of $\frac{1}{100}$

5. Fill in the blanks:

   a) $\frac{3}{5} + \boxed{} = 1$

   b) $\frac{4}{12} + \boxed{} = 1$

   c) $\frac{44}{44} + \boxed{} = 1$

   d) $\frac{1}{150} + \boxed{} = 1$

   e) $\frac{101}{101} + \boxed{} = 1$

   f) $\frac{98}{99} + \boxed{} = 1$

6. a) How many tenths make 1 whole?

b) How many sevenths make 1 whole?

c) How many lots of $\frac{1}{5}$ make 1 whole?

d) Explain why $\frac{3}{3}$ = 1

e) $\frac{1}{5}$ + _____ = 1

f) _____ + $\frac{4}{10}$ = 1

g) $\frac{1}{4}$ + _____ = 1

h) $\frac{1}{10}$ + $\frac{3}{10}$ + _____ = 1

i) $\frac{7}{5}$ - _____ = 1

j) $\frac{5}{3}$ - _____ = 1

k) _____ + $\frac{4}{9}$ = 1

l) 1 - _____ = $\frac{2}{3}$

m) 1 - _____ = $\frac{7}{10}$

n) $\frac{3}{3}$ + _____ = 1

o) 1 - _____ = $\frac{5}{5}$

p) _____ lots of $\frac{1}{8}$ = 1

7. Calculate:

a) $1 - \frac{1}{10}$

b) $1 - \frac{3}{8}$

c) $1 - \frac{7}{7}$

d) $1 - \frac{4}{15}$

e) $1 - \frac{3}{90}$

f) $1 - \frac{6}{40}$

8. Calculate $\frac{100}{101}$ + $\frac{1}{101}$

9. Complete these statements with >, < or =

a) $\frac{3}{5}$ ◯ 1

b) $\frac{5}{3}$ ◯ 1

c) $\frac{3}{3}$ ◯ 1

d) $\frac{5}{6}$ ◯ 1

e) $\frac{1}{5}$ + $\frac{3}{5}$ ◯ 1

f) $\frac{2}{3}$ + $\frac{5}{3}$ ◯ 1

g) $\frac{6}{5}$ - $\frac{1}{5}$ ◯ 1

h) $\frac{1}{3}$ + $\frac{4}{3}$ ◯ 1

i) $\frac{5}{4}$ - $\frac{2}{4}$ ◯ 1

- -

challenge

$\frac{6}{5}$ + _____ = 1

$\frac{8}{6}$ + _____ = 1

$\frac{9}{5}$ + _____ = 1

More, Less or Equal to 1 Whole?

Decide whether each card is more than, less than or equal to 1 whole and record your answers in a table like the one below.

A $\dfrac{5}{9}$

B $\dfrac{1}{4} + \dfrac{3}{4}$

C $\dfrac{6}{5}$

D $\dfrac{7}{7}$

E $\dfrac{8}{10} - \dfrac{1}{10}$

F $\dfrac{1}{5} + \dfrac{4}{5}$

G $1 - \dfrac{1}{10}$

H $\dfrac{1}{7}$

I $\dfrac{1}{19} + \dfrac{10}{19}$

J $\dfrac{3}{2}$

K $\dfrac{1}{3} + \dfrac{1}{3} + \dfrac{1}{3}$

L $\dfrac{2}{18} + \dfrac{3}{18}$

M $\dfrac{15}{15}$

N $\dfrac{18}{17}$

O $\dfrac{6}{5} - \dfrac{1}{5}$

P $\dfrac{1}{1}$

Q $\dfrac{2}{15} + \dfrac{6}{15} + \dfrac{1}{15}$

R $\dfrac{12}{11} - \dfrac{1}{11}$

S $\dfrac{22}{22}$

T $\dfrac{1}{4} + \dfrac{1}{4} + \dfrac{1}{4}$

U $\dfrac{12}{10} - \dfrac{2}{10}$

V $\dfrac{0}{4}$

W $\dfrac{12}{20} + \dfrac{8}{20} - \dfrac{1}{20}$

X $\dfrac{5}{4} + \dfrac{1}{4}$

Y $\dfrac{165}{164}$

Less than 1 Whole	Equal to 1 Whole	More than 1 Whole

improper fractions and mixed numbers

learn by heart

Proper Fraction: e.g. $\frac{4}{10}$, denominator > numerator

Improper Fraction: e.g. $\frac{10}{4}$, numerator ≥ denominator

Mixed Number: e.g. $3\frac{4}{5}$ (integer + fraction)

more than 1 whole

exercise 4c

1. Write as a fraction:

   a) Seven Quarters

   b) Nine fifths

   c) Five quarters

   d) Eight eighths

2. Circle the **improper** fractions:

   a) $\frac{3}{7}$ b) $\frac{5}{2}$ c) $\frac{7}{1}$ d) $\frac{100}{100}$ e) $\frac{9}{10}$

3. Write as a mixed number:

   a) 4 wholes + 2 thirds

   b) 5 wholes + 3 tenths

   c) 6 wholes + 4 fifths

   d) 1 whole + 3 halves

4. Write $6\frac{1}{3}$ in words

5. Circle the mixed numbers:

   a) $\frac{9}{4}$ b) 3   c) $4\frac{2}{5}$ d) $\frac{1}{2}$ e) $1\frac{1}{4}$

6. Which of these are more than 1 whole? Circle all that apply.

   a) $\frac{4}{5}$ b) $2\frac{1}{7}$ c) 4   d) $\frac{9}{5}$ e) $2\frac{3}{4}$

7. True or false: All mixed numbers are bigger than 1 whole

8. Decide which number on the right is being described:

Less than 1	A mixed number
Equals 1 Whole	An improper fraction

A $\frac{4}{4}$	B $\frac{4}{9}$
C $\frac{9}{4}$	D $1\frac{4}{9}$

9. Which numbers do the arrows point to? Give your answer as a fractions, integers or mixed number.

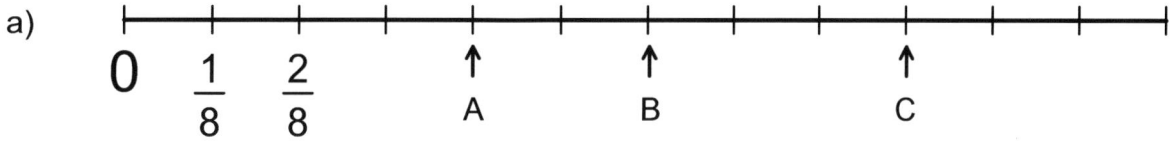

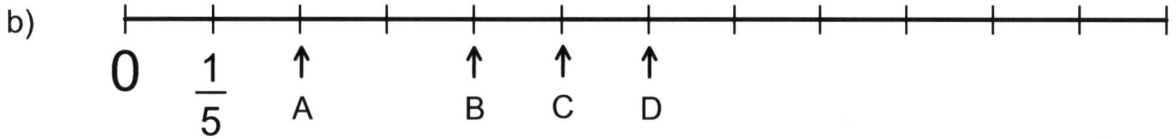

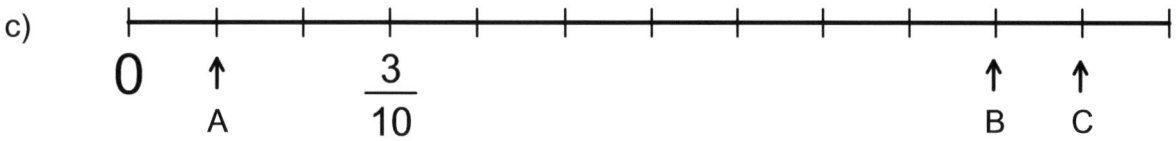

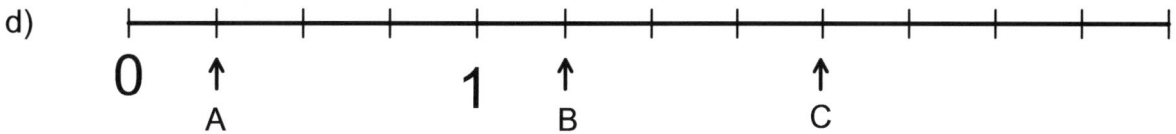

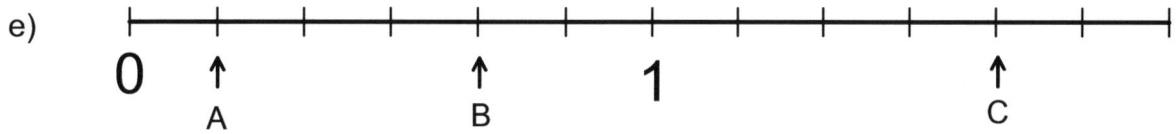

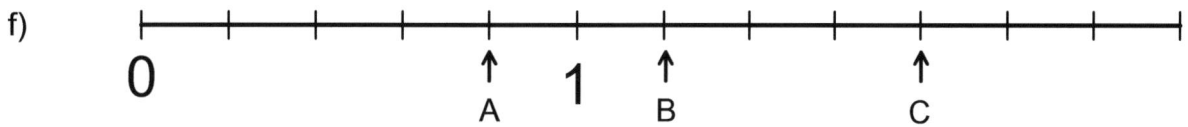

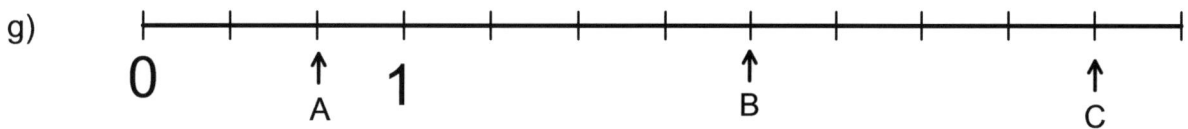

a)

$$0 \quad \frac{1}{8} \quad \frac{2}{8} \qquad A \qquad B \qquad C$$

b)

$$0 \quad \frac{1}{5} \quad A \qquad B \quad C \quad D$$

c)

$$0 \quad A \qquad \frac{3}{10} \qquad\qquad B \quad C$$

d)

$$0 \quad A \qquad 1 \quad B \qquad C$$

e)

$$0 \quad A \qquad B \quad 1 \qquad C$$

f)

$$0 \qquad A \quad 1 \quad B \qquad C$$

g)

$$0 \qquad A \quad 1 \qquad B \qquad C$$

h)

0   A   B $1\frac{1}{4}$ C

i)

0   A   B $1\frac{2}{3}$ C   D

j)

0   A   B $1\frac{3}{4}$ C   D

k)

0   A $1\frac{1}{2}$ B   C   D

- -

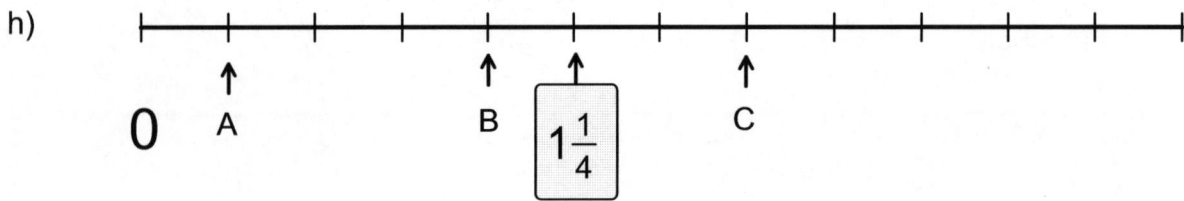

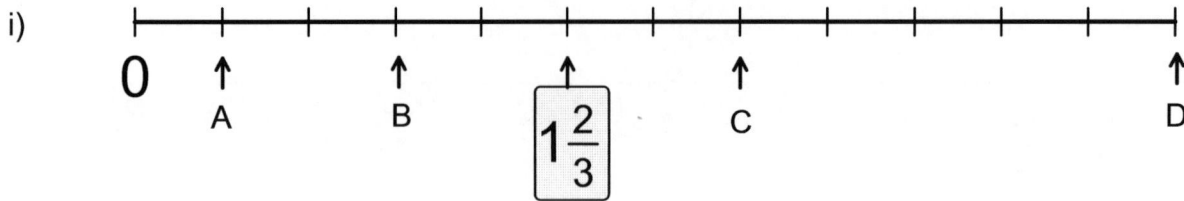

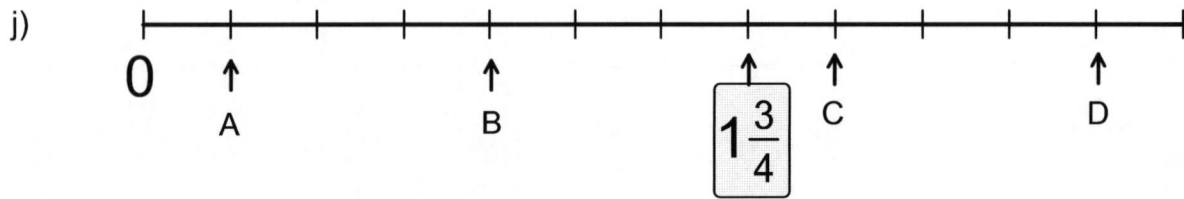

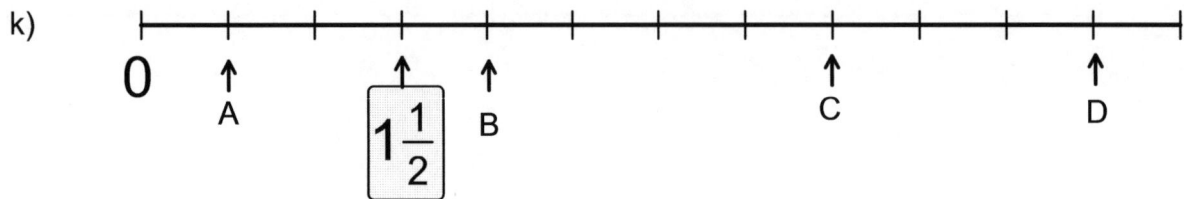

negative numbers recap

1. Calculate:

a) -2 - 1

b) 5 - 6

c) -2 × -3

d) 2 + -3

e) 5 + -1

f) -3 + 1

g) 4 - 4

h) -2 + -3

i) -6 - 2

j) 4 + -4

k) -3 × 4

l) 10 + -2

converting improper fractions & mixed numbers

examples

Write $\frac{4}{3}$ as a mixed number

since $\frac{3}{3} = 1$, $\frac{4}{3} = 1\frac{1}{3}$

Write $2\frac{3}{5}$ as an improper fraction

each whole $= \frac{5}{5}$, so $2\frac{3}{5} = \frac{13}{5}$

exercise 4d

1. Write as a mixed number:

a) $\frac{5}{4}$ d) $\frac{3}{2}$ g) $\frac{10}{6}$ j) $\frac{11}{3}$

b) $\frac{10}{9}$ e) $\frac{7}{5}$ h) $\frac{11}{9}$ k) $\frac{12}{5}$

c) $\frac{10}{7}$ f) $\frac{7}{3}$ i) $\frac{11}{6}$ l) $\frac{14}{6}$

2. Write as an improper fraction:

a) $1\frac{3}{4}$ c) $5\frac{1}{2}$ e) $2\frac{1}{6}$ g) $1\frac{1}{3}$

b) $3\frac{1}{9}$ d) $3\frac{1}{5}$ f) $3\frac{2}{6}$ h) $3\frac{3}{7}$

matching activity

Match each card on the left with an equivalent card from the right.

A $\frac{10}{8}$	B $\frac{12}{5}$	C $\frac{20}{3}$
D $\frac{18}{3}$	E $\frac{9}{2}$	F $\frac{10}{3}$
G $\frac{22}{6}$	H $\frac{30}{8}$	I $\frac{45}{4}$
J $\frac{15}{4}$	K $\frac{20}{2}$	L $\frac{18}{5}$

M $3\frac{4}{6}$	N 10	O 6
P $4\frac{1}{2}$	Q $11\frac{1}{4}$	R $1\frac{2}{8}$
S $2\frac{2}{5}$	T $3\frac{3}{5}$	U $3\frac{6}{8}$
V $3\frac{3}{4}$	W $3\frac{1}{3}$	X $6\frac{2}{3}$

A	B	C	D	E	F	G	H	I	J	K	L

fraction of an amount

learn by heart

Finding $\frac{1}{4}$ of an amount is the same as dividing by 4, so for example $\frac{1}{4}$ of 20 is 20 ÷ 4 = 5

This works for all unit fractions, so finding $\frac{1}{10}$ is the same as dividing by 10, e.g. $\frac{1}{10}$ of 18 = 1.8

For other fractions, such as to find $\frac{2}{5}$ of an amount, divide the amount into 5 equal parts and then select 2 of those parts

examples

Calculate $\frac{1}{3}$ of 21

= 21 ÷ 3 = 7

Calculate $\frac{2}{3}$ of 21

= 21 ÷ 3 × 2 = 14

divide into 3 equal parts, then select 2

Shade $\frac{2}{5}$

First split the amount into 5 equal parts. Then shade 2 of those parts.

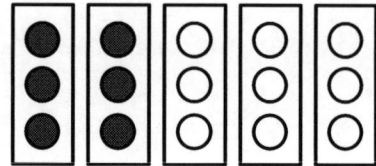

exercise 4e

1. To work out $\frac{1}{12}$ of an amount, we should:

   a) multiply by 12   b) add 12   c) divide by 12

2. Work out $\frac{1}{5}$ of

   a) 5   b) 30   c) 25   d) 0

3. Calculate:

   a) $\frac{1}{4}$ of 20   e) $\frac{1}{3}$ of 24   i) $\frac{1}{5}$ of 25

   b) $\frac{1}{3}$ of 30   f) $\frac{1}{4}$ of 24   j) $\frac{1}{4}$ of 40

   c) $\frac{2}{3}$ of 30   g) $\frac{2}{3}$ of 36   k) $\frac{2}{3}$ of 27

   d) $\frac{3}{4}$ of 20   h) $\frac{2}{5}$ of 30   l) $\frac{2}{5}$ of 35

4. Copy each diagram and shade $\frac{1}{5}$:

a)
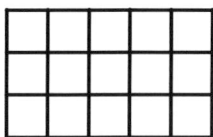

b)
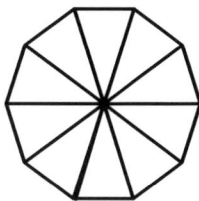

c)
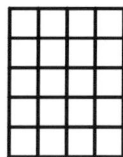

d)
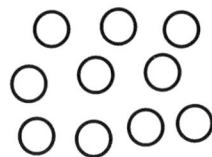

5. Copy each diagram and shade $\frac{1}{3}$

a)
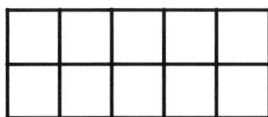

b)
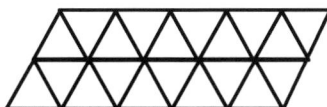

c)
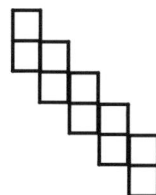

6. Copy each diagram and shade $\frac{1}{10}$

a)
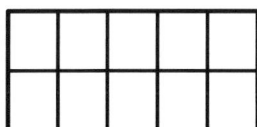

b)

c)
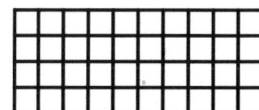

7. Copy each diagram and shade $\frac{2}{5}$:

a)
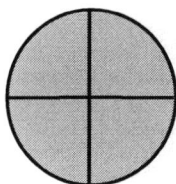

b)
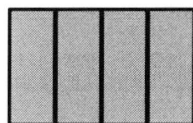

c)
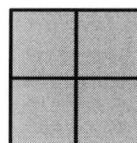

8. What fraction is shaded?

a)

b)

c)

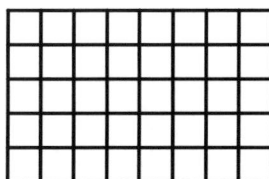

9. Copy the diagram and shade $\frac{1}{5}$

equivalent fractions

learn by heart

Equivalent fractions: *have the same value*
They are created by multiplying or dividing both
numerator and denominator by the same number

$$\times 2$$

$$\frac{3}{5} = \frac{6}{10}$$

$$\times 2$$

*Both parts of
the fraction are
multiplied (or
divided) by the
same number*

exercise 4f

1. Decide whether these statements are true or false:

a) $\frac{2}{5} = \frac{4}{7}$

d) $\frac{2}{10} = \frac{1}{5}$

g) $\frac{4}{25} = \frac{8}{50}$

b) $\frac{3}{8} = \frac{6}{10}$

e) $\frac{3}{7} = \frac{15}{21}$

h) $\frac{1}{5} = \frac{3}{10}$

c) $\frac{1}{4} = \frac{3}{12}$

f) $\frac{6}{10} = \frac{3}{7}$

i) $\frac{4}{3} = \frac{44}{33}$

2. Work out the value of the ?s to make each pair of fractions equivalent:

a) $\frac{3}{5} = \frac{15}{?}$

d) $\frac{5}{9} = \frac{?}{27}$

g) $\frac{1}{4} = \frac{?}{20}$

b) $\frac{6}{10} = \frac{?}{20}$

e) $\frac{20}{25} = \frac{?}{5}$

h) $\frac{6}{10} = \frac{?}{5}$

c) $\frac{1}{7} = \frac{3}{?}$

f) $\frac{18}{10} = \frac{?}{5}$

i) $\frac{4}{50} = \frac{2}{?}$

3. Find 10 fractions in the grid that are equivalent to $\frac{3}{5}$.

1	2	3	4	5	6	7	8
$\frac{6}{10}$	$\frac{31}{51}$	$\frac{20}{40}$	$\frac{60}{100}$	$\frac{2}{5}$	$\frac{90}{150}$	$\frac{5}{15}$	$\frac{15}{20}$
9	10	11	12	13	14	15	16
$\frac{9}{20}$	$\frac{8}{15}$	$\frac{9}{15}$	$\frac{10}{25}$	$\frac{5}{8}$	$\frac{13}{23}$	$\frac{40}{60}$	$\frac{300}{500}$
17	18	19	20	21	22	23	24
$\frac{12}{30}$	$\frac{18}{30}$	$\frac{130}{150}$	$\frac{1}{4}$	$\frac{45}{75}$	$\frac{12}{20}$	$\frac{50}{75}$	$\frac{13}{20}$
25	26	27	28	29	30	31	32
$\frac{3}{500}$	$\frac{15}{100}$	$\frac{25}{55}$	$\frac{60}{100}$	$\frac{75}{300}$	$\frac{15}{250}$	$\frac{30}{50}$	$\frac{12}{25}$

learn by heart

The simplest form of a fraction is when :
the numerator and denominator have no common factors (they cannot be divided further)

example

Simplify $\frac{4}{10}$

Divide numerator & denominator by 2, so $\frac{2}{5}$

exercise 4g

1. Simplify the following fractions as far as possible:

   a) $\frac{3}{9}$ d) $\frac{8}{16}$ g) $\frac{10}{25}$

   b) $\frac{4}{20}$ e) $\frac{3}{15}$ h) $\frac{6}{30}$

   c) $\frac{4}{12}$ f) $\frac{25}{100}$ i) $\frac{12}{36}$

2. Simplify $\frac{24}{30}$ fully. Find your answer below.

   a) $\frac{12}{15}$ b) $\frac{1}{2}$ c) $\frac{6}{7.5}$ d) $\frac{4}{5}$

3. Which of these fractions cannot be simplified?

   a) $\frac{3}{10}$ b) $\frac{7}{7}$ c) $\frac{5}{12}$ d) $\frac{6}{9}$ e) $\frac{10}{4}$ f) $\frac{27}{30}$

find the halves

In this grid there are 10 fractions that equal $\frac{1}{2}$. Can you find them?

1	2	3	4	5	6	7	8
$\frac{1}{4}$	$\frac{3}{5}$	$\frac{12}{24}$	$\frac{2}{5}$	$\frac{11}{20}$	$\frac{6}{12}$	$\frac{5}{15}$	$\frac{7}{14}$
9	10	11	12	13	14	15	16
$\frac{9}{20}$	$\frac{7}{15}$	$\frac{10}{22}$	$\frac{5}{8}$	$\frac{1}{3}$	$\frac{13}{23}$	$\frac{8}{10}$	$\frac{50}{100}$
17	18	19	20	21	22	23	24
$\frac{6}{7}$	$\frac{3}{7}$	$\frac{3}{6}$	$\frac{1}{9}$	$\frac{15}{30}$	$\frac{8}{16}$	$\frac{21}{50}$	$\frac{6}{10}$
25	26	27	28	29	30	31	32
$\frac{20}{40}$	$\frac{6}{9}$	$\frac{4}{16}$	$\frac{25}{50}$	$\frac{3}{30}$	$\frac{4}{20}$	$\frac{14}{28}$	$\frac{5}{25}$

Which Fraction is Left?

Use the clues to work out which fraction is left over.

Cross Out:

a. All the fractions that have an odd number denominator

b. All the fractions that equal one whole

c. All the fractions that equal $\frac{1}{2}$

d. All the fractions that are greater than 1

e. All the unit fractions

f. All the fractions that can be simplified

$\frac{1}{2}$	$\frac{2}{8}$	$\frac{5}{10}$	$\frac{9}{9}$	$\frac{5}{5}$
$\frac{15}{17}$	$\frac{12}{24}$	$\frac{1}{10}$	$1\frac{1}{3}$	$\frac{1}{9}$
$\frac{4}{9}$	$\frac{4}{4}$	$\frac{8}{16}$	$\frac{3}{4}$	$\frac{2}{1}$
$\frac{6}{4}$	$\frac{9}{8}$	$\frac{7}{3}$	$\frac{60}{120}$	$\frac{1}{7}$
$\frac{6}{12}$	$\frac{10}{20}$	$\frac{1}{122}$	$\frac{2}{5}$	$\frac{8}{8}$

- -

mixed review matching activity

Match these cards into pairs that are equal.
You may need to simplify fractions or change mixed numbers into improper fractions.

A	$\frac{2}{3}$	F	$\frac{3}{7} + \frac{2}{7}$	K	$\frac{1}{5} + \frac{2}{5}$	P	$\frac{11}{4}$
B	$\frac{8}{5}$	G	$1 - \frac{1}{7}$	L	1	Q	$\frac{11}{5}$
C	$3\frac{4}{5}$	H	$\frac{10}{15}$	M	$\frac{9}{5}$	R	$\frac{18}{10}$
D	$2\frac{1}{5}$	I	$1\frac{3}{5}$	N	$\frac{6}{7}$	S	$\frac{19}{5}$
E	$\frac{1}{5} + \frac{4}{5}$	J	$2\frac{3}{4}$	O	$\frac{3}{5}$	T	$\frac{5}{7}$

A	
B	
C	
D	
E	
F	
G	
J	
K	
M	

recap: converting fractions and decimals (using place value)

recall

tens	units	●	tenths	hundredths	thousandths
10	1		$\frac{1}{10}$ = 0.1	$\frac{1}{100}$ = 0.01	$\frac{1}{1000}$ = 0.001

Recall from chapter 1, we can use place value to write fractions as decimals, for example: $\frac{4}{10}$ = 0.4 $1\frac{19}{100}$ = 1.19 $\frac{6}{1000}$ = 0.006

exercise 4h

1. Write as a decimal: *watch out!*

   a) 3 tenths

   b) 7 hundredths

   c) 9 thousandths

   d) 3 tens

   e) $\frac{5}{10}$

   f) $\frac{8}{100}$

   g) $\frac{1}{10}$

   h) $\frac{3}{1000}$

   i) $\frac{9}{100}$

2. Write as a fraction:

   a) 0.9   b) 0.01   c) 0.005   d) 0.0007

3. Which of these is 4 tens + 4 hundredths?

   a) 0.44   b) 0.404   c) 4.4   d) 40.4   e) 40.04   f) 40.44

4. Which of these is 7 hundreds + 3 tenths?

   a) 0.37   b) 0.73   c) 7.3   d) 700.3   e) 700.03

5. Write as a decimal number:

   a) 5 tens + 3 tenths

   b) 2 units + 6 hundredths

   c) 8 tens + 1 tenth

   d) 5 hundreds + 3 hundredths

   e) 9 units + 3 tenths

   f) 1 thousand + 4 thousandths

6. Which of these is 3.06?

   a) $3\frac{6}{10}$ b) $3\frac{6}{100}$ c) $3\frac{6}{1000}$ d) $30\frac{6}{10}$ e) $30\frac{6}{100}$

7. Write as a decimal:

a) $4\frac{1}{10}$

b) $20\frac{1}{100}$

c) $3\frac{4}{100}$

d) $\frac{7}{1000}$

e) $100\frac{2}{100}$

f) $5\frac{1}{10}$

g) $1\frac{7}{100}$

h) $17\frac{6}{10}$

8. True or False?

a) $0.3 = \frac{1}{3}$

b) 4 tens = 0.4

c) $6.6 = 6 + \frac{6}{10}$

9. Write these fractions as decimals:

a) $\frac{71}{100}$

b) $\frac{901}{1000}$

c) $\frac{1}{1000}$

d) $\frac{37}{100}$

e) $\frac{9}{10}$

f) $\frac{409}{1000}$

g) $\frac{2}{10}$

h) $\frac{28}{1000}$

i) $\frac{8}{100}$

10. What is 0.45 as a fraction? Circle your answer.

a) $4\frac{5}{100}$

b) $\frac{45}{10}$

c) $\frac{45}{100}$

d) $\frac{45}{1000}$

e) $\frac{4.5}{100}$

11. The value of the digit 9 in the number 4.0**9** is:

a) 9 tens

b) 9 tenths

c) 9 hundredths

d) 9 thousandths

12. Which of these is largest?

a) 4 tens

b) 4 tenths

c) 4 hundreds

d) 4 thousandths

13. In each pair, decide which is the **larger** number:

a) 3 tens or 3 hundreds

b) 5 tenths or 5 tens

c) $\frac{7}{10}$ or 7 tens

d) $\frac{3}{100}$ or 3 thousandths

14. True or false?

a) $\frac{309}{1000} = 0.39$

b) $\frac{2}{100} = 0.2$

c) $\frac{48}{1000} = 0.048$

15. Which calculation equals zero?

a) $0.7 - \frac{7}{10}$

b) $0.7 - \frac{7}{100}$

c) $0.7 - \frac{7}{1000}$

d) $0.7 - 7$

converting fractions and decimals (using equivalent fractions)

learn by heart

If the denominator of a fraction is a factor of 10, 100 or 1000, we can use equivalent fractions to help us write it as a decimal.

It is helpful to know these factors of 100: | $2 \times 50 = 100$ | $4 \times 25 = 100$ | $5 \times 20 = 100$

examples

Write $\frac{4}{5}$ as a decimal

$$\frac{4}{5} = \frac{8}{10} = 0.8$$

Write $\frac{4}{50}$ as a decimal

$$\frac{4}{50} = \frac{8}{100} = 0.08$$

Write $\frac{7}{20}$ as a decimal

$$\frac{7}{20} = \frac{35}{100} = 0.35$$

exercise 4j

1. Write these fractions as decimals:

a) $\frac{3}{50}$

b) $\frac{1}{5}$

c) $\frac{1}{20}$

d) $\frac{22}{50}$

e) $\frac{6}{50}$

f) $\frac{10}{25}$

g) $\frac{12}{50}$

h) $\frac{22}{200}$

i) $\frac{3}{20}$

j) $\frac{24}{200}$

k) $\frac{6}{250}$

il) $\frac{405}{500}$

2. Match pairs of equivalent fractions and decimals.

A $\frac{3}{100}$	B $\frac{11}{50}$	C $\frac{3}{1000}$	D $\frac{14}{200}$

M 0.6	N 0.8	O 0.07	P 0.3

E $\frac{22}{50}$	F $\frac{3}{5}$	G $\frac{1}{5}$	H $\frac{3}{50}$

Q 0.2	R 0.202	S 0.03	T 0.22

I $\frac{10}{25}$	J $\frac{3}{10}$	K $\frac{4}{5}$	L $\frac{202}{1000}$

U 0.003	V 0.44	W 0.4	X 0.06

A	B	C	D	E	F	G	H	I	J	K	L

converting fractions & decimals (all types)

examples

Type 1: Denominator is 10, 100, 1000 etc..	Type 2: Denominator is a factor of 10,100,1000 etc..	Type 3: Other denominators
Write $\frac{23}{100}$ as a decimal Use place value – this is 23 hundredths = $\underline{0.23}$	Write $\frac{7}{25}$ as a decimal Use equivalent fractions $\frac{7}{25} = \frac{28}{100} = \underline{0.28}$	Write $\frac{1}{8}$ as a decimal Use short division $1 \div 8 = \underline{0.125}$

learn by heart

$\frac{1}{2} = 0.5$	$\frac{3}{4} = 0.75$	$\frac{1}{9} = 0.\dot{1}$	$\frac{1}{5} = 0.2$
$\frac{1}{4} = 0.25$	$\frac{1}{3} = 0.\dot{3}$	$\frac{2}{9} = 0.\dot{2}$	$\frac{2}{5} = 0.4$

exercise 4k

1. Write as a decimal:

   a) $\frac{9}{100}$ e) $\frac{9}{10}$ i) $\frac{8}{50}$ m) $\frac{6}{20}$

   b) $\frac{1}{50}$ f) $2\frac{1}{100}$ j) $\frac{4}{9}$ n) $\frac{7}{9}$

   c) $\frac{1}{5}$ g) $\frac{6}{50}$ k) $\frac{9}{25}$ o) $\frac{2}{25}$

   d) $\frac{2}{3}$ h) $\frac{3}{5}$ l) $\frac{18}{200}$ p) $\frac{4}{200}$

2. Convert these fractions to decimals. Which ones are recurring decimals?

   a) $\frac{1}{2}$ b) $\frac{1}{3}$ c) $\frac{1}{4}$ d) $\frac{1}{5}$ e) $\frac{1}{6}$ f) $\frac{1}{7}$

3. True or false?

   a) $\frac{1}{8} = 0.8$ c) $\frac{1}{5} = 0.2$ e) $\frac{12}{12} = 1.0$

   b) $\frac{1}{9} = 0.999...$ d) $\frac{2}{5} = 0.25$ f) $\frac{8}{100} = 0.8$

Odd One Out

In each group of three, one number is not equal to the others.
Can you work out which one?

A	$\frac{1}{2}$	0.5	0.2

B	$\frac{3}{10}$	0.$\dot{3}$	0.3

C	$\frac{1}{9}$	$\frac{9}{10}$	0.9

D	0.2	$\frac{1}{5}$	0.5

E	$\frac{3}{5}$	0.3	0.6

F	$\frac{3}{50}$	0.03	0.06

G	$\frac{6}{100}$	0.6	$\frac{6}{10}$

H	1.1	$1\frac{1}{10}$	$1\frac{1}{100}$

I	$\frac{1}{20}$	0.5	0.05

J	0.7	0.$\dot{7}$	$\frac{7}{9}$

K	0.4	0.40	$\frac{1}{4}$

L	$\frac{3}{6}$	$\frac{1}{2}$	0.3

M	0.8	$\frac{1}{8}$	$\frac{8}{10}$

N	$\frac{6}{20}$	0.6	0.3

O	$\frac{1}{5}$	$\frac{5}{5}$	1

P	$\frac{14}{20}$	0.28	0.7

Converting Fractions & Decimals Code Breaker

Write each of the following as a decimal and find your answer in the code box. Write the words down to reveal a message!

code box

0.015 = but	0.15 = safe	$0.\dot{4}$ = at	0.8 = half
0.023 = it	0.2 = through	0.45 = cat	0.99 = under
0.1 = and	0.23 = dance	0.46 = that	1.02 = always
0.12 = A	0.28 = sails	0.6 = is	1.15 = is
0.125 = ship	0.3 = not	0.65 = dress	1.25 = built
0.13 = water	$0.\dot{3}$ = shore	$0.\dot{7}$ = dizzy	1.8 = was
0.14 = sand	0.4 = what	0.79 = around	2 = for

a) $\dfrac{12}{100}$ = 0.12 = **A**

b) $\dfrac{1}{8}$ = _____ =

c) $\dfrac{3}{5}$ = _____ =

d) $1\dfrac{2}{100}$ = _____ =

e) $\dfrac{3}{20}$ = _____ =

f) $\dfrac{4}{9}$ = _____ =

g) $\dfrac{1}{3}$ = _____ =

h) $\dfrac{15}{1000}$ = _____ =

i) $\dfrac{23}{50}$ = _____ =

j) $1\dfrac{15}{100}$ = _____ =

k) $\dfrac{60}{200}$ = _____ =

l) $\dfrac{2}{5}$ = _____ =

m) $\dfrac{23}{1000}$ = _____ =

n) $1\dfrac{8}{10}$ = _____ =

o) $1\dfrac{1}{4}$ = _____ =

p) $\dfrac{20}{10}$ = _____ =

– Quote by Albert Einstein

learn by heart

Type 1: Same denominators	Type 2: Related denominators	Type 3: Different denominators
$\frac{2}{5} + \frac{1}{5}$	$\frac{5}{8} - \frac{1}{4}$	$\frac{2}{3} + \frac{1}{5}$
Add numerators	Convert one fraction to the denominator of the other	Convert both fractions to the same denominator
$\frac{2}{5} + \frac{1}{5} = \frac{3}{5}$	$\frac{5}{8} - \frac{2}{8} = \frac{3}{8}$	$\frac{10}{15} + \frac{3}{15} = \frac{13}{15}$

exercise 41

1. True or false? $\frac{1}{2} + \frac{1}{4} = \frac{2}{6}$

2. Work out, giving your answers in the simplest form:

    a) $\frac{1}{5} + \frac{1}{3}$ b) $\frac{3}{4} + \frac{1}{6}$

    c) $\frac{2}{3} - \frac{1}{12}$ d) $\frac{2}{5} - \frac{1}{4}$

    e) $\frac{2}{9} + \frac{3}{5}$ f) $\frac{5}{6} - \frac{1}{2}$

3. Match each of the cards A-L with one of the cards M-X.

A	B	C
$\frac{3}{10} + \frac{1}{5}$	$\frac{5}{6} - \frac{1}{4}$	$\frac{2}{3} + \frac{1}{4}$

D	E	F
$\frac{1}{2} - \frac{1}{3}$	$\frac{9}{10} - \frac{7}{10}$	$\frac{1}{2} + \frac{1}{6}$

G	H	I
$1 - \frac{7}{12}$	$\frac{3}{8} + \frac{3}{8}$	$\frac{5}{6} - \frac{1}{8}$

J	K	L
$\frac{1}{3} - \frac{1}{4}$	$\frac{3}{2} - \frac{2}{3}$	$\frac{7}{10} - \frac{3}{10}$

M	N	O
$\frac{1}{6}$	$\frac{3}{4}$	$\frac{2}{3}$

P	Q	R
$\frac{1}{12}$	$\frac{5}{6}$	$\frac{1}{2}$

S	T	U
$\frac{11}{12}$	$\frac{2}{5}$	$\frac{7}{12}$

V	W	X
$\frac{1}{5}$	$\frac{17}{24}$	$\frac{5}{12}$

A	B	C	D	E	F	G	H	I	J	K	L

multiplying fractions ⭐ extra challenge

learn by heart

Multiplying Fractions: Multiply numerators and denominators

examples

Evaluate $\frac{1}{2} \times \frac{3}{5}$

$= \frac{3}{10}$

Evaluate $5 \times \frac{3}{4}$

$= \frac{5}{1} \times \frac{3}{4} = \frac{15}{4}$

Evaluate $\frac{2}{5} \times 25$

$= \frac{2}{5} \times \frac{25}{1} = \frac{50}{5} = 10$

This is the same as finding $\frac{2}{5}$ of 25

exercise 4m

1. Calculate the following and simplify your answers:

   a) $\frac{1}{5} \times \frac{3}{4}$

   b) $\frac{1}{8} \times 5$

   c) $\frac{2}{5} \times 2$

   d) $\frac{1}{4} \times \frac{3}{5}$

   e) $20 \times \frac{2}{9}$

   f) $5 \times \frac{2}{7}$

   g) $\frac{1}{4} \times \frac{1}{2}$

   h) $3 \times \frac{3}{8}$

   i) $\frac{6}{5} \times 6$

2. Fill in the blanks:

   a) $\frac{4}{5} \times \boxed{} = \frac{8}{20}$

   b) $\frac{1}{3} \times \boxed{} = \frac{4}{6}$

   c) $\frac{2}{5} \times \boxed{} = \frac{20}{5}$

   d) $\frac{5}{9} \times \boxed{} = \frac{15}{18}$

   e) $4 \times \boxed{} = \frac{8}{3}$

   f) $5 \times \boxed{} = \frac{5}{7}$

   g) $\frac{3}{7} \times \boxed{} = \frac{12}{7}$

   h) $\frac{1}{10} \times \boxed{} = \frac{3}{10}$

3. Calculate:

   a) $\frac{2}{3} \times \frac{1}{3} \times \frac{1}{5}$

   b) $\frac{1}{5} \times \frac{1}{2} \times \frac{2}{3}$

4. Calculate the following and simplify your answers. What do you notice?

a) $\frac{3}{5} \times \frac{5}{3}$

c) $\frac{2}{5} \times \frac{5}{2}$

e) $\frac{8}{3} \times \frac{3}{8}$

b) $\frac{4}{10} \times \frac{10}{4}$

d) $\frac{2}{3} \times \frac{3}{2}$

f) $\frac{6}{4} \times \frac{4}{6}$

5. Calculate the following and simpify your answers. What do you notice?

a) $2 \times \frac{1}{2}$

c) $3 \times \frac{1}{3}$

e) $\frac{1}{10} \times 10$

b) $6 \times \frac{1}{6}$

d) $\frac{1}{5} \times 5$

f) $8 \times \frac{1}{8}$

6. True or false?

a) $\frac{2}{3} \times \frac{3}{4} = \frac{5}{7}$

c) $\frac{4}{5} \times 3 = \frac{12}{15}$

b) $\frac{1}{5} \times \frac{1}{5} = \frac{1}{10}$

d) $\frac{2}{7} \times 3 = \frac{6}{7}$

7. True or false:
to multiply fractions we first need to make a common denominator

mixed multiplications & additions

8. Calculate the following and simplify your answers:

a) $\frac{1}{5} + \frac{1}{5}$

d) $\frac{4}{5} + \frac{1}{5}$

g) $\frac{1}{4} + \frac{1}{5}$

b) $\frac{1}{5} \times \frac{1}{5}$

e) $\frac{9}{10} - \frac{1}{10}$

h) $\frac{1}{4} \times \frac{1}{5}$

c) $\frac{2}{3} \times \frac{3}{4}$

f) $\frac{4}{5} \times 3$

i) $\frac{1}{3} - \frac{1}{5}$

Mixed Up Multiplications ⭐ extra challenge

Complete these calculations and find your answer at the bottom.
Record your answers in a table.

A	B	C	D
$\frac{1}{5} \times \frac{2}{3}$	-3 × -7	0.2 × 0.3	$4 \times \frac{2}{7}$

E	F	G	H
-5 × 3	0.6 × 10	$\frac{3}{5} \times 4$	1.2 × 3

I	J	K	L
0.07 × 100	8 × -2	0.8 × 3	$\frac{3}{4} \times \frac{4}{3}$

M	N	O	P
0.24 × 1000	$6 \times \frac{2}{3}$	-2 × -12	6 × 0.3

Q	R	S	T
90 × 0.3	$\frac{4}{5}$ of 25	-16 × 0	80 × 0.1

U	V	W	X
$\frac{1}{3} \times 4$	$0.7 \times \frac{3}{4}$	$0.8 \times \frac{1}{10}$	3 × 0.9

----

jumbled answers

3.6 20 2.7

2.4 $\frac{2}{15}$ 4 24 -15

0 0.06 $\frac{4}{3}$ 0.08 -16 7 8

30 $\frac{12}{5}$ $\frac{21}{40}$ 21 240 $\frac{8}{7}$ 6 1 1.8

A	
B	
C	
D	
E	
F	
G	
H	
I	
J	
K	
L	
M	
N	
O	
P	
Q	
R	
S	
T	
U	
V	
W	
X	

fractions & decimals mixed practice

examples

Calculate $\frac{1}{5} + \frac{1}{3}$

$$= \frac{3}{15} + \frac{5}{15}$$

$$= \frac{8}{15}$$

Calculate $0.8 + 0.2$

$$= \frac{8}{10} + \frac{2}{10}$$

$$= 1$$

Calculate $\frac{1}{5} + 0.3$

$$= \frac{1}{5} + \frac{3}{10}$$

$$= \frac{2}{10} + \frac{3}{10}$$

$$= \frac{5}{10}$$

exercise 4n

1. Calculate the following. Give your answer as a fraction or decimal:

   a) $\frac{1}{9} + \frac{1}{9}$

   b) $0.6 - 0.1$

   c) $\frac{1}{5} + \frac{1}{5} + \frac{1}{5}$

   d) $2.5 + 0.1$

   e) $\frac{4}{10} - \frac{1}{10}$

   f) $\frac{1}{5} + \frac{3}{10}$

   g) $0.1 + 0.1 + 0.1$

   h) $1.5 - 0.1$

   i) $\frac{2}{5} - \frac{1}{3}$

   j) $0.9 + 0.1$

   k) $\frac{3}{10} + \frac{1}{10}$

   l) $\frac{1}{8} + \frac{1}{8} + \frac{1}{8}$

2. True or false?

   a) $\frac{1}{10} + \frac{1}{10} = \frac{1}{20}$

   b) $\frac{1}{10} + \frac{1}{10} = \frac{1}{100}$

   c) $\frac{1}{10} + \frac{1}{10} = \frac{2}{10}$

   d) $0.3 + 0.7 = 0.10$

   e) $\frac{3}{10} + \frac{3}{10} = 0.6$

   f) $1 - 0.1 = \frac{9}{10}$

3. Calculate the following, giving your answer as a **decimal**:

   a) $0.3 + \frac{1}{10}$

   b) $\frac{4}{10} + 0.1$

   c) $0.6 - \frac{3}{10}$

   d) $\frac{1}{5} + 0.1$

   e) $\frac{1}{4} + 0.2$

   f) $\frac{1}{2} + 0.6$

   g) $1.2 - \frac{2}{10}$

   h) $0.4 - \frac{4}{20}$

   i) $1 - \frac{1}{5}$

4. In the grid below there are five boxes that equal $\frac{1}{2}$. Can you find them?

A $\frac{1}{4} + \frac{1}{4}$	B $\frac{1}{8} + \frac{1}{2}$	C $\frac{6}{10} - 0.1$	D $0.1 + \frac{3}{10}$
E $0.7 - 0.2$	F $1 - \frac{1}{5}$	G $\frac{1}{100} + \frac{1}{100}$	H $1 - 0.05$
I $\frac{12}{24}$	J $\frac{1}{10} + 0.2$	K $\frac{5}{4}$	L $\frac{1}{5} + \frac{3}{10}$

5. Fill in the blanks with fractions or decimals:

a) 0.1 + _____ = 1

e) 0.5 + _____ = 1.5

b) 1 - _____ = $\frac{1}{8}$

f) $\frac{3}{8}$ + _____ = 1

c) _____ + $\frac{4}{12}$ = 1

g) 0.1 + $\frac{1}{2}$ = _____

d) 1 - _____ = 0.7

h) _____ + $\frac{1}{99}$ = 1

6. Write each of these as a decimal:

a) $\frac{1}{5}$

c) $\frac{1}{3}$

e) $\frac{4}{9}$

g) $\frac{4}{5}$

b) $\frac{3}{10}$

d) $\frac{1}{4}$

f) $\frac{2}{50}$

h) $\frac{8}{20}$

7. Calculate the following and give your answer **as a decimal**:

a) $\frac{4}{5}$ - 0.1

d) 1 - $\frac{1}{4}$

g) $\frac{1}{5}$ + $\frac{4}{5}$

b) $\frac{1}{8}$ + 0.1

e) $\frac{1}{2}$ - $\frac{1}{4}$

h) $\frac{2}{3}$ - 0.$\dot{3}$

c) $\frac{3}{5}$ + 0.2

f) 0.7 - $\frac{1}{10}$

i) 0.4 + $\frac{6}{50}$

fractions, decimals & negatives mixed practice

examples

Calculate...

-4 + -3	-4 × -3	0.4 + 0.3	$\frac{1}{4} + \frac{1}{3}$
= -7	= 12	= 0.7	= $\frac{7}{12}$

exercise 40

1. Calculate:

   a) -5 + -2

   b) 0.7 - 0.2

   c) -6 + 1

   d) $\frac{1}{3} + \frac{1}{3}$

   e) 1 - 0.1

   f) -3 - 2

   g) 1 - $\frac{9}{10}$

   h) -4 × -2

   i) 0.3 × 2

   j) 8 - -2

   k) 2.5 + 0.5

   l) -6 ÷ 2

2. Fill in the blanks:

   a) -6 × _____ = 36

   b) 0.4 + _____ = 1

   c) 1 - _____ = $\frac{2}{3}$

   d) 15 ÷ _____ = -3

   e) 6 + _____ = 4

   f) -2 + _____ = -10

   g) 1 - _____ = 0.4

   h) $\frac{3}{10}$ + _____ = 1

3. Write each of these as a decimal:

   a) $\frac{3}{10}$

   b) $\frac{2}{5}$

   c) $\frac{1}{2}$

   d) $\frac{1}{3}$

   e) $\frac{4}{50}$

   f) $\frac{1}{9}$

   g) $\frac{6}{100}$

   h) $1\frac{3}{10}$

4.   Calculate:

a) 0.2 × 10

b) -7 × -3

c) $\frac{1}{4}$ + $\frac{1}{10}$

d) 12 ÷ 10

e) 400 ÷ 100

f) $\frac{1}{9}$ + $\frac{1}{9}$ + $\frac{1}{9}$

g) 0.42 × 100

h) -1 × -1

i) 15 ÷ -5

j) $\frac{3}{12}$ - $\frac{1}{12}$

k) 420 ÷ 10

l) -16 × 1000

5.   Which of these fractions equal 1 whole?

a) $\frac{12}{13}$ b) $\frac{15}{15}$ c) $\frac{6}{1}$ d) $\frac{1}{6}$ e) $\frac{19}{19}$

6.   True or false:

a) -4 × 4 = 16

b) 15 ÷ 100 = 0.15

c) 0.6 × 0.6 = 3.6

d) $\frac{1}{10}$ + 0.1 = $\frac{2}{10}$

7.   Calculate:

a) $\frac{3}{12}$ - $\frac{1}{6}$

b) 0.1 × 4

c) $\frac{3}{5}$ + 0.2

d) $\frac{4}{10}$ - 0.1

e) -0.6 × 100

f) -5 ÷ 10

four operations puzzle

8.   Use 8 of the numbers below to make the sums on the right true:

-7	9	5
-4	7	2
3	18	-6

☐ - ☐ = -2

☐ + ☐ = 0

☐ × ☐ = -8

☐ ÷ ☐ = -3

Same, or Different?

Without calculating any answers, decide whether each card shows two calculations with the same answer, or with different answers.

A	
$\frac{1}{5}$ of 35	$35 \div 5$

I	
$-12 \div 3$	$12 \div -3$

B	
$1 - 0.1$	$1 - \frac{1}{10}$

J	
$\frac{5}{4}$	$1\frac{3}{4}$

C	
-3×-5	3×5

K	
$0.4 + 0.5$	$\frac{4}{10} + \frac{5}{10}$

D	
$\frac{12}{15}$	$\frac{4}{5}$

L	
$2 - -3$	$2 + 3$

E	
$6 \div 2$	$6 \div -2$

M	
$\frac{1}{10}$ of 30	$30 \div 10$

F	
$6 + -4$	$6 - 4$

N	
$1\frac{1}{5}$	$\frac{6}{5}$

G	
$\frac{4}{4}$	1

O	
$8 - 9$	$9 - 8$

H	
$\frac{1}{3}$	0.3

P	
0.03×5	$5 \times \frac{3}{100}$

The cards with DIFFERENT calculations are : ____   ____   ____   ____

chapter review

exercise 4p

1. Write three fifths as a fraction.

2. Calculate $1 - \frac{1}{5}$

3. Calculate $\frac{1}{3} + \frac{2}{3}$

4. Write $\frac{5}{4}$ as a mixed number.

5. Simplify $\frac{8}{10}$

6. Copy the diagram and shade $\frac{5}{6}$

7. A cake is cut into 8 equal pieces.
   3 children take a slice.
   What fraction is left?

8. What fraction is shaded?

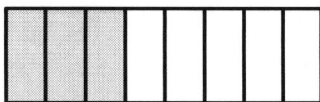

9. Write $2\frac{1}{2}$ as an improper fraction.

10. Calculate $\frac{4}{7} - \frac{1}{7}$

11. Calculate $\frac{3}{5}$ of 20

12. True or false: $\frac{15}{15} = 1$

13. How many fifths make 1?

14. How many lots of $\frac{1}{8}$ make 1?

15. Copy the diagram and shade $\frac{2}{3}$

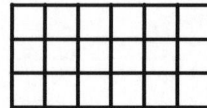

16. Calculate $\frac{1}{3} + \frac{1}{3} + \frac{2}{3}$

17. Complete the calculation:

    $\frac{4}{10} + $ _____ $ = 1$

18. Work out the value of ? so
    these fractions are equivalent:

    $\frac{2}{3} = \frac{?}{36}$

19. Calculate $\frac{2}{3}$ of 18

20. Calculate $1 - \frac{3}{5}$

21. Calculate $\frac{1}{4} + \frac{3}{4}$

22. Calculate $\frac{6}{5} - \frac{3}{5}$

23. Simplify $\frac{18}{20}$

24. Which number does each arrow point to?
    Write your answers as mixed numbers.

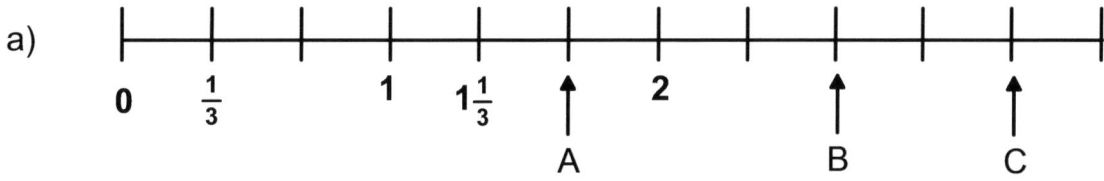

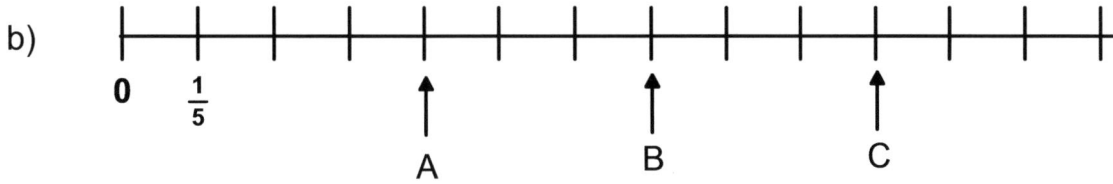

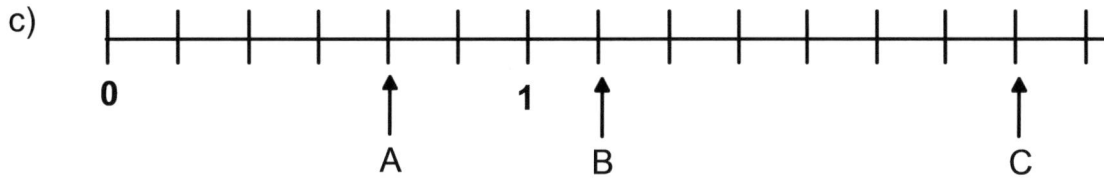

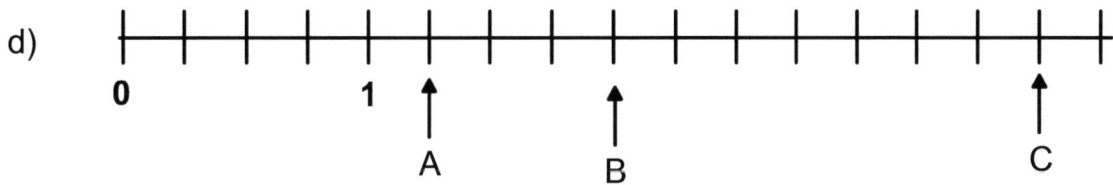

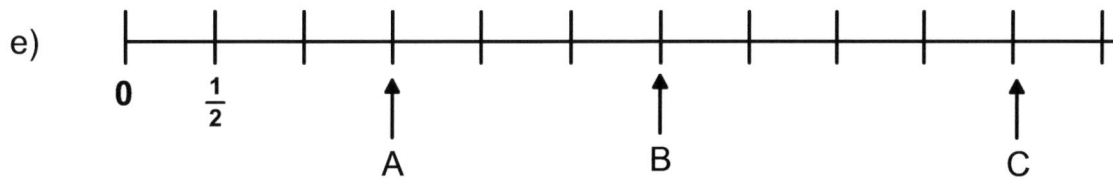

a)

$0 \qquad \frac{1}{3} \qquad\qquad 1 \qquad 1\frac{1}{3} \qquad A \qquad 2 \qquad\qquad B \qquad\qquad C$

b)

$0 \qquad \frac{1}{5} \qquad\qquad A \qquad\qquad B \qquad\qquad C$

c)

$0 \qquad\qquad A \qquad 1 \qquad B \qquad\qquad C$

d)

$0 \qquad\qquad 1 \qquad A \qquad\qquad B \qquad\qquad C$

e)

$0 \qquad \frac{1}{2} \qquad A \qquad\qquad B \qquad\qquad C$

25. Calculate:

a) $\frac{1}{4} + \frac{1}{3}$

b) $0.1 + 0.9$

c) $\frac{2}{18} + \frac{3}{18}$

d) $1 - \frac{3}{4}$

e) $1 - 0.6$

f) $\frac{1}{3} + \frac{1}{3} + \frac{1}{3}$

g) $\frac{4}{10} - \frac{1}{5}$

h) $1.5 + 0.5$

i) $1 - 0.1$

j) $\frac{3}{4} + \frac{1}{4}$

k) $\frac{1}{50} + \frac{1}{100}$

l) $\frac{1}{9} - \frac{1}{9}$

26. Work out the missing numbers to make these fractions equivalent:

a) $\frac{2}{5} = \frac{\square}{15}$

b) $\frac{3}{4} = \frac{9}{\square}$

c) $\frac{8}{10} = \frac{4}{\square}$

d) $\frac{5}{25} = \frac{1}{\square}$

e) $\frac{4}{6} = \frac{20}{\square}$

f) $\frac{9}{10} = \frac{90}{\square}$

27. Which of these are equal to 0.7? Circle two answers.

a) 0.70   b) $\frac{7}{10}$ c) 0.07   d) $\frac{7}{100}$ e) 7.0

28. Match pairs of equivalent fractions and decimals.

A $\frac{1}{5}$	B $1\frac{3}{10}$	C $\frac{3}{5}$	D $\frac{4}{50}$	M 0.6	N 0.$\dot{3}$	O 0.75	P 0.2
E $\frac{4}{100}$	F $\frac{1}{4}$	G $\frac{3}{10}$	H $\frac{3}{4}$	Q 0.3	R 1.3	S 0.8	T 0.04
I $\frac{1}{3}$	J $\frac{3}{100}$	K $\frac{4}{5}$	L $\frac{33}{100}$	U 0.08	V 0.33	W 0.25	X 0.03

A	B	C	D	E	F	G	H	I	J	K	L

Odd One Out

In each box, find pairs of equivalent numbers. Cover them up
and find the odd one out – the number in each box that has no pair.

A

$\frac{1}{3}$	$\frac{1}{4}$	$\frac{4}{8}$
$\frac{1}{2}$	$\frac{1}{5}$	$\frac{2}{6}$
$\frac{3}{12}$	$\frac{1}{10}$	$\frac{5}{25}$

B

$\frac{2}{5}$	$\frac{1}{10}$	$\frac{3}{4}$
$\frac{6}{24}$	$\frac{12}{16}$	$\frac{4}{10}$
$\frac{2}{8}$	$\frac{3}{5}$	$\frac{4}{40}$

C

$\frac{4}{3}$	$\frac{7}{8}$	$\frac{5}{4}$
$1\frac{1}{5}$	$1\frac{1}{2}$	$1\frac{1}{3}$
$\frac{6}{5}$	$1\frac{1}{4}$	$\frac{3}{2}$

D

$\frac{1}{5}$	$\frac{1}{4}$	$0.\dot{3}$
0.25	$\frac{1}{10}$	0.1
$\frac{1}{3}$	$\frac{1}{2}$	0.5

E

$2\frac{1}{5}$	$2\frac{2}{3}$	$\frac{7}{4}$
$\frac{7}{5}$	$1\frac{3}{4}$	$\frac{11}{5}$
$\frac{9}{5}$	$1\frac{2}{5}$	$\frac{8}{3}$

F

$\frac{3}{5}$	$\frac{2}{3}$	0.6
$\frac{4}{50}$	$\frac{2}{10}$	0.4
$0.\dot{6}$	0.08	0.2

G

$\frac{9}{9}$	$1\frac{9}{100}$	1
0.9	$\frac{9}{100}$	1.09
$1\frac{9}{10}$	1.9	0.09

H

$\frac{12}{15}$	$\frac{21}{30}$	$\frac{15}{20}$
$\frac{3}{4}$	$\frac{4}{5}$	$\frac{3}{10}$
$\frac{2}{3}$	$\frac{7}{10}$	$\frac{20}{30}$

I

$\frac{4}{100}$	0.6	0.06
0.40	0.3	$\frac{6}{10}$
$\frac{6}{100}$	0.4	$\frac{3}{10}$

J

$1\frac{1}{9}$	$3\frac{1}{5}$	$\frac{11}{4}$
$2\frac{3}{4}$	$\frac{10}{9}$	$\frac{23}{10}$
$\frac{16}{5}$	$\frac{4}{5}$	$2\frac{3}{10}$

K

$\frac{7}{100}$	$\frac{3}{3}$	$\frac{5}{3}$
$1\frac{2}{3}$	$\frac{12}{24}$	0.70
1	$\frac{1}{2}$	0.7

L

$\frac{1}{9}$	$\frac{5}{9}$	$0.\dot{1}$
$\frac{2}{9}$	$\frac{1}{3}$	$0.\dot{5}$
$0.\dot{3}$	$0.\dot{2}$	$0.\dot{4}$

exercise 4q

1. Calculate:

   a) 5 - 8

   b) 18 - 10

   c) 3 - 4

   d) 6 - 10

   e) 2 - 10

   f) 9 - 10

   g) -3 - 5

   h) 10 - 2

   i) -5 - 1

   j) -6 - 3

   k) 5 - 10

   l) 20 - 30

2. Write three million, eight thousand and seven in digits

3. Circle all the numbers that are more than 1 whole:

   a) $\frac{4}{5}$ b) $\frac{8}{9}$ c) $1\frac{1}{3}$ d) $\frac{7}{10}$ e) $\frac{12}{6}$

4. Fill in the blanks:

   a) -4 + _____ = 0

   b) -12 + _____ = 1

   c) -104 + _____ = 0

   d) 6 - _____ = -1

   e) -7 + _____ = 1

   f) 54 - _____ = 0

5. Which is larger, 0.403 or 0.42?

6. Work out half of each of these numbers:

   a) 42

   b) 5

   c) 50

   d) 46

   e) 70

   f) 92

   g) 84

   h) 120

   i) 186

7. True or False: $\frac{5}{15}$ is equivalent to $\frac{6}{16}$ because 1 has been added to both the numerator and denominator.

8. What fraction of this shape is shaded?

   a) $\frac{1}{2}$ b) $\frac{2}{5}$ c) cannot tell

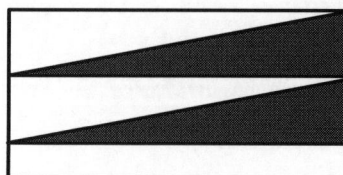

9. Write these decimals as fractions or mixed numbers:

    a) 0.27   b) 0.3   c) 0.4

    d) 0.04   e) 1.1   f) 0.17

    g) 0.009   h) 0.909   i) 0.099

10. Round each number as shown:

    a) 2.45 (1 decimal place)   e) 35 (nearest ten)

    b) 471 (nearest hundred)   f) 1.081 (2 decimal places)

    c) 0.333 (2 decimal places)   g) 12.5 (nearest whole number)

    d) 1,400 (nearest thousand)   h) 4,820 (nearest thousand)

11. Put these numbers in order, starting with the smallest: -4   3   -9   0

12. Put these numbers in order, starting with the smallest: 0.11   0.2   0.101

13. Calculate:

    a) 1.4 + 0.6   d) $\frac{4}{10}$ + 0.5   g) 3 + -3

    b) 1 - $\frac{1}{9}$ e) 0.6 × 100   h) 0.2 × 7

    c) $\frac{1}{4}$ + $\frac{3}{4}$ f) -5 × -2   i) 14 ÷ 10

14. Simplify fully $\frac{8}{100}$

15. Round 3.99 to 1 decimal place.

negative numbers practice

exercise 4r

1. Calculate

   a) -4 × -2

   b) -6 + -2

   c) -3 × -1

   d) 20 ÷ -5

   e) 6 ÷ -3

   f) 8 × -2

   g) 4 × -3

   h) -5 + -5

   i) -6 - 3

   j) 10 - 12

   k) -2 × -2

   l) 7 + -3

   m) 5 - - 2

   n) -2 + 5

   o) 14 ÷ -7

2. Fill in the blanks:

   a) When two negative numbers are added, the answer is _____

   b) When two negative numbers are multiplied, the answer is _____

3. Which of these calculations have a **negative** answer? Circle all that apply.

   a) -3 + 6

   b) -3 × 6

   c) -4 × -5

   d) -4 + -5

   e) -10 - 5

   f) -10 ÷ -5

   g) -2 + -6

   h) -2 × -6

4. Calculate:

   a) 7 - - 3

   b) -8 - 2

   c) -5 × -5

   d) -12 × 3

   e) -2 + -8

   f) 35 ÷ -5

   g) -4 - - 4

   h) -6 - 10

four operations puzzle

Choose 8 of the numbers below to make the sums correct:

-8	-11	-4
5	-4	-9
10	8	1

☐ - ☐ = -10

☐ + ☐ = 18

☐ × ☐ = -55

☐ ÷ ☐ = 2

chapter 5: indices

[Recommended Time: 10 - 14 hours]

Contents

learn by heart

2 × 2 × 2 is not the same as 2 × 3
2 × 2 × 2 = 8 (work it out one bit at a time)

recall

A negative × a negative = a positive

Product = the result of multiplying,
e.g. the product of 6 and 2 is 12

examples

Calculate....

3 × 3 × 3	-2 × -2 × -2 × -2
= 27	= 16

*If an **even** number of negatives are multiplied, the product is positive*

exercise 5a

1. Work out:

    a) 2 × 2 × 2   d) 3 × 3   g) 2 × 2 × 2 × 2

    b) 1 × 1 × 1 × 1   e) -3 × -3   h) 5 × 5 × 5

    c) -5 × -5   f) -1 × -1 × -1   i) -10 × -10

2. True or False: 2 × 2 × 2 = 6

3. Work out 1 × 1 × 1 × 1 × 1 × 1 × 1 × 1 × 1 × 1

4. Calculate:

    a) -2 × -2 × -2   b) 0 × 0 × 0 × 0 × 0   c) 3 × 3 × 3

5. True or False:

    a) 5 × 5 = 10   c) -4 × -4 = -16

    b) 1 × 1 × 1 = 3   d) -2 × -2 × -2 = -6

6. Work out:

    a) -3 × -3 × -3   b) -1 × -1 × -1   c) -2 × -2 × -2 × -2

7. Work out 1 × 1 × 1 × 1 × 1 × 1 × 1 × 1 × 1 × 1 × 1 × 1 × 1 × 1

8. Work out 2 × 2 × 2 × 2 × 2 × 2 × 2

6. Calculate each of the following:

    a) -1 × -1

    b) -1 × -1 × -1

    c) -1 × -1 × -1 × -1

    d) -1 × -1 × -1 × -1 × -1

    e) -1 × - 1 × -1 × -1 × -1 × -1

    f) -1 × -1 × -1 × -1 × -1 × -1 × -1

    g) -1 × -1 × -1 × -1 × -1 × -1 × -1 × -1

    h) -1 × -1 × -1 × -1 × -1 × -1 × -1 × -1 × -1

7. Fill in the blanks with positive or negative:

    a) When **3** negatives are multipled, the answer is _____

    b) When **4** negatives are multiplied, the answer is _____

    c) When **5** negatives are multiplied, the answer is _____

    d) When **99** negatives are multiplied, the answer is _____

8. Given that 6 × 6 × 6 = 216, work out -6 × -6 × -6

9. Calculate:

    a) 2 × 2 × 3

    b) 1 × 1 × 1 × 1 × 1 × 1 × 4

    c) 3 × 3 × 1 × 1 × 1

    d) 2 × 2 × 2 × 11

    e) 3 × 3 × 3 × 1 × 1 × 1

    f) 10 × 10 × 10

    g) -5 × -5 × 2

    h) 3 × 3 × 3 × 3 × 3 × 3 × 0

    i) 3 × 3 × 10 × 10

    j) -2 × -2 × -2 × -10 × -10 × -10

10. Which calculation will have a **negative** answer?

    a) -5 × -5   b) -5 × -5 × -5 × -5   c) 5 × 5 × 5   d) -5 × -5 × -5

11. Which of these is 1 million?

    a) 10 × 10 × 10 × 10

    b) 10 × 10 × 10 × 10 × 10 × 10

index notation: positive bases

learn by heart

To show repeated multiplication we use a base and an index.

The base is the number being multiplied, the index shows how many times to multiply.

An index of 1 is not written, so $4 = 4^1$

People use many different names for 'index', including 'exponent' and 'power'

An index of 2 is pronounced 'squared', so 3^2 is read 'three squared'. The result is called a square number.

An index of 3 is pronounced 'cubed', so 5^3 is read 'five cubed'. The result is called a cube number.

Higher indices are read as 'to the power of', so 3^5 is read '3 to the power of 5'

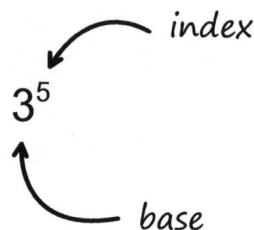

3^5

index

base

examples

Evaluate 2^3

$2 \times 2 \times 2 = 8$

Write $7 \times 7 \times 7 \times 7$ using indices

$= 7^4$

exercise 5b

1. Write using indices:

   a) Five to the power nine

   b) Three to the power four

   c) Seventeen squared

   d) Forty one cubed

2. Write the following using indices:

   a) $4 \times 4 \times 4$

   b) $3 \times 3 \times 3 \times 3$

   d) $10 \times 10 \times 10 \times 10 \times 10$

   e) 9

3. Evaluate:

   a) 3^2

   b) 2^3

   c) 10^2

   d) 2^4

   e) 0^4

   f) 3^3

   g) 4^2

   h) 10^3

   i) 2^1

   j) 10^4

   k) 1^8

   l) 5^2

   m) 5^3

   n) 1^{400}

   o) 400^1

   p) 2^6

4. True or false:

a) $3^3 = 9$

c) $4^2 = 4 \times 2$

b) $2 \times 2 \times 2 \times 2 = 2^4$

d) $2 \times 2 \times 2 = 6$

5. Write $1 \times 1 \times 1 \times 1 \times 1 \times 1 \times 1 \times 1$ using indices.

6. Fill in the missing numbers:

a) $\boxed{}^2 = 49$

d) $\boxed{}^{10} = 1$

b) $\boxed{}^3 = 8$

e) $\boxed{}^1 = 10$

c) $6^{\boxed{}} = 36$

f) $3^{\boxed{}} = 27$

7. Evaluate:

a) 2^3

d) 3^3

g) 6^2

j) 3^1

b) 1^4

e) 2^4

h) 3^2

k) 8^2

c) 5^2

f) 1^{10}

i) 4^3

l) 1^{100}

8. Fill in the blanks with >, < or =

a) 2^3 _____ 3^2

c) 4^2 _____ 3^3

e) 2^4 _____ 4^2

b) 1^4 _____ 1^7

d) 0^4 _____ 1^3

f) 8^1 _____ 1^8

9. Calculate:

a) $3^2 - 2^2$

d) $10^2 \times 3$

g) $3^2 + 4^2$

b) $4^2 \times 1^3$

e) $4^2 + 2^2$

h) $10^2 \times 7^2$

c) $10^2 - 1^2$

f) $5^2 \times 2^2$

i) $10^3 \times 2^3$

10. What is 1 to the power 1 million?

index notation: square and cube numbers

learn by heart

Square Numbers: the answer when a positive whole number is squared, for example $3^2 = 9$, so the third square number is 9

Cube Numbers: the answer when a positive whole number is cubed, for example $2^3 = 8$, so the second cube number is 8

exercise 5c

1. Write down the first 12 square numbers.

2. Write down the first 6 cube numbers.

3. Which of the following is 2 cubed?

   a) 2×3 b) 2^4 c) 3^2 d) 2^3 e) 2^5

4. Write using indices:

   a) 4 squared = _____   c) 12 squared = _____

   b) 1 cubed = _____   d) 5 cubed = _____

5. In the box, find all the square numbers:

1	7	15	4	10	2	6	20	9
11	100	99	50	12	3	16	36	18
49	20	8	13	23	64	25	5	40

6. Evaluate:

   a) 7^2 c) 1^2 e) 2^3 g) 6^2

   b) 4^2 d) 3^3 f) 9^2 h) 1^3

7. What is the tenth square number?

8. What is the first cube number?

9. In the box, find all the **cube** numbers:

1	3	5	9	12	2	8	20	9
11	100	27	125	30	64	16	36	216

10. Give an example of a number that is both a square number and a cube number.

11. For each card, work out which numbers are being described:

A | A cube number + a square number = 10   .... and ....

B | A square number + a square number = 25   .... and ....

C | An odd number + a cube number = 30   .... and ....

D | A square number + a cube number = 17   .... and ....

E | A square number × a square number = 100   .... and ....

F | A cube number + a cube number = 9   .... and ....

G | A square number × a cube number = 32   .... and ....

H | A square number + a square number = 104   .... and ....

index notation: negative bases

learn by heart

If the base number is negative, it requires a bracket, so -3 × -3 = (-3)^2

If the base is negative, and the index is **even**, the answer will be a **positive** number.

examples

Evaluate (-3)^2

-3 × -3
= 9

Evaluate (-1)^5

-1 × -1 × -1 × -1 × -1
= -1

If the base is negative, and the index is **odd**, the answer will be a **negative** number.

exercise 5d

1. Evaluate:

    a) $(-7)^2$ c) $(-3)^3$ e) $(-2)^3$ g) $(-4)^2$

    b) $(-5)^2$ d) $(-1)^3$ f) $(-10)^2$ h) $(-2)^4$

2. True or False: $(-3)^2$ = -9

3. Copy and complete the table to show what happens for the powers of -1:

$(-1)^1$	$(-1)^2$	$(-1)^3$	$(-1)^4$	$(-1)^5$	$(-1)^6$	$(-1)^7$	$(-1)^8$	$(-1)^9$	$(-1)^{10}$	$(-1)^{11}$

4. Which of these equal -1?

    a) $(-1)^{18}$ b) $(-1)^{19}$ c) $(-1)^{20}$ d) $(-1)^{21}$

5. If we multiply **31** negative numbers, the answer will be _____ (choose positive or negative)

6. Which of the following will have a positive answer? Circle all that apply:

    a) 1^4 b) $(-2)^2$ c) 3^1 d) $(-3)^3$ e) $(-2)^3$

7. Evaluate:

    a) 3^3 b) $(-3)^3$ c) $(-4)^2$ d) 1^3

8. Given that 6^4 = 1296, work out $(-6)^4$

exercise 5e : mixed positive & negative bases

1. Evaluate:

   a) 2^3

   b) 1^4

   c) 5^2

   d) 3^1

   e) 3^3

   f) 2^4

   g) 1^{10}

   h) 7^1

   i) 6^2

   j) $(-4)^2$

   k) 4^3

   l) $(-2)^2$

   m) $(-1)^3$

   n) 8^2

   o) $(-3)^3$

   p) $(-5)^1$

2. Work out the missing indices:

   a) $6^? = 36$

   b) $4^? = 4$

   c) $5^? = 125$

   d) $2^? = 8$

   e) $(-3)^? = 9$

   f) $2^? = 32$

3. There are 6 false statements in this grid. Can you find them?

A $5^2 = 10$	F $2 \times 3 = 2^3$	K $2^3 = 8$	P $3 \times 3 \times 3 = 9$
B $2^5 = 32$	G $9^2 = 3$	L $2^2 \times 2 = 2^3$	Q $4^2 = 2^4$
C $(-1)^5 = -1$	H $7^6 > 7^5$	M $10^3 = 1{,}000$	R $1^1 = 1$
D $1^5 = 5$	I $3^3 = 27$	N $10^4 = 10{,}000$	S $(-3)^2 = 3^2$
E $8^2 = 64$	J $10^6 = 1$ million	O $3^4 = 12$	T $9^2 = 81$

4. Put these in order of size, starting with the smallest:

   A $(-2)^2$ B -8 C 3^2 D $(-3)^3$

   ____ ____ ____ ____

5. Put these in order of size, starting with the smallest:

   A 1^5 B 3^1 C 0^2 D $(-2)^3$

   ____ ____ ____ ____

6. Annie says that $(-2)^{13} = 8192$. Explain why she must be wrong.

7. Evaluate $(-1)^{1{,}000{,}000}$

index notation: the power 0 & mixed practice

learn by heart

Any base to the power 0 is 1 ⟶ *e.g. $100^0 = 1$* ↘ (except 0^0)

exercise 5f

1. Copy and complete these power tables. The first one is started for you:

a)

2^3	
2^2	
2^1	2
2^0	1

b)

3^3	
3^2	
3^1	
3^0	

c)

5^3	
5^2	
5^1	
5^0	

d)

10^3	
10^2	
10^1	
10^0	

2. Evaluate:

a) 6^0

b) $(-1)^0$

c) 400^0

d) 0.8^0

e) 5^1

f) 7^2

g) 2^3

h) $(-5)^2$

i) 10^3

3. Which of the following means 2^4?

a) 2×4 　　　　 b) $2 + 2 + 2 + 2$ 　　　　 c) $2 \times 2 \times 2 \times 2$

4. Evaluate:

a) 3^2

b) $(-3)^2$

c) $(-1)^3$

d) 1^5

e) 6^1

f) 2^5

5. Will the answer to $(-1)^{10}$ be positive or negative? Explain your answer.

6. Evaluate $(-2)^5$

7. What's missing? Work out the missing indices:

a) $2^a = 8$

b) $2^b = 16$

c) $2^c = 32$

d) $3^d = 27$

e) $4^e = 4$

f) $10^f = 10,000$

g) $8^g = 64$

h) $3^k = 27$

i) $2^l = 1$

Two Lies & a Truth

In each row, two statements are false and one is true.

Can you find the **true** statement?

	A	B	C
1	$2 \times 2 \times 2 = 6$	$2 \times 2 \times 2 = 8$	$2 \times 2 \times 2 = 10$
2	3^2 means 3×3	3^2 means $3 + 3$	3^2 means $3 - 3$
3	$(-3)^2 = 6$	$(-3)^2 = -9$	$(-3)^2 = 9$
4	$2^3 = 6$	$2^3 = 8$	$2^3 = -8$
5	$(-10)^2 = -20$	$(-10)^2 = 20$	$(-10)^2 = 100$
6	$1^5 = 1$	$1^5 = 5$	$1^5 = -1$
7	$3^3 = 9$	$3^3 = 27$	$3^3 = 6$
8	$6^1 = 36$	$6^1 = \frac{1}{6}$	$6^1 = 6$
9	$(-2)^3 = -8$	$(-2)^3 = 6$	$(-2)^3 = -6$
10	$(-3)^3 = -9$	$(-3)^3 = 9$	$(-3)^3 = -27$
11	$1^{400} = 1,400$	$1^{400} = 1$	$1^{400} = 400$
12	$5^2 = 10$	$5^2 = 7$	$5^2 = 25$
13	$(-3)^4 = -12$	$(-3)^4 = -81$	$(-3)^4 = 81$

Indices Match

Evaluate each card and then find a matching card at the bottom.

A	B	C	D
6^2	2^3	$(-3)^2$	$(-2)^3$

E	F	G	H
6^0	$3^2 \times 2$	$3^2 + 4^2$	7×3^0

I	J	K	L
3^3	2^4	$5^2 - 2^2$	$(-3)^3$

M	N	O	P
$2^3 - 2^2$	$1^5 \times 5^1$	$10^2 - 5^2$	12^1

Q	R	S	T
4×2^3	$(-3)^2 \times 10$	$(-12)^2$	10^3

U	V	W	X
$2^2 - 3^2$	$12^0 - 12^1$	$2^3 + (-2)^3$	$(-3)^3 \div 9$

- -

answers

5	18	-11	0	1	27	-27	25	4	21	144	12

-5	36	32	7	-3	16	90	8	1000	75	9	-8

multiplying with indices

$3^{10} \times 3^2 = 3^{12}$

Multiplication Law: *when multiplying with the same base, add the indices*

examples

Write $7^2 \times 7^4$ as a power of 7	Write $5^{-6} \times 5$ as a power of 5
$= 7^{2+4} = 7^6$	$= 5^{-6+1} = 5^{-5}$

exercise 5g

1. Write as a power of 3:

   a) $3^2 \times 3^2$

   b) 3×3^2

   c) $3^2 \times 3^2$

   d) $3^7 \times 3$

   e) $3^3 \times 3$

   f) $3^5 \times 3^4$

   g) $3^4 \times 3^2 \times 3$

   h) $3^7 \times 3 \times 3^1$

   i) $3^8 \times 3 \times 3 \times 3$

2. Simplify the following, where possible.
   Two statements cannot be simplified using the multiplication law. Which two?

   a) $5^{10} \times 5^{-3}$

   b) $(-4)^2 \times (-4)^3$

   c) $4^5 - 4^2$

   d) $3^0 \times 3^0$

   e) $3^4 + 3^2$

   f) $(-3)^2 \times (-3)^5$

   g) $6^{-2} \times 6^2$

   h) $5^{-4} \times 5^4$

   i) $8^{-2} \times 8^5$

3. True or false?

   a) $6^7 + 6^7 = 6^{14}$

   b) $6^7 \times 6^7 = 6^{49}$

   c) $6^7 \times 6^7 = 6^{14}$

   d) $6^7 \times 6^7 = 36^{14}$

4. Write as a power of 3, if possible:

   a) $3^5 \times 3^2$

   b) $3^{-2} \times 3^4$

   c) $3^{-1} \times 3^3$

   d) $3^{-2} \times 3^2$

   e) $3^1 \times 3$

   f) $3^{-2} \times 3^{-6} \times 3^{-1}$

   g) $3^0 \times 3^4$

   h) $3^2 \times 3 \times 3^3$

   i) $3^2 + 3^2$

5. Work out the missing numbers:

A
$$3^4 \times 3^{\square} = 3^{14}$$

B
$$2^5 \times 2^{\square} = 2^4$$

C
$$5 \times 5^{\square} = 5^7$$

D
$$4^{\square} \times 4^{-2} = 4^6$$

E
$$2^{\square} \times 2^7 = 2^4$$

F
$$7^{-3} \times 7^{\square} = 7^0$$

G
$$3^{\square} \times 3^8 = 3^9$$

H
$$(-2)^7 \times (-2)^{\square} = (-2)^{10}$$

I
$$5^{-5} \times 5^{\square} = 5^{-7}$$

J
$$2^{\square} \times 2^{-5} = 2^{-1}$$

K
$$8^{-9} \times 8^{\square} = 8^{-1}$$

L
$$6^{-3} \times 6^{\square} = 6^6$$

clever calculations

6. Use the laws of indices to help you calculate the value of these expressions:

a) $7^{50} \times 7^{-48}$

b) $5^{45} \times 5^{-43}$

c) $1^{427} \times 1^3$

d) $15^9 \times 15^{-8}$

e) $2^{16} \times 2^{-13}$

f) $(-4)^7 \times (-4)^{-5}$

dividing with indices

learn by heart

$$3^{10} \div 3^2 = 3^8$$

Division Law: *when dividing with the same base, subtract the indices*

examples

Write $5^8 \div 5^2$ as a power of 5

$$= 5^{8-2} = 5^3$$

Write $\dfrac{2^4}{2^{-3}}$ as a single power

$$= 2^{4--3} = 2^7$$

exercise 5h

1. Write as a single power:

   a) $3^5 \div 3^1$

   b) $4^{10} \div 4^3$

   c) $3^8 \div 3^2$

   d) $3^8 \div 3^8$

   e) $4^3 \div 4^4$

   f) $8^5 \div 8^2$

   g) $6^4 \div 6^8$

   h) $5^4 \div 5^6$

   i) $8^{-2} \div 8^3$

2. True or False:

   a) $5^{10} \div 5^5 = 5^2$

   b) $10^7 \div 10^5 = 1^2$

   c) $\dfrac{5}{5^2} = 5 \div 5^2$

   d) $15^7 \div 5^3 = 3^4$

   e) $8^6 - 8^4 = 8^2$

   f) $10^5 \div 2^3 = 5^2$

3. Write as a single power of 2, if possible:

   a) $2^5 \div 2^2$

   b) $2^1 \div 2^4$

   c) $2^3 \div 2^5$

   d) $2^0 \div 2^3$

   e) $2^{-6} \div 2^5$

   f) $2^{-2} \div 2^5$

   g) $2^{-3} \div 2^3$

   h) $2^{-1} \div 2^5$

   i) $2^{-3} \div 2^5$

   j) $2^{-7} \div 2^3$

   k) $\dfrac{2^6}{2^2}$

   l) $\dfrac{2^5}{2^3}$

   m) $\dfrac{2^5}{2^4}$

   n) $\dfrac{2^5}{2^0}$

   o) $\dfrac{2^{-2}}{2^5}$

   p) $\dfrac{2^3}{2^{-2}}$

   q) $\dfrac{2}{2^{-4}}$

   r) $\dfrac{2^3}{2^{-2}}$

mixed multiplication & division practice

exercise 5i

1. Simplify using the laws of indices:

   a) $3^7 \div 3^2$

   b) $2^5 \times 2^3$

   c) $3^5 \times 3^{-2}$

   d) $4^4 \div 4^0$

   e) $5^6 \times 6^5$

   f) $3^8 \times 3^2$

   g) $10^2 \div 10^5$

   h) $8^2 \times 8^{-4}$

   i) $6^4 \times 6$

   j) $3^0 \times 3^{-4}$

   k) $5^{-2} \div 5^2$

   l) $8^3 \div 8^{10}$

   m) $6^3 \div 6$

   n) $(-5)^9 \times (-5)^4$

   o) $\dfrac{2^4}{2}$

2. There are 5 false statements in this grid. Find them.

a $4^3 = 12$	e $3^2 \times 3^4 = 3^8$	i $2^8 \div 2^4 = 2^4$	m $6^2 = 36$
b $2^3 \times 2 = 2^4$	f $9^2 \div 9^3 = 9^1$	j $4^3 + 4^5 = 4^8$	n $8^0 = 1$
c $3^5 \div 3^5 = 3^0$	g $6^2 \div 6^4 = 6^{-2}$	k $8^5 \times 8^3 = 8^8$	o $2^{15} \div 2^3 = 2^5$
d $6^2 - 6 = 30$	h $8^3 \div 8 = 8^2$	l $4^1 \times 5 = 20$	p $4^2 \div 4^3 = 4^{-1}$

3. True or False: $3 \times 3 \times 3 \times 3 = 4^3$

4. True or False: $2 \times 2 \times 2 \times 2 = 2^3$

5. Simplify $4^2 \times 4^2 \times 4^2$

6. Which of the following is the same as 6^8?

   a) $6^2 + 6^6$ b) $6^2 \times 6^4$ c) $2^2 \times 3^6$ d) $6^2 \times 6^6$

7. Work out the missing powers to make each of these statments true:

   a) $3^6 \times 3^? = 3^{10}$

   b) $(-4)^8 \times (-4)^? = (-4)^5$

   c) $10^4 \div 10^? = 10^4$

   d) $5^8 \times 5^? = 5^7$

   e) $6^4 \times 6^3 \div 6^2 = 6^?$

   f) $4^3 \times 4^? = 4^2$

index laws (power law)

learn by heart

$(2^3)^5 = 2^{15}$

Power Law: When a base is raised to more than one index, multiply the indices

exercise 5j

1. Which of the following is 2^8?

   a) $(2^6)^2$ b) $(2^4)^4$ c) $(2^2)^4$ d) $(2)^4$

2. Write as a single power:

   a) $(2^2)^4$ b) $(4^3)^2$ c) $(5^4)^5$

   d) $(2^2)^2$ e) $(5^8)^0$ f) $(6^{-2})^3$

   g) $(3^4)^{-5}$ h) $(6^9)^1$ i) $(3^{-1})^{-2}$

   j) $(5^{-3})^{-2}$ k) $(2^{-4})^3$ l) $(4^0)^7$

3. Write as a single power of 5:

   a) $(5^{0.1})^2$ b) $(5^3)^{0.2}$ c) $(5^3)^{0.2}$ d) $(5^{100})^1$

matching activity

Match each card on the left with its answer on the right:

A $5^3 \times 5^2$	**B** $(5^5)^2$	**C** $\dfrac{5^6}{5^2}$
D $(5^{-2})^2$	**E** $5^{-4} \times 5^2$	**F** $5^7 \times 5^{-1}$
G $(5^4)^{-3}$	**H** $\dfrac{5^8}{5^2}$	**I** $5^6 \times 5$
J $\dfrac{5^6}{5^3}$	**K** $\dfrac{5^7}{5^7}$	**L** $(5^{-1})^{-1}$

Answer cards:

5^3	5^{-4}
1	5^7
5^6	5
5^6	5^{-12}
5^4	5^5
5^{-2}	5^{10}

A	B	C	D	E	F	G	H	I	J	K	L

Mixed Laws of Indices Code Breaker

Write each of the following as a single power using the laws of indices.
Find your answer in the code box.
Write down the words to reveal a hidden joke!

code box

5^{-11} = don't	5^{-3} = will	5^4 = hair	5^{11} = a
5^{-10} = forever	5^{-2} = and	5^5 = on	5^{12} = you
5^{-9} = over	5^{-1} = never	5^6 = talk	5^{13} = can
5^{-8} = to	5^0 = go	5^7 = drink	5^{14} = cake
5^{-7} = decimal?	5 = ever!	5^8 = wish	5^{15} = Because
5^{-6} = paper	5^2 = Why	5^9 = should	5^{16} = cable
5^{-4} = they	5^3 = book	5^{10} = recurring	5^{17} = What

a) $5^7 \div 5^5 =$ ___5^2___ = **Why**

b) $(5^3)^3 =$ _____ =

c) $5^{10} \times 5^2 =$ _____ =

d) $5^3 \times 5^{-4} =$ _____ =

e) $\dfrac{5^8}{5^2} =$ _____ =

f) $(5^4)^{-2} =$ _____ =

g) $5^{10} \times 5 =$ _____ =

h) $\dfrac{5^{11}}{5} =$ _____ =

i) $5^{-2} \div 5^5 =$ _____ =

j) $(5^{-3})^{-5} =$ _____ =

k) $5 \div 5^5 =$ _____ =

l) $(5^3)^{-1} =$ _____ =

m) $5^7 \times 5^{-7} =$ _____ =

n) $\dfrac{5^4}{5^{-1}} =$ _____ =

o) $5^{-3} \times 5^{-7} =$ _____ =

p) $\dfrac{5^8}{5^{10}} =$ _____ =

q) $\dfrac{5^7}{5^6} =$ _____ =

learn by heart

Square Numbers: 1, 4, 9, 16, 25, 36, 49, 64, 81, 100, 121, 144

Cube Numbers: 1, 8, 27, 64, 125, 216, 343

$\sqrt{}$ is read 'square root' $\sqrt[3]{}$ is read 'cube root'

examples

Evaluate $\sqrt{36}$
= 6

Evaluate $\sqrt[3]{27}$
= 3

This means, which number, to the power 3, equals 27?

exercise 5k

1. Show how to write each of these. The first one is done for you.

Symbol	In Words
$\sqrt{36}$	Square root of 36
	Square root of 49
	Cube root of 27
	Cube root of 0

Symbol	In Words
	Cube root of 1
	Five cubed
	Nine squared
	Three cubed

2. Evaluate:

a) $\sqrt{25}$

b) $\sqrt{49}$

c) $\sqrt[3]{8}$

d) $\sqrt{4}$

e) $\sqrt[3]{27}$

f) $\sqrt{16}$

g) $\sqrt{100}$

h) $\sqrt{9}$

i) $\sqrt[3]{125}$

j) $\sqrt{144}$

k) $\sqrt{0}$

l) $\sqrt{1}$

m) $\sqrt[2]{1}$

n) $\sqrt[3]{1}$

o) $\sqrt[3]{0}$

3. True or false: $\sqrt{9} = 4.5$

4. Find all the square numbers in this grid:

A 8	E 4	I 5	M 100	Q 40	U 11
B 7	F 20	J 25	N 32	R 38	V 13
C 2	G 6	K 9	O 10	S 49	W 1000
D 1	H 3	L 90	P 12	T 26	X 36

5. Which of these are cube numbers?

   a) 1   b) 2   c) 3   d) 8   e) 9   f) 27

6. Work out:

   a) the square root of 9   b) 9 squared

   c) the cube root of 8   d) the square root of 100

   e) 3 cubed   f) 1 to the power 4

   g) 4 squared   h) the cube root of 27

   i) the square root of 4   j) 8 squared

7. Evaluate:

   a) 4^2 f) $\sqrt{36}$ k) $\sqrt{16}$ p) 10^3

   b) 6^2 g) 1^3 l) $\sqrt[3]{1}$ q) $\sqrt{4}$

   c) 2^3 h) 5^2 m) $\sqrt{25}$ r) $\sqrt[3]{8}$

   d) $(-3)^2$ i) 4^3 n) 9^2 s) $(-2)^3$

   e) $\sqrt{49}$ j) 3^3 o) $\sqrt[3]{27}$ t) $\sqrt[3]{125}$

challenge

8. Which of these is impossible? Explain your answer.

   a) $\sqrt{1}$ b) $\sqrt{0}$ c) $\sqrt{-9}$ d) $\sqrt{16}$

exercise 51 (further practice with squares, cubes & roots)

1. Find all the cube numbers in this grid:

A 8	E 4	I 5	M 100	Q 216	U 11
B 7	F 125	J 25	N 27	R 38	V 13
C 2	G 6	K 9	O 10	S 49	W 1000
D 1	H 3	L 90	P 12	T 64	X 36

2. Work out:

a) $\sqrt{25}$　　　　　b) $\sqrt{49}$　　　　　c) $\sqrt[3]{8}$　　　　　d) 3^3

3. Decide whether these statements are true or false:

a) $\sqrt{49} = 7$　　　　　e) $\sqrt{20} = 10$　　　　　i) $\sqrt{100} = 10$

b) $\sqrt[3]{9} = 3$　　　　　f) $\sqrt[3]{8} = 2$　　　　　j) $\sqrt{50} = 25$

c) $\sqrt[4]{16} = 4$　　　　　g) $2^3 = 8$　　　　　k) $4^2 = 16$

d) $5^3 = 15$　　　　　h) $10^2 = 20$　　　　　l) $5^3 = 125$

matching activity

4. Match these cards into pairs that are equivalent.
Record your pairs in a table.

A	5²	B	(-3)²	C	6²
D	10	E	(-2)²	F	3
G	$\sqrt{25}$	H	$\sqrt{64}$	I	$\sqrt[3]{1}$

J	4	K	$\sqrt[3]{27}$	L	1
M	$\sqrt{100}$	N	9	O	25
P	5	Q	8	R	36

A	
B	
C	
D	
E	
F	
G	
H	
I	

5. Which of these are square numbers? Circle three answers.

   a) 1   b) 2   c) 5   d) 8   e) 9   f) 100

6. Evaluate:

   a) 9^2 e) 3^3 i) 1^5 m) 6^3

   b) $\sqrt[3]{1000}$ f) $\sqrt[3]{125}$ j) 0^3 n) $(-3)^3$

   c) $(-3)^2$ g) $\sqrt[4]{16}$ k) $\sqrt{25}$ o) 5^1

   d) $\sqrt{64}$ h) 2^3 l) $\sqrt[3]{8}$ p) $\sqrt{144}$

7. Put these in order of size, starting with the smallest:

A	B	C	D
$\sqrt{36}$	3^3	2^4	$\sqrt[3]{64}$

   ____ ____ ____ ____

8. Calculate:

   a) $\sqrt{4} \times 3^2$ d) $\sqrt[3]{27} \div 3$ g) $9 \div \sqrt{9}$

   b) $\sqrt{36} \times 2^3$ e) $18 \div \sqrt{81}$ h) $2^3 \div \sqrt[3]{8}$

   c) $4^1 \times \sqrt{25}$ f) $1^5 + 1^3$ i) $2^4 \div \sqrt{16}$

9. Fill in the blanks with >, < or =

   a) 2^3 _____ 3^2 c) $\sqrt{9}$ _____ 4^2 e) $\sqrt{1}$ _____ $\sqrt[3]{1}$

   b) 2^4 _____ 4^2 d) $\sqrt[3]{64}$ _____ $\sqrt{64}$ f) 1^9 _____ 8^1

10. If $\sqrt{a} = \sqrt[3]{a}$, what could a be?

learn by heart

Addition and subtraction have equal & lowest priority. When a calculation only involves adding and subtracting, just read from left to right.

B ()

I ^{2} $\sqrt{}$

DM × ÷

AS - +

Divisions and multiplications have more impact on the size of the answer, so they have higher priority. Calculate these **before** additions and subtractions.

Divisions can be written with a fraction bar, e.g. $\frac{5 \times 3}{6 - 1}$
In this case, calculate numerator and denominator seprately and then divide

examples

Calculate 30 - 3 × 5

$$= 30 - 15 = 15$$

Calculate 4 - 2 + 1

$$= 3$$

Calculate $\frac{4 + 8}{2}$

$$= 12 \div 2 = 6$$

Work out the multiplication first, so replace 3 × 5 with 15, then read from left to right

Just read from left to right – addition and subtraction have equal priority.

exercise 5m

1. Work out:

   a) 10 - 8 + 2

   b) 4 + 3 × 2

   c) 20 ÷ 4 - 2

   d) 10 - 6 ÷ 2

   e) 3 × 5 + 4

   f) 10 - 8 ÷ 2

2. Work out:

   a) 10 + 5 ÷ 5

   b) $\frac{10 + 5}{5}$

   c) $\frac{10}{5}$ + 5

   d) 8 - 4 + 2

   e) $\frac{20}{4 - 3}$

   f) 3 × 2 + 5

   g) 5 + 24 ÷ 4 + 2

   h) 24 ÷ 2 + 4 × 3

   i) 3 × 4 - 7

   f) $\frac{9 - 3}{3}$

   i) 2 × 4 × 5

   l) 18 ÷ 2 - 3

3. True or false: 9 - 3 + 2 = 4

165

4. Calculate:

a) $\dfrac{5 \times 6}{3} - 4$

b) $\dfrac{18 - 2}{10 - 6}$

c) $12 - \dfrac{9}{3}$

d) $\dfrac{20 - 2}{9} - 10$

e) $\dfrac{18}{5 - 2} - 7$

f) $\dfrac{15}{3} + 4 \times \dfrac{10}{2}$

g) $5 - \dfrac{8 + 2}{3 - 1}$

h) $\dfrac{16}{2} \times \dfrac{25 - 3}{10 + 1}$

i) $9 - \dfrac{30}{2 \times 3} - 2$

j) $4 - \dfrac{8}{5 - 4} + 3 \times \dfrac{5}{5}$

k) $6 \times \dfrac{6}{2} - 6 \div \dfrac{9}{3}$

l) $20 - \dfrac{16 + 4}{3 - 4}$

Order of Operations Puzzle

Can you use the numbers in the grid below to complete the empty boxes and make the sums true?

18	4	10	2
3	5	6	8
2	8	6	5

A $\boxed{2}$ + $\boxed{3}$ × $\boxed{}$ = $\boxed{17}$

B $\boxed{3}$ + $\boxed{}$ × $\boxed{4}$ = $\boxed{11}$

C $\boxed{5}$ + $\boxed{}$ ÷ $\boxed{5}$ = $\boxed{7}$

D $\boxed{}$ + $\boxed{5}$ ÷ $\boxed{5}$ = $\boxed{}$

E $\boxed{}$ − $\boxed{2}$ × $\boxed{5}$ = $\boxed{8}$

F $\boxed{}$ − $\boxed{8}$ ÷ $\boxed{}$ = $\boxed{2}$

G $\boxed{}$ − $\boxed{5}$ + $\boxed{}$ = $\boxed{6}$

H $\boxed{8}$ × $\boxed{}$ ÷ $\boxed{}$ = $\boxed{8}$

learn by heart

Indices, including roots, have a bigger impact than the four operations ($+ - \div \times$) so they have higher priority and should be calculated first.

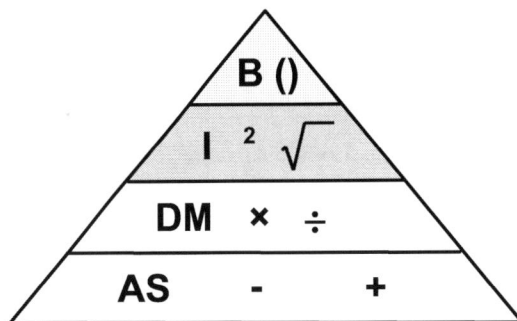

```
          B ()
        I  ² √‾
     DM  ×  ÷
   AS  -    +
```

Brackets create a group of calculations that should be given highest priority.

examples

Calculate $(9 - 1) \times 2$

$$= 8 \times 2 = 16$$

Start with the bracket first $(9 - 1)$

Calculate $3 + 2^2$

$$= 3 + 4 = 7$$

exercise 5n

1. Work out:

    a) $4 + 3^2$

    b) 2×3^2

    c) $16 - 3^2$

    d) $5 - 1^2$

    e) $10 - 2^3$

    f) $20 - 3^3$

    g) $20 \div 2^2$

    h) $2^3 + 3^2$

    i) $3^2 - 2^2$

    j) $(10 - 3)^2$

    k) $(1 + 2 \times 3)^2$

    l) $(9 - 4) \times 3^2$

2. Calculate:

    a) $6 \times (3 + 5)$

    b) $20 \div (4 + 1)$

    c) $\sqrt{9} + 7$

    d) $(3 + 2) \times (5 - 2)^2$

    e) $10 \div (3 - 2)^2$

    f) $4 - (5 - 10)$

    g) $(-6 + 3) \times (-2 - 1)$

    h) $4 - (2 + 10)$

    i) $(\sqrt{4} + 5)^2$

    j) $10 \times (3 + 2^2)$

    k) $(-3 - 5) \times (8 - 10)$

    l) $4 + (3 - 9)$

3. Put brackets into each of these calculations to make them true, if required:

a) $3 \times 5 + 4 = 27$

b) $4 + 3 \times 5 + 1 = 20$

c) $8 - 2 \times 6 = 36$

d) $10 - 4^2 = 36$

e) $18 - 9 \div 3 = 15$

f) $7 \times 3 \times 2 = 42$

g) $20 - 6 + 3 = 11$

h) $15 - 6 \div 3 = 3$

i) $8 - 3^2 = 25$

j) $5 + 3 \times 2^2 = 41$

k) $5 + 2 \times 3 + 1 = 28$

l) $3 + 4^2 = 49$

4. Use the numbers on the right to make this calculation true:

$$\boxed{} \times \boxed{} - (\boxed{} \times \boxed{} + \boxed{}) = 7$$

$\boxed{1}$ $\boxed{2}$ $\boxed{4}$

$\boxed{6}$ $\boxed{8}$

more challenging

5. Work out:

a) $-3 \times 4 + 2$

b) $-1 + 2 \times -3$

c) $9 - -1 \times 6$

d) $12 \div -3 + -1$

e) $(-6)^2 + -6$

f) $5 + -5 \times -7$

g) $(-5 + -3) \times 4$

h) $8 - (-2 + -2)$

i) $(-2 + 5)^2$

----

chapter review

exercise 50

1. Write as a single power of 2:

a) $2^4 \times 2^3$

d) $2^5 \div 2$

g) $\dfrac{2^{10}}{2^2}$

b) $2^8 \div 2^2$

e) $2 \times 2^2 \times 2^3$

h) $2^6 \div 2^7$

c) $(2^3)^2$

f) $(2^4)^{-3}$

i) $2^5 \times 2^{-5}$

2. Evaluate:

a) 10^2

b) 2^3

c) 5^0

d) $6^1 \times 6$

e) 10^3

f) $\sqrt{36}$

g) $\sqrt[3]{27}$

h) 5^3

i) $(-1)^3$

j) $\sqrt{49}$

k) $2^4 \div 2^4$

l) 8^2

m) 1^4

n) $\sqrt{25}$

o) $6^2 \div 6$

p) $\sqrt[3]{8}$

q) 42^1

r) $2^3 + 2$

3. What is the value of 3000^0?

a) 30,000   b) 3000   c) 1   d) 0

4. True or false: $5^6 \times 5^2 = 25^8$

5. Write down the first 12 square numbers.

6. Write down the first 5 cube numbers.

7. Decide whether the answer will be positive or negaive:

a) $(-4)^2$

b) $(-3)^3$

c) $(-2)^3$

d) $(-1)^5$

e) $(-2)^4$

f) $(-1)^{52}$

8. Calculate

a) $3 + 5 \times 2$

b) $3 \times 7 - 2$

c) $20 \div 5 - 5$

d) $5 + 6 - 2$

e) $5 + 18 \div 2$

f) $3 \times 2 + 5 \times 2$

g) $8 \times 5 - 6 \times 2$

h) $8 + 4 \times 6 - 2$

9. Fill in the missing numbers:

a) $\boxed{}^2 = 100$ b) $\boxed{}^3 = -8$ c) $3^{\boxed{}} = 27$

Odd One Out

In each box, cover up pairs of numbers that are equal and
find the number that is left over.

A

2^2	3^2	25
5^2	6^2	4
9	36	6

B

$\sqrt{49}$	50	$\sqrt{25}$
$\sqrt{100}$	$\sqrt{4}$	7
5	10	2

C

0^3	6^1	$(-2)^2$
1	6^0	0
4	6	-4

D

2^3	16	8
1^3	6^2	4^2
36	12	1

E

3^3	1^8	5^2
25	8	27
2^4	1	16

F

$\sqrt[3]{27}$	5^3	$\sqrt{25}$
15	5	$(-5)^2$
215	25	3

G

49	81	11^2
12^1	121	5^3
7^2	125	3^4

H

2^4	10^3	8
4^3	32	64
1000	2^3	2^5

I

$(-2)^3$	-1	2^0
$\sqrt[3]{8}$	$(-1)^3$	2
1	-2	-8

J

$(-1)^3$	8	4
$(-2)^2$	$(-1)^{10}$	-8
1	$(-2)^3$	-1

K

0^4	1	4
$(-1)^{19}$	19	0
5^0	19^1	-1

L

$\sqrt{1}$	$\sqrt[3]{64}$	$\sqrt[3]{1}$
$\sqrt{9}$	8	$\sqrt{64}$
4	10	3

Power Puzzles

Work out the missing numbers.

1 positive integers

A
$(3 + \underline{})^2 = 25$

B
$4^3 + \underline{}^2 = 73$

C
$100 - \underline{}^2 = 36$

D
$\underline{}^3 + \underline{}^2 = 10$

E
$(7 - \underline{})^3 = 27$

F
$\underline{}^2 - 3 \times 4 = 13$

G
$2^{\square} + 3^2 = 25$

H
$\underline{}^2 \div 5^2 = 4$

I
$4 \times \underline{}^2 = 64$

J
$(12 - \underline{})^2 = 81$

K
$(\underline{} \times 2)^3 = 1000$

L
$(3 + \underline{})^3 = 64$

2 positive and negative integers

A
$\underline{}^3 + 2 = -6$

B
$(-2)^2 + \underline{} = 12$

C
$(4 - \underline{})^3 = -1$

D
$\underline{}^3 + (-2)^3 = -16$

E
$(4 - 2 \times 3)^2 = \underline{}$

F
$5 \times \underline{}^3 = -40$

G
$(-1 \times \underline{})^3 = 27$

H
$(-5)^2 + \underline{}^3 = 26$

I
$(-8)^2 \div \underline{} = 32$

J
$(\underline{} + 1)^5 = -32$

K
$(-10)^{\square} = -1000$

L
$(-3)^2 \times \underline{}^3 = -72$

M
$\underline{}^3 - 4 = 4$

N
$\underline{} - 10^2 = -100$

O
$10^3 - (-10)^2 = \underline{}$

cumulative review (chapters 1-5)

exercise 5p

1. Write 3 million, eight thousand and four in digits.

2. In each number, state the value of bold digit. The first one is done for you.

   a) **4**08.6

   ↑

   four hundreds

   b) 26.0**8**4

   ↑

   c) 2**3**,801

   ↑

   d) **3**,005,005

   ↑

   e) 9.**8**65

   ↑

   f) 23,**4**08,300

   ↑

3. Write each of these as decimals:

   a) $\frac{3}{10}$

   b) $\frac{5}{100}$

   c) $\frac{12}{100}$

   d) $\frac{2}{50}$

   e) $1\frac{3}{10}$

   f) $\frac{12}{1000}$

   g) $\frac{1}{8}$

   h) $\frac{1}{9}$

4. Calculate 19.6 - 2.35

5. Calculate 84.306 × 100

6. Calculate $\sqrt{49}$

7. Calculate:

   a) $(-2)^2$

   b) $(-2)^3$

   c) $(-2)^4$

matching activity

8. Match these cards into pairs that are equivalent.
   Record your pairs in a table.

A	-3 + 2	B	-2 - 4	C	10 -15
J	0	K	-6	L	-5
D	-1 - - 1	E	6 - 8	F	6 - - 3
M	-1	N	3	O	4
G	-2 + -2	H	4 + -1	I	-2 + 6
P	9	Q	-2	R	-4

A	
B	
C	
D	
E	
F	
G	
H	
I	

9. Calculate:

a) -3 - 3

b) -4 + 4

c) 48 ÷ 2

d) 0.4 × 3

e) $\frac{1}{4} + \frac{3}{4}$

f) 4^2

g) 12 × 5

h) 426 - 19

i) -20 ÷ 5

10. Copy these diagrams and shade $\frac{1}{2}$:

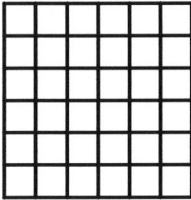

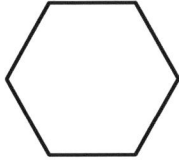

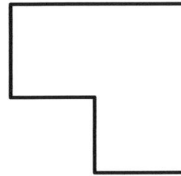

11. Which of the following are true? Circle 2 answers.

a) 14 < 15

b) -3 < 0

c) -4 < -5

d) -2 > 2

12. Calculate:

a) -5 × 2

b) -3 × -4

c) $\frac{1}{9} + \frac{4}{9}$

d) 20 ÷ -2

e) 1 - 0.2

f) -6 × 10

g) $\frac{1}{3}$ of 18

h) 40 ÷ -5

i) $\frac{1}{4} + \frac{3}{8}$

j) -2 × 10

k) $1 - \frac{1}{9}$

l) -8 × -3

m) 0.04 × 100

n) -25 ÷ -5

o) -6 ÷ -1

13. Write each fraction as a decimal:

a) $\frac{7}{100}$

b) $\frac{3}{5}$

c) $\frac{1}{4}$

d) $\frac{1}{1000}$

e) $\frac{4}{10}$

f) $\frac{3}{50}$

g) $\frac{1}{3}$

h) $\frac{1}{2}$

i) $\frac{1}{9}$

chapter 6: intro to algebra

[Recommended Time : 12 - 14 hours]

Contents

174

variables & like terms

learn by heart

Variable: a letter that stands for a number, which can vary

$1a$ is written simply as a and the letter x is written so that it looks different to a × symbol

The times sign is not used, so $a + a$ is written $2a$, which means 2 lots of a

Like terms: are multiples of the same variable, such as $3b$ and $5b$

Simplify: add together like terms (only like terms can be collected)

examples

Simplify $a + 4a - 2a$
$$= 3a$$

Simplify $6b - 10b$
$$= -4b$$

exercise 6a

1. Simplify:

    a) $b + b + b$

    b) $4b + 2b$

    c) $8y + y$

    d) $y + 3y + y$

    e) $10y - 4y$

    f) $4y - 10y$

    g) $9y - y$

    h) $4y + 5y - 3y$

    i) $b + 4b - 2b$

    j) $8b - 3b - 5b$

    k) $2b - b - b$

    l) $b - 2b$

2. Which of these is the same as $1x$?

    a) $1y$

    b) 24

    c) x

    d) $x + 1$

3. Circle the pairs which are like terms:

    a) $4a$ & $5a$

    b) $3x$ & $3y$

    c) y & $4y$

    d) $2p$ & $6p$

    e) $9d$ & 9

    f) t & $4t$

4. True or False?

    a) $8a + 8 = 16a$

    b) $4a - a = 4$

    c) $8a + 8b = 16ab$

    d) $10y + 10y = 20y$

    e) $100y - y = 99y$

    f) $6a - 7a = a$

5. Simplify, **if possible**:

a) $w + w + w =$ _____

b) $y + y + 2y =$ _____

c) $8a - 2a - a =$ _____

d) $2y + 4y - 6y =$ _____

e) $3p - 6p =$ _____

f) $4b + b - b =$ _____

g) $6t - t =$ _____

h) $4p + 6 =$ _____

6. Explain why this expression cannot be simplified: $3a + 4b + 5c + 6d$

7. Simplify: $5a + 4a + 3a + 2a + a$

8. Which of these **cannot** be simplified?

a) $6b + 4b$

b) $6b + 4a$

c) $4b - 6b$

d) $4b + 4$

e) $3b - b$

f) $b + 6$

9. Simplify, **if possible:**

a) $8a - 10a$

b) $8a - a$

c) $8a - 8$

d) $8a + -8a$

e) $-8a + 8$

f) $-8a - 8a$

10. Simplify $b - b - b$

11. Which of these equals $2b$? Circle all that apply.

a) $1 + b$

b) $3 - b$

c) $3b - b$

d) $2 + b$

12. Fill in the blanks:

a) $4t +$ _____ $= 5t$

b) $2t +$ _____ $= 0$

c) $t -$ _____ $= 2t$

d) $8t -$ _____ $= 10t$

e) $12t +$ _____ $= 10t$

f) $6t -$ _____ $= -2t$

g) $-3t +$ _____ $= 0$

h) $4t -$ _____ $= -10t$

13. Simplify:

a) $-3y + 2y$

b) $-9d - d$

c) $-10d + d$

14. Simplify: $6a - a + 5a - a + 4a - a + 3a - a + 2a - a$

176

collecting like terms

examples

If like terms get separated, we can still add or subtract them....

$4a + 5 + 2a$

$= 6a + 5$ ← the 5 cannot be added because its not a like term

Simplify: $6a - 3 - 2a$

Circle each term, including its sign:

$(6a)(- 3)(-2a)$

Add or subtract like terms, to get **4a - 3**

exercise 6b

1. Simplify:

    a) $b + 5 + b$

    b) $7b + 4 + 2b$

    c) $3b + a + 2b$

    d) $5y - 2 + 3y$

    e) $8y - 4 - 2y$

    f) $6y - 5 - y$

    g) $8a + 5b - 3b$

    h) $6y - 4y - 6$

    i) $9a + a - 2a$

2. True or false?

    a) $2b + 3 = 5b$

    b) $5a - 1 = 4a$

    c) $3x + 4x = 7x^2$

    d) $3a + 5 + 2a = 10a$

3. Simplify:

    a) $10y + 4 - 3y$

    b) $4a + 3a - a$

    c) $5y + b - 5y$

    d) $9a - 3a - 5$

    e) $5b - 4b + 8$

    f) $6t - 2 - t$

    g) $4p + 1 - 3p$

    h) $3y + 2 - 3y$

    i) $y + 4 - 3y$

4. Which of these **cannot** be simplified?

    a) $a + b + c$ b) $2a + b + a$ c) $3y - y - 1$ d) $4c - 5c$

5. Simplify $a + 1 + 2a + 2 + 3a + 3$

6. Simplify each of these expressions:

   a) $a + a + a$ d) $3y - y$

   b) $4b + 5b$ e) $10t + 2 - 4t$

   c) $6y + 5 + 2y$ f) $9p - 10p$

7. Which of these is the same as $3a + a$?

   a) $3a^2$ b) a^3 c) $4a$ d) $2a$ e) $3a^3$

8. Which of these cannot be simplified? Circle all that apply.

   a) $3a + 4b + 2$ c) $2b + 2a$

   b) $6a - 10a$ d) $4b + 3 + 5b$

9. Simplify each of these expressions, **if possible:**

   a) $4b + a + 2b$ d) $9a - 5 - 2a - 3$

   b) $6a - 10a$ e) $9 - a + 3 + a$

   c) $a + 2b + 6$ f) $20a - 4 - 5a + 5$

10. True or false?

    a) $6a + a = 6a^2$ c) $2a + b = 2ab$

    b) $a - a - a = -3a$ d) $5a - a = 5$

11. Simplify:

    a) $a - a - a$ e) $2x - 3x$

    b) $2a + 6 + 3a$ f) $8b - 3 - 2b + 1$

    c) $4y - 3 + 2y - 2$ g) $9 - 7f + f - 3$

    d) $6y + 1 - 5y + 2$ h) $3 + b - 2 + 2b - 1 - 3b$

12. Which of these cannot be simplifed?

    a) $8y - 2y$ b) $4b + 2b$ c) $9y - 3 + 2x$

Expression Pyramids

Complete the pyramids by adding together
two side by side blocks to make the block directly above

Pyramid 1 (bottom row): $x + 2$ | $3x + 1$ | x

Pyramid 2 (bottom row): $5x$ | $2x - 1$ | $4x + 5$

Pyramid 3 (bottom row): 5 | $3x + 2$ | $4x - 2$

Pyramid 4: middle-left: $5x + 8$; bottom row: $3x + 5$ | (blank) | $x + 2$

Pyramid 5: middle-left: $4x + 3$; bottom row: $8x - 3$ | $2x - 1$ | (blank)

Pyramid 6: middle-left: $6x + 1$; bottom row: $5x + 1$ | (blank) | $2x - 1$

- -

Make the Total ⭐ extra challenge

Arrange the cards into three groups, so that each group has the total indicated.
You must use all the cards.

| $-4x$ | -6 | 5 | $3x$ | $3x$ | 4 | 1 | -4 | x | $-2x$ | $-x$ |

Total: $x - 5$	**Total: $2x + 1$**	**Total: $4 - 3x$**

example

Simplify $4a - 6 + 3a - 5a - 2$

Circle each term with the sign attached:

$(4a)(- 6)(+ 3a)(- 5a)(- 2)$

Add like terms:
$4a + 3a - 5a = 2a$
$-6 - 2 = -8$

Final answer $= 2a - 8$

exercise 6c

1. Simplify

    a) $4a + 3a + 2 - a$

    b) $2a + 5 - a - 3$

    c) $7a - 2 - 5a - 5$

    d) $4a + 1 - 5a + 3$

    e) $-3a - 5a$

    f) $10 - 2a + 5 - 3a$

    g) $-5a + 8a - 3$

    h) $6 + 5a - 3 - a$

    i) $9a - 5 - 10a - 2$

2. Match the cards on the left with their counter part on the right.
    Record your answers in a table.

A	$6a + 3a - 5$

G	$7a + 1 - 5a - 1$

B	$-3a + 4a$

H	$3 - 2a - 3 - 5a$

C	$2a - 5 + 3a$

I	$-5a + 5 + 12a - 2$

D	$6 + 3a - a - 4$

J	$-4a - 4a - 4a$

E	$8a - 10a$

K	$2a - 3 - a + 6$

F	$6 - 3a + 5 - 2a$

L	$7 - 8a + 3 - 2a$

M	$2 + 2a$	S	$11 - 5a$
N	$2a$	T	$a + 3$
O	$-7a$	U	$5a - 5$
P	$9a - 5$	V	$10 - 10a$
Q	$-12a$	W	a
R	$-2a$	X	$7a + 3$

A	B	C	D	E	F	G	H	I	J	K	L

multiplying variables

learn by heart

We don't use the × sign with algebra, variables are placed next to each other in alphabetical order.

$y × b × a = aby$

A single number is placed at the front (unless it is 1, which we don't write)

$y × 3 = 3y$

If more than 1 number is being multiplied, we write their product at the front

$2 × y × 4 = 8y$

examples

$a × 2$ $= 2a$	$a × b$ $= ab$	$3 × b × 4 × a$ $= 12ab$	$e × f × -5$ $= -5ef$	$4y × 3x$ $= 12xy$

exercise 6d

1. Write more simply:

   a) $8 × p$

   b) $a × b × c$

   c) $f × a$

   d) $2 × y × 5$

   e) $10 × a × 4$

   f) $3 × 4 × p$

   g) $a × 4 × y$

   h) $3 × x × 4 × y$

   i) $2 × y × 4 × p$

2. True or false?

   a) $2p × 4 = 8p$

   b) $4 × 3a = 43a$

   c) $y + a = ay$

   d) $y × 2 × 3 = 23y$

   e) $5p × 3 = 8p$

   f) $p × 4 × y = 4py$

3. Simplify:

   a) $2y × 5$

   b) $3a × 2$

   c) $p × 4y$

   d) $a × 1 × y$

   e) $2y × 5 × p$

   f) $3y × 4 × a$

4. Which of these is the same as $3 × p × 4$?

   a) $34 × p$ b) $3p × 4$ c) $3 + p + 4$ d) $43p$

5. Which of these is the correct way to simplify $4y \times 2a$?

    a) $4y2a$ b) ay^8 c) $8ya$ d) $8ay$

6. Fill in the blanks:

    a) _____ $\times 2p = 14p$ d) $3 \times$ _____ $= 6ab$

    b) _____ $\times 3y = 21ay$ e) _____ $\times 8ab = 16abc$

    c) _____ $\times 10 = 40x$ f) $10y \times$ _____ $= 100xy$

7. Write simply:

    a) $m \times 3$ e) $b \times 3 \times a$ i) $2 \times a \times 4 \times b$

    b) $h \times g$ f) $a \times -3b$ j) $3b \times 5a$

    c) $k \times -3$ g) $w \times x \times d$ k) $-4a \times -2b$

    d) $5 \times p \times q$ h) $t \times 2 \times 5 \times a$ l) $-6p \times 3$

8. Which of these is the correct simplification of $-4 \times a \times b \times -3$?

    a) $12ab$ b) $-12ab$ c) $ab12$ d) $-43ab$

9. Simplify $4a \times 3b \times 2c$

10. True or false?

    a) $2 \times a = a2$ b) $4y \times 5a = 45ay$ c) $-3y \times 4x = 12yx$

11. Which of these **cannot** be written more simply?

    a) $a \times 4$ b) $3y \times 2$ c) $8ab$ d) $p \times -3$

12. Complete the gaps:

    a) _____ $\times -5b = 10b$ d) $6p \times$ _____ $= -24p$

    b) _____ $\times -3 = -18b$ e) $-5a \times$ _____ $= 25ab$

    c) _____ $\times 2y = 22xy$ f) $2d +$ _____ $= 8d$

13. Simplify $-3x \times -3y \times -3z$

multiplying variables - index notation

learn by heart

If a variable is multiplied repeatedly, an index is used to show how often, e.g. $a \times a \times a = a^3$

An index of 1 is not written, so $a^1 = a$

If numbers are being multiplied, their product is written at the front as a coefficient

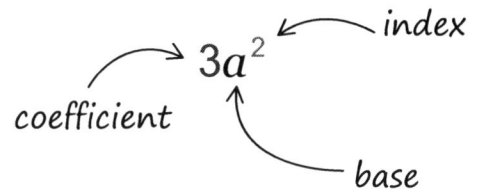

$3a^2$

coefficient

index

base

examples

Write in index form:

| $y \times y = y^2$ | $a \times b \times b \times a = a^2b^2$ | $2 \times y \times 5 \times y = 10y^2$ | $3a \times 5a = 15a^2$ |

exercise 6d

1. Simplify:

    a) $b \times b$

    b) $d \times d \times d$

    c) $e \times e \times f \times f$

    d) $3 \times y \times y$

    e) $4 \times a \times 2 \times a$

    f) $10 \times a \times a \times a$

    g) $2 \times b \times b$

    h) $a \times b \times a \times b$

    i) $a \times b \times b \times 3$

2. Which of these is the correct way to write $a \times a \times a$?

    a) $3a$ b) a^3 c) $a3$ d) $a + 3$

3. When simplified, $y + y =$ _____ and $y \times y =$ _____.

4. Simplify

    a) $2a \times a$

    b) $5y \times y \times y$

    c) $4a \times 2a$

    d) $p \times 7 \times p$

    e) $4y \times 3y$

    f) $6 \times a \times b \times b$

5. Write in index form:

    a) $a \times a \times a \times a$

    b) $b \times c \times b \times c$

    c) $2 \times a \times 7 \times a$

    d) $y \times y \times 5 \times y$

    e) $4a \times 5a$

    f) $3 \times a \times 3a$

    g) $x \times 2x$

    h) $4ab \times 4ab$

    i) $2y \times 2y \times 2y \times 2y$

6. True or false?

   a) $4 \times y = y^4$

   b) $2 \times a \times b = ab^2$

   c) $3 \times a \times 2 \times a = 32a^2$

   d) $3a \times 4a = 12a$

   e) $b \times a \times b \times a = a^2b^2$

   f) $a \times a \times a = a^3$

7. Which of the following is the best simplification of $2 \times a \times b \times a \times 5$?

   a) $10aba$　　　　b) $10aab$　　　　c) $10a^2b$　　　　d) $7a^2b$　　　　e) $7a^2 + b$

8. Which of the following statements is true?

   a) $a + a + a = a^3$

   b) $x + y = xy$

   c) $y + y = y2$

   d) $s \times 4 \times s = 4s^2$

9. Simplify $b \times b \times b \times b \times d \times d \times d \times d \times d$

10. Simplify:

   a) $3 \times 4a \times a$

   b) $1 \times p$

   c) $a^1 \times a$

   d) $y \times -3 \times y$

   e) $2x \times 0$

   f) $-7a \times -3b$

   g) $-4p \times -2p$

   h) $d \times -2 \times d \times -8$

   i) $-2b \times 3b$

mixed multiplications and additions

11. Simplify:

   a) $n + n + n$

   b) $n \times n \times n$

   c) $4 \times y$

   d) $y \times y \times y \times y$

   e) $2y + 3y$

   f) $a - a$

   g) $4a - 3a$

   h) $4a \times 3a$

   i) $6 + 3p + p$

11. Which of these cannot be simplified?

   a) $3a + 2b$　　　　b) $3a \times 2b$　　　　c) $3a \times a$　　　　d) $3a + a$

12. Simplify $2a + 5 + 3a + 5$

13. Simplify $10a - a$

Expressions Code Breaker

Simplify the following and find your answer in the code box.
Write the words down to reveal an inspirational message!

code box

$-10a$ = citizens	a = the	$21a$ = of	$7a^2$ = it
$-5a$ = thing	$2a$ = doubt	$10a$ = is	$10a^2$ = group
$-4a$ = true	$4a$ = thoughtful,	$-12a^2$ = only	$21a^2$ = world.
$-3a$ = through	$5a$ = can	$-7a^2$ = that	$-a^3$ = door
$-2a$ = deep	$6a$ = small	$-4a^2$ = ever	a^3 = a
$-a$ = Indeed	$7a$ = that	a^2 = Never	$12a^3$ = pen.
0 = the	$8a$ = committed	$4a^2$ = change	$4a^3$ = has.

a) $a \times a$ = __a^2__ = **Never**

b) $a + a$ = _____ =

c) $a \times 7$ = _____ =

d) $a \times a \times a$ = _____ =

e) $2 \times a \times 3$ = _____ =

f) $5 \times a \times 2 \times a$ = _____ =

g) $7a \times 3$ = _____ =

h) $7a - 3a$ = _____ =

i) $7a + a$ = _____ =

j) $-2a \times 5$ = _____ =

k) $6a - a$ = _____ =

l) $a \times 4a$ = _____ =

m) $9a - 8a$ = _____ =

n) $3a \times 7a$ = _____ =

o) $3a - 4a$ = _____ =

p) $a \times 7 \times a$ = _____ =

q) $a \times 2 \times 5$ = _____ =

r) $a - a$ = _____ =

s) $-3a \times 4a$ = _____ =

t) $5a - 10a$ = _____ =

u) $a \times -7a$ = _____ =

v) $2a \times -2a$ = _____ =

w) $4a \times a \times a$ = _____ =

– Quote by Margaret Mead

multiplying variables - using index laws

recall

Multiplication Law (add the indices): $a^3 \times a^4 = a^7$

Power Law (multiply the indices): $(a^5)^3 = a^{15}$

examples

Simplify $a^6 \times a^4 \times a$

Add the indices $= a^{11}$

Simplify $(a^6)^{-3}$

Multiply the indices $= a^{-18}$

exercise 6e

1. Simplify, if possible:

    a) $a^2 \times a^4$

    b) $b^6 \times b$

    c) $y^7 \times y^{-3}$

    d) $p^{-5} \times p^{-3}$

    e) $y^3 \times y^{-6}$

    f) $p^5 \times p \times p^3$

    g) $p^{-2} \times p^3$

    h) $a^8 \times b^4$

    i) $a^2 \times a$

    j) $s^{-4} \times s^{-5}$

    k) $y^{-10} \times y^4$

    l) $x^4 \times x^{-4}$

2. Simplify

    a) $(y^3)^5$

    b) $(a^4)^{-3}$

    c) $(y^{-4})^{-3}$

    d) $(y^3)^0$

    e) $(a^3)^{-2}$

    f) $(y^2)^5$

    g) $(y^{-5})^3$

    h) $(p^{-5})^{-3}$

    i) $(a^4)^1$

3. Match expressions on the left and right that have the same answer:

A	
B	
C	
D	
E	
F	

A $(a^5)^2$

B $(a^2)^{-3}$

C $(a^9)^1$

D $(a^{-2})^{-3}$

E $(a^2)^{-2}$

F $(a^2)^0$

G $a^3 \times a^3$

H $a^7 \times a^3$

I $a^2 \times a^{-6}$

J $a \times a^8$

K $a^5 \times a^{-5}$

L $a^{-2} \times a^{-2} \times a^{-2}$

5. Fill in the blanks:

a) $x^7 \times$ _____ $= x^{14}$

b) $x^4 \times$ _____ $= x^3$

c) $x \times$ _____ $= x^{12}$

d) $x^{-4} \times$ _____ $= x^0$

6. Simplify:

a) $(y^4)^3$

b) $y^7 \times y^3$

c) $y \times y^8$

d) $y \times y \times y^2$

e) $(y^8)^{-2}$

f) $y^{-4} \times y^5$

g) $(y^{-3})^{-10}$

h) $y^4 \times y^0$

i) $(y^4)^0$

j) $y^3 \times y^{-1}$

k) $y \times 2 \times y$

l) $2y \times 3y$

True or False?

In the grid there are 6 true statements. Can you find them?

A	B	C	D
$5b + 1 = 6b$	$b \times b = 2b$	$b - 1 = 1$	$b - 1 = 0$
E $4b - b = 4$	**F** $b \times b \times b = b^3$	**G** $b = 1b$	**H** $b \times 4 = b^4$
I $2b \times 3b = 6b$	**J** $b^4 \times b = b^5$	**K** $(b^4)^3 = b^7$	**L** $b^5 \times b = 2b^6$
M $b + b = b^2$	**N** $6b + b = 7b^2$	**O** $2b + b = 3b$	**P** $b^4 \times b^4 = b^{16}$
Q $(b^{-2})^{-3} = b^6$	**R** $2b \times b = 3b$	**S** $(b^5)^2 = b^{25}$	**T** $3b - 4b = -b$

The true statements are: _____ _____ _____ _____ _____ _____

exercise 6f: mixed multiplications and additions

1. Simplify

   a) $a + a + a$

   b) $a^3 \times a^3$

   c) $3a + a$

   d) $3a + 3a$

   e) $a \times a \times a$

   f) $5a + b - a$

   g) $y^4 \times y^5$

   h) $(y^4)^2$

   i) $2y - 3y$

   j) $2y \times 3y$

   k) $10a - 3 - 2a$

   l) $y \times y \times y \times y$

   m) $y + y + y + y$

   n) $4a - a$

   o) $4a \times a$

2. Fill in the blanks:

   a) $a \times \underline{\quad} = ab$

   b) $3y \times \underline{\quad} = 21y^2$

   c) $t + \underline{\quad} = 3t$

   d) $t \times \underline{\quad} = 3t$

   e) $4a \times \underline{\quad} = 12ab$

   f) $x \times \underline{\quad} = 3x^2$

3. Simplify:

   a) $y^2 \times y^2$

   b) $2y + 2y$

   c) $2 \times y^2$

4. Simplify $y - y - y$

5. Simplify $y \times y \times y \times y \times y \times y \times y \times y$

- -

Mixed Operations Puzzle

Use 8 of the expressions below to make these statements true:

$3x$	x^6	x	$4x$
x^2	$2x$	4	x^4
x^3	5	$9x$	$5x$

$$\boxed{} - \boxed{} = -2x$$

$$\boxed{} + \boxed{} = 10x$$

$$\boxed{} \times \boxed{} = 8x^2$$

$$\boxed{} \times \boxed{} = x^9$$

Mixed Up Expressions

Simplify each expression and find your answer at the bottom.
Record your answers in a table.

A	$a + a + a$
B	$a \times a \times a$
C	$2a + 8a$
D	$(a^4)^2$

E	$7a + a$
F	$a^4 \times a^3$
G	$5a - 3a$
H	$(a^{-2})^{-3}$

I	$2a \times 3a$
J	$a + a + 4$
K	$a \times a$
L	$a \times -3$

M	$(a^3)^{-1}$
N	$5a - a$
O	$a \times a^3 \times a$
P	$8a + 1 - 3a$

Q	$4a + a - 2$
R	$-2 \times 4a$
S	$(a^5)^0$
T	$a \times a^9$

U	$-5a \times -5a$
V	$4a - 10a$
W	$3a - 2 + a$
X	$4a \times a \times -3$

jumbled answers

$-3a$ $-12a^2$ $-8a$

a^{10} $5a - 2$ $6a^2$ $4a - 2$ $25a^2$

a^2

a^5 a^3 a^{-3} a^0 $10a$ a^6

$2a$

$-6a$ $2a + 4$ $4a$ $8a$ $5a + 1$ a^8 a^7 $3a$

A	
B	
C	
D	
E	
F	
G	
H	
I	
J	
K	
L	
M	
N	
O	
P	
Q	
R	
S	
T	
U	
V	
W	
X	

learn by heart

Dividing Variables: *the ÷ sign is not used, a ÷ 3 is written* $\frac{a}{3}$

examples

$a \div 2$ $\quad = \frac{a}{2}$	$(a \times 2) \div b$ $\quad = \frac{2a}{b}$

$d \times d$ $\quad = d^2$

$e \times f \times e$ $\quad = e^2 f$

exercise 6g

1. Write each of these more simply:

    a) $b \times 3 =$ _____

    b) $t \times t =$ _____

    c) $p \div q =$ _____

    d) $w \times w \times d =$ _____

    e) $y \div 5 =$ _____

    f) $5 \div y =$ _____

    g) $x \times y \times x \times y =$ _____

    h) $(3 \times y) \div p =$ _____

2. Which of these means $4 \div a$?

    a) $\frac{4}{a}$ b) a^4 c) $4a$ d) $\frac{a}{4}$

3. How do we write $y \times y$?

    a) $2y$ b) $y + y$ c) yy d) y^2

4. Which of these means y multiplied by 4?

    a) $y + 4$ b) y^4 c) $4y$ d) $\frac{y}{4}$

5. Which of these is the correct way to write $a \times a \times a$?

    a) $3a$ b) $a3$ c) $3(a)$ d) a^2 e) a^3

6. True or false?

    a) $x + y = xy$ b) $b^4 = b + b + b + b$

7. Match each expression on the left with one on the right:

A	G		M	T
n add 4	4 divided by n		$-4n$	$4n^2$

B	H		N	U
n times 4	n squared times 4		n^3	$\dfrac{n}{4}$

C	I		O	V
n minus 4	n squared times n		$\dfrac{4+n}{n}$	$n + 4$

D	J		P	W
4 minus n	n squared + 4		$\dfrac{4}{n}$	$n - 4$

E	K		R	X
n times -4	n - 4 divided by n		$n^2 + 4$	$\dfrac{n-4}{n}$

F	L		S	Y
n divided by 4	4 + n divided by n		4 - n	$4n$

Record the letters of your matching pairs in a table:

A	B	C	D	E	F	G	H	I	J	K	L

8. Write each of these as an algebraic expression:

a) I think of a number, n, and multiply it by 5

b) I think of a number, y, add on 3 and then divide by 4

c) I think of a number, b, times by 2 and then divide by 6

d) I think of a number, a, square it and then subtract 10

e) I think of a number, x, divide by 4 and then subtract 8

f) I think of a number, p, square it and then add 5

g) I think of a number, m, divide by 2 and then add 5

h) I think of a number, d, square it, then add 7

i) I think of a number, c, subtract 15, then divide by 2

Flow Chart Expressions

Write an expression for each sequence of operations on the variable n:

a) n — $\times 4$ — $+ 1$ _____

b) n — $\times n$ — $- 6$ _____

c) n — $\times a$ — $\times 3$ _____

d) n — $+ 6$ — $\div y$ _____

e) n — $\div y$ — $+ 6$ _____

f) n — $\times 3$ — $- 4$ _____

g) n — $- 2$ — $\div 5$ _____

h) n — $\div 5$ — $- 2$ _____

i) n — $\times 4$ — $\times n$ _____

Now complete the empty flow charts to show how each expression is made:

a) n — ☐ — ☐ $3n - 8$

b) n — ☐ — ☐ $6n + 5$

c) n — ☐ — ☐ $n^2 + 1$

d) n — ☐ — ☐ $\dfrac{n}{3} + 5$

e) n — ☐ — ☐ $\dfrac{n + 5}{3}$

f) n — ☐ — ☐ $an - 6$

g) n — ☐ — ☐ $\dfrac{5n}{9}$

h) n — ☐ — ☐ — ☐ $\dfrac{2n - 5}{9}$

substitution (positive numbers)

examples

Given $y = 3$, evaluate:

$y + 7$ $= 3 + 7$ $= 10$	$2y + 5$ $= 2 \times 3 + 5$ $= 6 + 5$ $= 11$	$2(y + 5)$ $= 2 \times (3 + 5)$ $= 2 \times 8$ $= 16$

exercise 6h

1. Given that $a = 3$, evaluate:

   a) $10a$ e) $4a + 2$ i) $5 - a$

   b) a^2 f) $7 + a$ j) a^3

   c) $\frac{a}{3}$ g) $7a$ k) $4 + 2a$

   d) $5a - 1$ h) $2a + 5$ l) $3a - 2$

2. If $x = 10$, which of these is smallest?

   a) $2x$ b) $x + 2$ c) $\frac{x}{2}$ d) x^2

3. If $x = 2$, evaluate:

   a) $3(x + 1)$ d) $4(x - 2)$ g) $(x + 8)^2$

   b) $5(x + 2)$ e) $3(4 + x)$ h) $(x - 2)^2$

   c) $6(x - 1)$ f) $(x + 3)^2$ i) $(3x)^2$

4. Complete each table for the value of a given:

   a)

$a = 2$
$a^1 =$
$a^2 =$
$a^3 =$

   b)

$a = 3$
$a^1 =$
$a^2 =$
$a^3 =$

   c)

$a = 1$
$a^1 =$
$a^2 =$
$a^3 =$

   d)

$a = 5$
$a^1 =$
$a^2 =$
$a^3 =$

Substitution Mystery Grid

Use the clues to complete the grid:

$$a = 2 \qquad b = 3 \qquad c = 5$$

The number in the top left is $4b - 1$

The number above 3 is $6b$

The number next to 18 is $b + c$

The number below 2 is $5c + 1$

The number below 11 is $6c - 3$

The number above 1 is $3c + a$

The number in the bottom left corner is $b - a$

The number below 4 is ab

The number next to 17 is c^2

Each diagonal adds up to 40

The number in the bottom right is $a - 2$

The number above 2 is a^3

The number below 12 is $b + 1$

The number next to 1 is $2(a + b)$

The numbers in the bottom row add up to $3c + b$

		2	

substitution with negatives

recall

| A negative × a positive = a negative | A negative × a negative = a positive |

examples

if $a = -4$, evaluate:

$2a$
$= 2 \times -4$
$= -8$

$-5a$
$= -5 \times -4$
$= 20$

$a - 5$
$= -4 - 5$
$= -9$

a^2
$= -4 \times -4$
$= 16$

exercise 6i

1. Given $a = -3$, work out:

   a) $2a$

   b) a^2

   c) $a + 4$

   d) $a - 1$

   e) $-4a$

   f) $5a$

   g) a^3

   h) $a + 3$

   i) $a - 5$

2. Given $x = -4$, evaluate:

   a) x^2

   b) $x + 4$

   c) $x - 1$

   d) $10x$

   e) $5x$

   f) $x + 8$

   g) $-3x$

   h) $3x - 1$

   i) $2x + 1$

   j) $x - 3$

   k) $(x + 1)^2$

   l) $(x - 1)^2$

3. Given $y = -3$, evaluate $5(x + 1)$

4. If $a = -2$, which of these is smallest?

   a) $2a$

   b) a^2

   c) $a + 2$

   d) $\frac{a}{2}$

5. If $b = -1$, evaluate:

   a) b^2

   b) b^3

   c) b^4

   d) b^5

expressions review

exercise 6j

1. Simplify, if possible:

    a) $y + y + y + y + y$ = _____

    b) $y \times y \times y \times y \times y$ = _____

    c) $2a - 3 + 4a$ = _____

    d) $5t - t$ = _____

2. If $a = 4$, evaluate:

    a) a^2 b) $3a$ c) $a + 10$ d) $2a + 3$

3. True or false: $5t - 3t = 2$

4. True or false: $3ab$ is the same as $3 + a + b$

5. The simplest ways of writing $4 \times a \times a$ is _____

6. True or false: g^3 is the same as $3g$

7. Simplify, if possible:

    a) $4a + 3a$

    b) $4a \times 3a$

    c) $a^{10} \times a^2$

    d) $(a^3)^2$

8. Write each of these in algebra

    a) n add 6 = _____

    b) n multiplied by n = _____

    c) n divided by 4 = _____

    d) n multiplied by 2, subtract 5 = _____

9. Write each of these more simply:

    a) $a \times a$ = _____

    b) $b \times b \times b$ = _____

    c) $4 \times a \times b$ = _____

    d) $7 \times a \times 2$ = _____

    e) $1 \times a \times a$ = _____

    f) $a \times 3 \times a \times 2$ = _____

solving one step equations (addition & subtraction)

learn by heart

Equation: *two expressions that are equal (=)*

Solution: *a value that makes the equation true*

examples

Solve $x + 5 = 2$
 -5 -5

$x = -3$

Solve $2 = y - 5$
 + 5 + 5

$y = 7$

*addition is the **inverse** of subtraction*

exercise 6k

1. Solve:

   a) $x + 4 = 10$

   b) $x - 4 = 10$

   c) $x + 3 = 0$

   d) $x - 0.3 = 1.2$

   e) $x + 7 = -2$

   f) $x - 9 = -4$

   g) $1.5 = x - 0.4$

   h) $-3 = x + 4$

   i) $x - 5 = -5$

   j) $10 = x + 6$

   k) $5 = x - 3$

   l) $0.2 + x = 0.5$

   m) $5 + x = -2$

   n) $9 = x - 2$

   o) $\frac{6}{10} = x + \frac{1}{10}$

   p) $6 + x = 4$

   q) $x - 3 = -2$

   r) $x + 5 = 0$

   s) $x - 8 = 1$

   t) $3 + x = -3$

   u) $5 = 7 + x$

   v) $7 + x = 4$

   w) $4 = x - 2.2$

   x) $18 = 19 + x$

2. For which of the following is $x = 8$ a solution? Tick all that apply.

   a) $2x = 16$

   b) $x + 2 = 10$

   c) $8 - x = 0$

   d) $x^2 = 16$

   e) $2(x + 1) = 20$

   f) $3 - x = -5$

solving one step equations (multiplication)

examples

Solve $2x = 16$	Solve $-5x = 20$	Solve $10x = 16$	Solve $5x = 51$
$\div 2 \quad \div 2$	$\div -5 \quad \div -5$	$\div 10 \quad \div 10$	$\div 5 \quad \div 5$
$x = 8$	$x = -4$	$x = 1.6$	$x = 10.2$

practice your short division here

exercise 61

1. Solve:

a) $4x = 8$

b) $10 = 2x$

c) $5x = 30$

d) $-2x = 20$

e) $15 = 3x$

f) $4x = -16$

g) $-4x = -16$

h) $10x = 500$

i) $2x = 25$

j) $10x = 77$

k) $-15 = 3x$

l) $3x = -9$

m) $-5x = 20$

n) $3x = 36$

o) $5x = 45$

p) $2x = 9$

q) $-7x = -49$

r) $-3x = 12$

s) $4x = 25$

t) $10x = 43$

u) $100x = 55$

v) $-5x = 50$

w) $100x = 623$

x) $9x = 50$

- -

Arrange the Digits ☆ extra challenge

`0` `1` `3` `4` `4` `5` `6`

Arrange the digits to make five correct equations.
The value of x is the same in all five equations.

$$\boxed{}x = 2\boxed{}$$

$$x = \boxed{}$$

$$x + \boxed{2} = \boxed{7}$$

$$x - \boxed{} = \boxed{}$$

$$\boxed{}x = \boxed{}0$$

solving one step equations (division)

Solve $\frac{x}{3}$ = 5

$\times$ 3 $\times$ 3

x = 15

Solve $\frac{x}{2}$ = -6

$\times$ 2 $\times$ 2

x = -12

Solve $\frac{x}{0.4}$ = 3

$\times$ 0.4 $\times$ 0.4

x = 1.2

exercise 6m

1. Solve:

a) $\frac{x}{2}$ = 6

b) $\frac{x}{2}$ = 50

c) -3 = $\frac{x}{3}$

d) $\frac{x}{0.1}$ = 4

e) 0 = $\frac{x}{5}$

f) -1 = $\frac{x}{2}$

g) $\frac{x}{-6}$ = -7

h) $\frac{x}{-3}$ = 2

i) $\frac{x}{0.4}$ = 4

j) 0.5 = $\frac{x}{5}$

k) $\frac{x}{3}$ = 1.2

l) $\frac{x}{3}$ = -12

m) $\frac{x}{3.5}$ = 2

n) $\frac{x}{2}$ = 0.7

o) 4.1 = $\frac{x}{1}$

p) $\frac{x}{-5}$ = -3

q) $\frac{x}{0.1}$ = 8

r) 5.2 = $\frac{x}{2}$

s) $\frac{x}{3}$ = 0

t) $\frac{x}{-5}$ = 0.7

u) 21 = $\frac{x}{-3}$

Arrange the Digits ⭐ extra challenge

| 0 | 1 | 2 | 3 | 5 | 6 | 7 |

Arrange the digits to make five correct equations.
The value of x is the same in all five equations.

$\dfrac{x}{\Box} = \Box$

$x + \Box = \Box$

$x = \Box$

$x - \boxed{8} = \boxed{-2}$

$\Box x = \boxed{3}\,\Box$

exercise 6n

1. Solve these equations:

    a) $x + 9 = 20$

    b) $x - 7 = 10$

    c) $x + 3 = 0$

    d) $x - 5 = 15$

    e) $x - 9 = 0$

    f) $3x = 12$

    g) $\frac{x}{2} = 12$

    h) $x - 8 = 12$

    i) $\frac{x}{-3} = -5$

2. Solve:

    a) $2x = 6$

    c) $10x = 15$

    e) $x + 6 = 0$

    b) $2x = 21$

    d) $8x = 64$

    f) $5x = 10$

mixed equations matching activity

Match each equation on the left with a solution from the right. Use each card once only.

A $x + 3 = 7$	B $4x = 12$	C $5 = x - 1$	$x = -7$	$x = 8$	$x = 5$
D $3x = -6$	E $x - 3 = -2$	F $\frac{x}{2} = 4$	$x = 0$	$x = -1$	$x = 4$
G $x - 2 = -2$	H $x - 3 = -1$	I $x + 2 = 9$	$x = -8$	$x = 6$	$x = 9$
J $\frac{x}{5} = 2$	K $15 = 6 + x$	L $5x = -35$	$x = 3$	$x = 10$	$x = 1$
M $x - 3 = -4$	N $-3x = -15$	O $\frac{x}{2} = -4$	$x = 2$	$x = 7$	$x = -2$

A	B	C	D	E	F	G	H	I	J	K	L	M	N	O

exercise 60

1. Solve each equation:

   a) $x + 3 = -4$

   b) $x - 5 = -1$

   c) $x + 1 = -4$

   d) $x - 2 = -6$

   e) $x + 10 = 4$

   f) $x - 8 = -2$

   g) $4 + x = -3$

   h) $x + 5 = 2$

   i) $x - 3 = 1$

2. Solve each equation:

   a) $x - 0.5 = 4$

   b) $x - 2.5 = 5$

   c) $x + 2 = 9$

   d) $3x = -33$

   e) $x + 5 = 1$

   f) $x - 3 = 0.1$

   g) $\dfrac{x}{2} = 3.5$

   h) $2x = 70$

   i) $\dfrac{x}{2} = 1.2$

matching activity

Match the equations on the left with their solutions on the right.

1	-10
0	7
6	3
-3	-1
-5	-4
4	-2

A $x + 4 = 1$

B $-2x = -14$

C $x + 3 = -1$

D $x - 1 = -3$

E $x - 10 = -7$

F $x - 5 = -5$

G $-4x = -4$

H $x - 6 = -2$

I $x + 1 = 0$

J $-2x = -12$

K $2x = -10$

L $x + 3 = -7$

A	B	C	D	E	F	G	H	I	J	K	L

examples

Solve $2x + 3 = 17$	Solve $2x + 3 = 17$
$\quad$ -3 $\quad$ -3	$\quad$ -3 $\quad$ -3
$\quad$ $2x = 14$	$\quad$ $2x = 14$
$\quad$ ÷2 $\quad$ ÷2	$\quad$ ÷2 $\quad$ ÷2
$\quad$ $x = 7$	$\quad$ $x = 7$

exercise 6p

1. Solve:

a) $2x + 5 = 19$

b) $3x - 2 = 10$

c) $10x + 3 = 83$

d) $5x - 5 = 35$

e) $6x + 3 = 33$

f) $9x + 2 = 20$

g) $4x + 1 = 29$

h) $9x + 9 = 81$

i) $4x - 8 = 0$

j) $2x + 5 = 17$

k) $4x - 1 = 11$

l) $3x + 1 = 22$

m) $8 + 3x = 11$

n) $16 = 4x - 4$

o) $10x - 8 = 82$

p) $8x + 12 = 76$

q) $65 = 15x + 5$

r) $29 = 4x - 15$

2. Spot the error. These equations have been solved incorrectly - circle the mistakes and state what should have been done.

a) $3x - 6 = 18$

$$3x - 6 = 18$$
$$3x = 12 \quad (-6)$$
$$x = 4 \quad (÷3)$$

b) $8 = 6x + 2$

$$8 = 6x + 2$$
$$6 = 6x \quad (-2)$$
$$x = 0 \quad (÷6)$$

c) $2 + 5x = 22$

$$2 + 5x = 22$$
$$2x = 17 \quad (-5)$$
$$x = 8.5 \quad (÷2)$$

exercise 6q

1. Simplify

    a) $3x + 5x$

    b) $3x + 5 + 5x$

    c) $3x \times 5x$

    d) $n \times 3$

    e) $n \times n \times n$

    f) $4 \times y \times y$

    g) $x + x + x$

    h) $7y - y$

    i) $(a^4)^2$

    j) $y \times y \times y \times y$

    k) $2y + 3y$

    l) $a - a$

    m) $3y - 2 - y$

    n) $a^4 \times a^6$

    o) $3a \times 3a$

    p) $4a - 3a$

    q) $4a \times 3a$

    r) $6 + 3p + p$

2. Solve these equations:

    a) $x + 4 = 7$

    b) $x - 5 = 19$

    c) $10x = 50$

    d) $\frac{x}{3} = 5$

    e) $\frac{x}{5} = 5$

    f) $x - 7 = 9$

    g) $6x = 36$

    h) $2x = 9$

    i) $10x = 55$

true or false? Find 4 true statements:

A $2 \times x$ is the same as x^2	B $x \times 2$ is written as: $x2$	C $x - y$ is the same as $y - x$	D $y \times y \times y$ is written y^3
E $x \times y \times x$ is written as: x^2y	F $2 \times y \times y$ is written as $2y$	G $y \times y$ is the same as $2y$	H $y \times 2$ is the same as $2y$
I $5y - 4$ simplifies to y	J $3 \times y \times 4$ is written as $34y$	K $\frac{x}{2}$ is the same as $x \div 2$	L $y + y$ is the same as y^2

3. True or False: $a + a + a + a$ is written as a^4

4. Which of these are the same as $6b^2$? Circle all that apply.

    a) $6 + b + b$ b) $3 \times b \times 3 \times b$ c) $2 \times b \times 3 \times b$

5. Which of these are like terms? Circle them.

    a) $8a$ b) $8b$ c) b^8 d) $18b$ e) b^2

6. True or false: $t \times t = 2t$

7. True or false: $t + t = 2t$

8. Which of these cannot be simplified?

    a) $3a + 2b$ b) $3a \times 2b$ c) $3a \times a$ d) $3a + a$

9. Simplify:

    a) $7a + 3a + 5 =$ _____   d) $8b + 2 + 3b =$ _____

    b) $12a - 10a - a =$ _____   e) $5b - 6b =$ _____

    c) $2m + 3m =$ _____   f) $2y - 5y =$ _____

matching activity

Match the equations on the left with their solutions on the right.

A	B	C
$7x = 21$	$x + 4 = 19$	$2x = 5$

D	E	F
$x - 5 = 12$	$2x = 12$	$x - 8 = 10$

G	H	I
$x + 9 = 0$	$x - 7 = 0$	$\frac{x}{5} = 4$

J	K	L
$\frac{x}{3} = 9$	$\frac{x}{2} = 13$	$x - 5 = 7$

2.5	27
12	3
-9	18
20	15
6	26
7	17

A	B	C	D	E	F	G	H	I	J	K	L

Algebra in Words

Match expressions on the left with their descriptions on the right.

1 $\dfrac{b}{a}$

2 $3a + 2b$

3 a^5

4 $\dfrac{ab}{5}$

5 a^2b^2

6 ab

7 $3 - b$

8 $3b$

9 $\dfrac{5}{a}$

10 $6a$

11 $(a + b)^2$

12 $5a$

13 $\dfrac{a}{b}$

14 a^4

15 $8a^2$

16 $b - 3$

17 b^0

18 $4x = -12$

19 b^3

20 $5b - b$

A The same as $b \times b \times b$

B a is divided by b

C This expression simplifies to $4b$

D a is multiplied by b

E An equation with a solution of -3

F Subtract b from 3

G An expression that cannot be simplified

H Subtract 3 from b

I The sum of $4a$ and $2a$

J The same as $b + b + b$

K The same as $a \times a \times b \times b$

L If $b = 100$, this expression equals 1

M b is divided by a

N The same as $4a \times 2a$

O a is multiplied by itself 5 times

P a is multiplied by 5

Q b is multiplied by a and the result is divided by 5

R The same as $a \times a \times a \times a$

S a and b are added together and the result is squared

T 5 is divided by a

A	B	C	D	E	F	G	H	I	J	K	L	M	N	O	P	Q	R	S	T

exercise 6r

1. Work out:

    a) -3 + 4   b) -8 + 3   c) 3 - 7   d) -2 - 1

    e) 4 - 6   f) -9 + 8   g) -6 + 8   h) -4 - 5

2. Which of the following have a **positive** answer? Choose all that apply.

A -4×-3	B 8×-5	C -3×9	D -1×-4
E $-20 \div 5$	F $8 \div -2$	G $-16 \div -4$	H $10 \div 10$

3. Which of these is the correct way to write $a \times 2$?

    a) $2a$ b) $a2$ c) a^2 d) $a + 2$

4. Write down the first 6 cube numbers.

5. Write $\frac{23}{4}$ as a mixed number.

6. Write as a decimal:

    a) $\frac{4}{100}$ b) $1\frac{3}{10}$ c) $\frac{4}{5}$ d) $\frac{1}{9}$

7. Calculate:

    a) 7 × 100   d) 240 ÷ 100   g) 0.6 × 100

    b) 0.4 × 10   e) 34 ÷ 10   h) 25 ÷ 100

    c) 16 ÷ 10   f) 1.9 × 10   i) 0.09 × 100

8. Fill in the blanks:

    a) 1 - _____ = $\frac{1}{10}$ b) 0.7 + _____ = 1   c) 0.3 × _____ = 0.9

9. Solve:

    a) $x - 4 = 7$ c) $3x = 27$ e) $\frac{x}{2} = 54$

    b) $\frac{x}{2} = 3.5$ d) $x + 6 = 11$ f) $2x = 23$

10. Evaluate:

    a) $\sqrt{25}$ c) 3^2 e) $(-2)^2$ g) $\sqrt[3]{8}$

    b) $\sqrt{49}$ d) 2^3 f) $(-1)^3$ h) $\sqrt{25}$

11. Calculate 46×31

12. Work out $\frac{1}{4} + \frac{1}{3}$

13. Work out:

    a) $-5 + 3$ c) $\frac{1}{5} + \frac{3}{5}$ e) 0.4×6

    b) $-7 - 7$ d) $1 - \frac{2}{5}$ f) $\frac{2}{3}$ of 15

14. Simplify:

    a) $6a - 3 + 3a$ c) $9a - 4 - 9a$

    b) $7a - 7a$ d) $8 - 2a + 2$

15. True or False: $-6 \times -3 = -18$

16. Which is the smallest?
    a) 0.3   b) 0.30   c) 0.207   d) 0.210

17. Which of these is the same as $4a - 5a$?

    a) $1a$ b) a c) $-a$ d) $9a$

18. Write more simply: $b + b + b =$ _____

19. Which of these are the same as $t + t + t + t$?

    a) t^4 b) $2t \times 2t$ c) $t \times t \times t \times t$ d) $4t$

20. Calculate:

    a) $-4 - 5$ c) $-4 + -5$ e) -4×-5

    b) $-4 + 5$ d) $4 + -5$ f) -4×5

21. Put these in order of size, starting with the smallest: 0.74   0.701 $\frac{7}{10}$

exercise 6s

1. Calculate:

   a) $\frac{2}{5} + \frac{3}{5}$

   b) $1 - \frac{1}{7}$

   c) $\frac{5}{8} - \frac{2}{8}$

   d) $1 - 0.9$

   e) $\frac{5}{10} - \frac{1}{5}$

   f) $\frac{1}{3} + \frac{1}{8}$

   g) $0.6 + \frac{1}{10}$

   h) $\frac{2}{5} - \frac{1}{4}$

   i) $\frac{1}{4} + \frac{1}{4} + \frac{1}{4} + \frac{1}{4}$

2. Write $\frac{3}{5}$ as a decimal.

3. Which of these fractions are equivalent to $\frac{3}{30}$? Circle all that apply.

   a) $\frac{2}{29}$

   b) $\frac{1}{2}$

   c) $\frac{1}{10}$

   d) $\frac{9}{90}$

   e) $\frac{6}{15}$

4. Which of these fractions cannot be simplifed? Circle all that apply.

   a) $\frac{4}{18}$

   b) $\frac{9}{10}$

   c) $\frac{3}{27}$

   d) $\frac{2}{5}$

   e) $\frac{9}{18}$

- -

Missing Numbers Puzzle

Use the numbers below to make the calculations on the right correct.

11	1
-1	-2
-3	-4
-5	-6
-7	-8

A [ ] + [-3] = [-6]

B [-5] + [-2] = [ ]

C [6] + [ ] = [5]

D [ ] - [ ] = [-5]

E [6] - [ ] = [ ]

F [ ] - [ ] = [ ]

208

chapter 7: working with measures

[Recommended Time : 11 - 15 hours]

Contents

The diagrams in this chapter are not drawn to scale

P For resources marked P, students will need a photocopy or print out of this activity to work on

rounding to 1 significant figure

examples

Round 482 to 1 significant figure (1.s.f)	Round 9.45 to 1 significant figure (1.s.f)
The first significant figure is 4, which is in the hundreds column, so round to the nearest hundred = 500	The first significant figure is 9, which is in the units column, so round to the nearest whole number = 9

exercise 7a

1. Round each of the following to 1 significant figure:

   a) 870

   b) 34

   c) 582

   d) 690

   e) 4,500

   f) 21

   g) 85

   h) 611

   i) 901

   j) 92

   k) 2,103

   l) 24,500

2. Round each of the following to 1 significant figure:

   a) 4.7

   b) 3.5

   c) 8.02

   d) 7.5

   e) 2.44

   f) 6.034

   g) 1.04

   h) 0.5

   i) 9.803

3. I'm thinking of a number. I round it to 1 significant figure. The answer is 80. Which of these could have been my number?

   a) 72   b) 79   c) 85   d) 800

4. I'm thinking of a number. I round it to 1 significant figure. The answer is 9. Which of these could have been my number?

   a) 8.2   b) 8.3   c) 8.4   d) 8.5

5. Paula rounds a number to one significant figure. She gets the answer 34. Explain how you know she has made a mistake.

estimating calculations

learn by heart

To estimate: *try rounding numbers to 1 significant figure before calculating*

≈ means 'is approximately'

examples

Estimate the answer to £423 × 42	Estimate the answer to 3.55 × 172
≈ £400 × 40 ≈ £16,000	≈ 4 × 200 ≈ 800

exercise 7b

1. Estimate the following:

    a) 793 × 22

    b) 102 × 3.8

    c) 426 × 2.6

    d) 1.009 × 4,099

    e) 22.8 × 650

    f) 3.05 × 29.7

    g) 690 + 114.7

    h) 5,120 + 2,289.9

    i) 19.7 × 526

    j) 24.7 × 35.9

    k) 2,320 × 2.3

    l) 340 × 7.888

2. Carly works out £821.50 × 13
    She gets an answer of £1,067,950
    Explain how you know that Carly's answer is definitely wrong.

3. Explain why the answer to 41.7 × 2.8 cannot be 11.676

4. Use estimations to work out which of these has the largest answer:

    a) 73 × 1.9   b) 57 × 2.78   c) 42 × 3.1

5. Estimate the answer to 420 + 18.9 × 5.9

Find the Correct Answer 📱

In each row, work out which is the correct answer
to the calculation by estimating.

	calculation	answer 1	answer 2	answer 3
A	147 × 2.9	4.263	42.63	426.3
B	11 × 19	209	2,090	20,900
C	399 × 3.4	13.566	135.66	1356.6
D	2.8 × 4.9	1.372	13.72	137.2
E	198 × 3.1	613.8	61.38	6.138
F	34.7 × 20.15	699.205	6,992.05	69,920.5
G	1,420 + 2,999	44.19	441.9	4,419
H	7.2^2	5.184	51.84	518.4
I	92 + 54 × 3.5	28.1	281	2,810
J	340 + 2.1 × 3	346.3	34.63	3.463
K	9.9^2	9.801	98.01	980.1
L	7.1 × 140 + 52	1046	10,460	104,600
M	2.1 + 3.8 × 4.2 + 1.9	0.996	1.996	19.96
N	-14.7 × -2.8	-41.16	-4.16	41.16

estimating heights & lengths

learn by heart

The metric measurements for length are mm, cm, m and km

| **millimetres** (mm) are small. 10mm make 1 cm. | **centimetres** (cm) 100 of them make 1 metre. | **metres** (m) A normal door is 2m. | **kilometres** (km) are big. 1 km = 1000 metres |

exercise 7c

1. Which of these are very unlikley measurements?

A A door that is 4km tall	B A real train that is 3cm wide	C A man that is 2m tall
D A pen that is 15cm long	E A book that is 4mm wide	F A classroom that is 3m high
G The distance from Sheffield to London is 30m	H The Shard skyscraper is 306m tall	I A TV that is 1m wide

2. Which of these are metric units for length? Circle 2 answers.

   a) mm   b) m^2 c) miles   d) km   e) litres   f) yards

3. Fill in the blanks with mm, cm, m or km:

   a) The length of a ruler is 30 _____.   b) The height of a door is 2 _____.

   c) The distance from the Earth to the Moon is 384,000 _____.

   d) A paperclip is 20 _____ tall.   e) A chair is 0.5 _____ tall.

   f) A house is 7_____ tall.   g) An ant is 8 _____ long.

   h) A laptop is 45 _____ wide.   i) A train is 1.2 _____ long

4. There are _____ metres in 1 kilometre.

5. Estimate the length of these objects using a sensible metric unit.

a) A hammer is _____ long.

b) A car is _____ tall.

c) The wing on a jumbo jet is _____ long.

d) A cat is _____ tall.

e) The average man is _____ tall.

6. There are _____ cm in a metre.

7. Which of these is likely to be tallest?

| A door | A bookcase | A giraffe | A window |

8. Which of these is longest?

| 1km | 1mm | 1cm | 1m |

9. Which of these could be the height of a house?

a) 8cm   b) 8kg   c) 8m   d) 8g

10. True or False?

a) A metre is the same as 100cm.

b) mm, cm, m and km are all metric measurements.

c) A metre is longer than a kilometre.

d) 10mm are the same as 1cm.

e) A kilometre equals 100 metres.

f) The distance from York to Sheffield would be best measured in millimetres.

11. Fill in the blanks:

a) 30cm + _____ = 1 metre

b) 500m + _____ = 1 kilometre

c) 3mm + _____ = 1 centimetre

d) 2m + _____ = 1 kilometre

12. Complete the blanks:

a) Half a centimetre is _____ mm.

b) Half a metre is _____ cm.

c) Half a kilometre is _____ m.

13. Which of these lengths is longest?

| 0.1km | 0.35km | 0.4km | 0.2km | 0.200km |

14. If you had to measure the following lengths, what units would you use for your answers? Choose **mm, cm, m or km:**

a) The distance from Edinburgh to London

b) The height of a book

c) The length of a fly

d) The height of a skyscraper

e) The height of a man

f) The distance around the Earth

---

matching activity

Match each object to its length:

A A ruler

B The length of the UK

C The length of a snake

D The height of a Lorry

E The height of a man

F A paperclip

G The length of a swimming pool

H The width of America

| 50m | 4,300km | 3cm | 175cm |

| 1,400km | 2.5m | 30cm | 450cm |

Object	Length
A	
B	
C	
D	
E	
F	
G	
H	

powers of 10 warm up

exercise 7d

1. Work out:

   a) 84 × 10
   b) 9.1 × 1000
   c) 60 × 100

   d) 1700 ÷ 100
   e) 45 ÷ 10
   f) 300 ÷ 1000

   g) 10,000 ÷ 100
   h) 120 ÷ 1000
   j) 907 ÷ 10

2. Work out the missing numbers:

   a) 65 × _____ = 6500
   b) 2710 ÷ _____ = 271

   c) _____ × 10 = 95,600
   d) _____ ÷ 100 = 20

   e) 450 ÷ _____ = 0.45
   f) 1000 × _____ = 29,000

3. Work out:

   a) 2.7 × 10
   c) 0.5 × 100
   e) 1.250 ÷ 10

   b) 902 ÷ 10
   d) 1.1 ÷ 10
   f) 0.007 × 100

4. If a zero is added to the end of one of these numbers, it doesn't get any bigger.
   Circle the number.

   a) 3
   b) 42
   c) 0.9
   d) 10

matching activity

Match these calculations to their answers:

A	B	C
0.45 × 10	20.6 ÷ 100	4.5 × 100

D	E	F
450 ÷ 1000	0.45 × 100	4.5 ÷ 100

G	H	I
4.5 × 1000	2.6 × 100	260 ÷ 1000

J	K	L
206 ÷ 100	2.06 × 100	0.026 × 1000

M	S
4500	0.045

N	T
450	45

O	U
4.5	0.45

P	V
26	2.06

Q	W
0.206	260

R	X
0.26	206

A	B	C	D	E	F	G	H	I	J	K	L

metric units of length: cm & mm

learn by heart

| 1cm = 10mm | 0.5cm = 5mm |

exercise 7e

1. Fill in the blank spaces:

   a) 3mm + _____ = 1cm

   b) 6mm + _____ = 1cm

2. Fill in the blank spaces. The first one is done for you.

   a) 2cm + 3mm = __2.3__ cm

   d) 6cm + 9mm = _____ cm

   b) 5cm + 1mm = _____ cm

   e) 8cm + 10mm = _____ cm

   c) 12cm + 8mm = _____ cm

   f) 9mm = _____ cm

3. Measure the length of each of these lines. Give your answer in cm.

   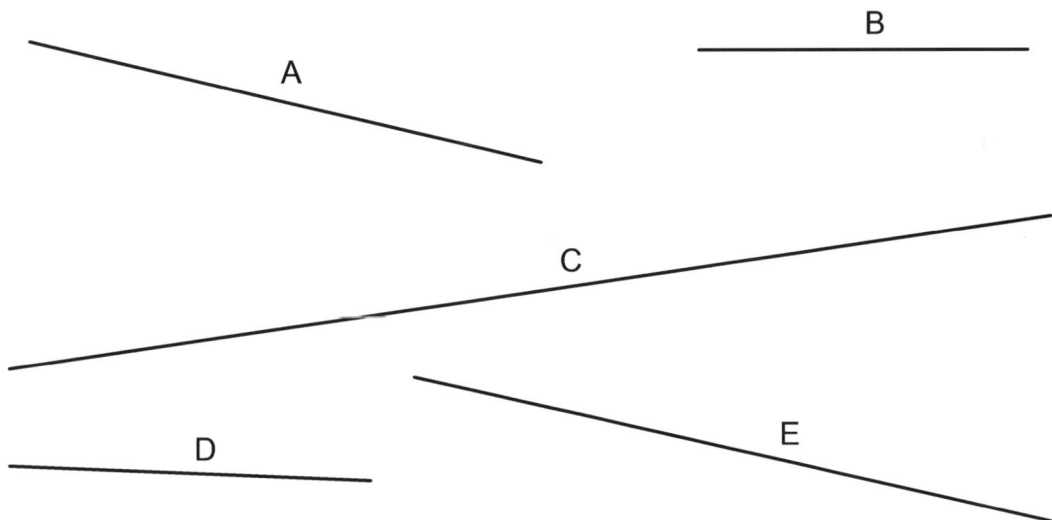

4. Complete these metric conversions

   a) 5cm = _____ mm

   c) 0.4cm = _____ mm

   e) 9.4cm = _____ mm

   b) 2.3cm = _____ mm

   d) 1.1cm = _____ mm

   f) 0.8cm = _____ mm

5. Round each of these lengths to the nearest cm:

   a) 3.8cm   c) 1.99cm   e) 18.6cm

   b) 4.5cm   d) 4.08cm   f) 109.85cm

6. 1cm is the same as _____mm

7. 3.5cm is the same as _____mm

8. Which is longer? Choose the larger length in each pair:

   a) 1cm or 1mm   e) 1cm or 12mm   g) 0.5cm or 9mm

   b) 1cm or 8mm   e) 0.5cm or 6mm   h) 0.2cm or 3mm

   c) 11mm or 1cm   f) 0.2cm or 1mm   i) 1.9cm or 20mm

9. Fill in the missing units with cm or mm.

   a) A ruler is 30_____ long.   d) A ruler is 300_____ long

   b) A door is 200_____ tall.   e) A bottle is 180_____ tall.

   c) A crayon is 75_____ long.   f) A nail is 5 _____long.

10. Which of these are unrealistic measurements?

   a) A table that is 100cm tall   d) A battery that is 50cm long

   b) A dice that is 1mm wide   e) A door that is 2000cm tall

   c) A plaster that is 50mm long   f) A pen that is 15mm long

11. Complete these metric conversions:

   a) 7cm = _____mm   d) 10mm = _____cm   g) 100cm = _____mm

   b) 0.5cm = _____mm   e) 25mm = _____cm   h) 95mm = _____cm

   c) 90cm = _____mm   f) 33mm = _____cm   i) 62mm = _____cm

metric units of length: cm & m

learn by heart: | 1 metre is 100cm |

0.9m is less than 1 metre, so your answer should be less than 100

examples

Convert 70cm into metres.

$$= 70 \div 100$$
$$= 0.7m$$

Convert 0.9m into centimetres.

$$= 0.9 \times 100$$
$$= 90cm$$

exercise 7f

1. Complete these statements:

   a) 200cm = _____ m

   b) _____ cm = 3m

   c) _____ cm = 3.5m

   d) 250cm = _____ m

   e) 90cm = _____ m

   f) 4.2m = _____ cm

   g) 105cm = _____ m

   h) 0.6m = _____ cm

   i) _____ m = 8cm

   j) _____ cm = 3.02m

multiple choice

Choose the correct answer, or answers, for each question.

1. Which of the following is equal to 100cm?

   a) 10m   b) 100m

   c) 1m   d) 1km

2. Which of the following is equal to 3.5m?

   a) 3500cm   b) 350cm

   c) 305cm   d) 30.5cm

3. Which of the following is the largest?

   a) 250cm   b) 2.9m

   c) 2.55m   d) 209cm

4. Which of the following is the smallest?

   a) 0.7m   b) 76cm

   c) 0.68m   d) 70.5cm

metric units of length: m & km

<u>learn by heart:</u> | 1 kilometre is 1000m |

0.04km is less than 1 km, so your answer should be less than 1000

examples

| Convert 820m into kilometres.

= 820 ÷ 1000
= 0.82km | Convert 0.04km into metres.

= 0.04 × 1000
= 40m |

exercise 7g

1. Complete these statements:

   a) 2000m = _____km

   b) _____m = 5km

   c) _____m = 1.5km

   d) 2600m = _____km

   e) _____m = 1.08km

   f) 2.75km = _____m

   g) 500m = _____km

   h) _____km = 2050m

   i) 0.65km = _____m

   j) 10,000m = _____km

matching activity

Find 12 pairs of matching lengths. Record your results in a table.

A 4m	B 3.5m	C 250m		M 35cm	N 0.5km	O 0.015km
D 500m	E 1.5m	F 2500m		P 1.05km	Q 400cm	R 0.25km
G 0.4m	H 0.35m	I 15m		S 350cm	T 40cm	U 105cm
J 1.05m	K 1050m	L 350m		V 0.35km	W 2.5km	X 150cm

A	B	C	D	E	F	G	H	I	J	K	L

converting metric lengths mixed practice

learn by heart

When converting to a larger unit, you will need a smaller number, so divide

When converting to a smaller unit, you will need a larger number, so multiply

examples

Convert 92cm into metres.

$92 \div 100$

$= 0.92m$

Convert 7m into kilometres.

$7 \div 1000$

$= 0.007km$

Convert 84cm into mm.

84×10

$= 840mm$

exercise 7h

1. Complete these statements:

   a) 300cm = _____ m

   b) 4cm = _____ mm

   c) 2km = _____ m

   d) 700mm = _____ cm

   e) 3,400m = _____ km

   f) 5m = _____ cm

   g) 2.5cm = _____ mm

   h) 3.1km = _____ m

   i) 6.4m = _____ cm

   j) 680m = _____ km

2. In each pair, decide which is longest (or state if they are equal):

   a) 3m or 200cm

   d) 9m or 8cm

   g) 45cm or 50mm

   b) 1km or 2m

   e) 5cm or 4m

   h) 2km or 2000m

   c) 30cm or 30mm

   f) 2.5m or 200cm

   i) 9mm or 1cm

3. True or false?

   a) There are 100 metres in a kilometre.

   c) A kilometre is longer than 100 metres.

   b) There are 10 centimetres in a millimetre.

   d) A metre is made of 100 centimetres.

4. Which of these are longer than 1 metre? Circle 2 answers.

    a) 20cm   b) 5mm   c) 0.5 km   d) 4.5cm   e) 105cm

5. A kilometre is the same as _____ metres.

6. True or false:

    a) 7cm = 70mm   d) 3mm = 0.3cm   g) 9km = 9000m

    b) 5m = 0.5km   e) 0.9m = 9cm   h) 8m = 800cm

    c) 200cm = 2m   f) 400m = 4km   i) 55mm = 5.5cm

7. Fill in the blanks:

    a) 80cm + _____ = 1 metre   c) 100m + _____ = 1 kilometre

    b) 3mm + _____ 1 centimetre   d) 4cm + _____ = 1 metre

8. Copy and complete the table to show equivalent lengths:

mm	cm	m	km
	600		
		80	
		1000	
2000			

9. True or false?

    a) 30m = 300cm   b) 5.4m = 54cm   c) 2.8cm = 280mm

10. Which of these equals 200cm? Circle two answers.

    a) 2000mm   b) 0.2km   c) 20m   d) 0.02km

11. challenge! Complete these conversions:

    a) 0.24km = _____cm   d) 52,000cm = _____km

    b) 3,400mm = _____m   e) 0.01m = _____mm

    c) 1.9m = _____mm   f) 290mm = _____m

Estimating Large & Small Lengths

Match the lengths given below to the items they describe.
Two cards are left blank. Estimate these lengths.

A Length of the UK	F Length of a pencil	K Size of a galaxy
B Distance across the earth	G Thickness of a credit card	L Height of Mount Everest
C Height of the Eifell Tower	H Distance from the earth to the sun	M Length of an egg
D Width of a red blood cell	I Height of a lamp post	N Length of a grain of rice
E Height of Big Ben	J Width of an atom	O Length of a marathon

1 8,800m	4 150,000,000km	7 96m	10 20cm	13 13,000km
2 0.007mm	5 1,400km	8 42km	11 320m	14
3 1,000,000,000, 000,000km	6 0.0000001mm	9 0.7mm	12 4.5m	15

A	B	C	D	E	F	G	H	I	J	K	L	M	N	O

perimeter

learn by heart

Perimeter: The distance around the edge of a shape

Sides with equal
lengths are marked
with dashes

examples

Work out the perimeter of these shapes. Give our answer as a decimal

4.6

$3\frac{3}{10}$

$4.6 + 4.6 + 3.3 + 3.3$
$= 15.8$

$\frac{1}{4}$

$0.25 + 0.25 + 0.25$
$= 0.75$

exercise 7i

1. In these diagrams, the lengths are all measured in cm. Calculate the perimeter:

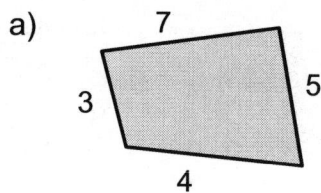

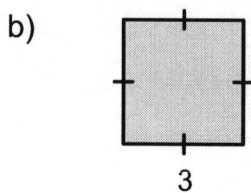

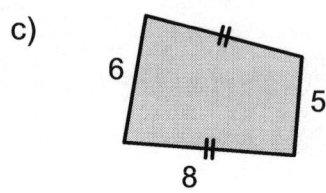

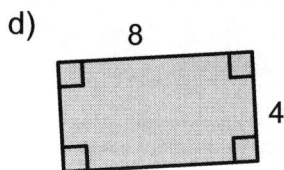

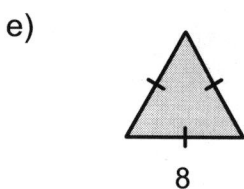

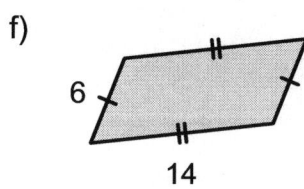

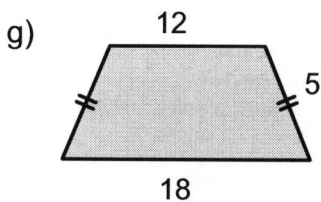

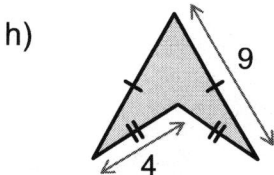

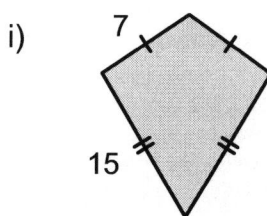

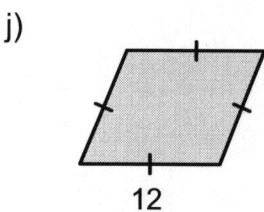

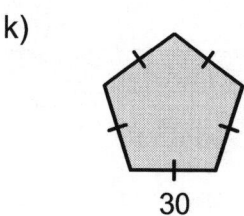

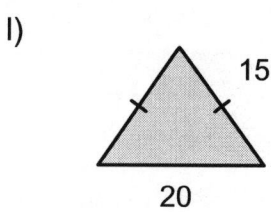

a)

7

3

5

4

b)

3

c)

6

5

8

d)

8

4

e)

8

f)

6

14

g)

12

5

18

h)

9

4

i)

7

15

j)

12

k)

30

l)

15

20

2. Complete the sentence using two of these words:

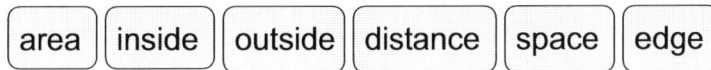

area inside outside distance space edge

Perimeter is the total _____ around the _____ of a shape.

3. These shapes are drawn on square grids. Work out their perimeters.

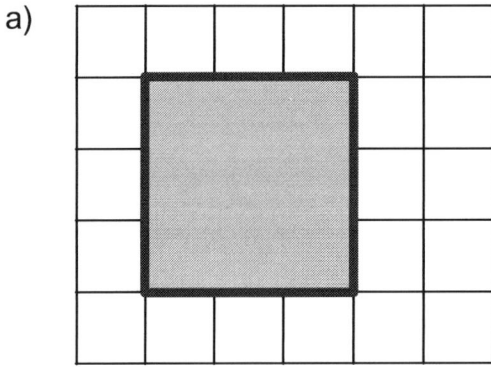

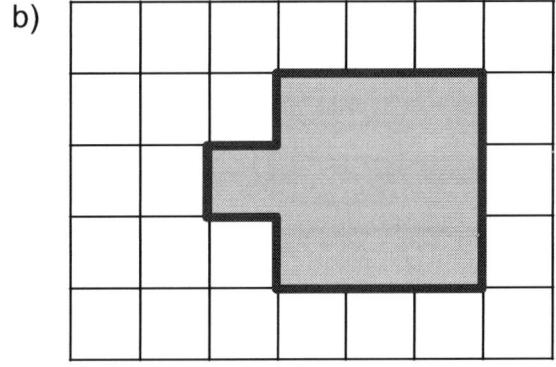

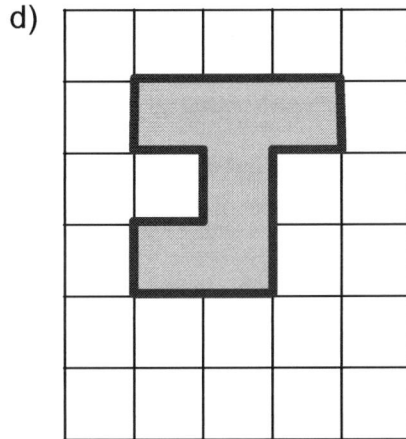

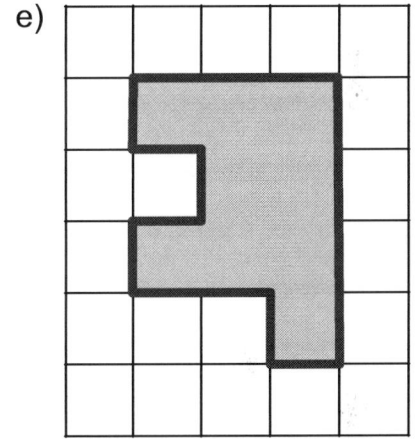

a)

b)

c)

d)

e)

4. On a square grid, draw two different shapes each with a perimeter of 10

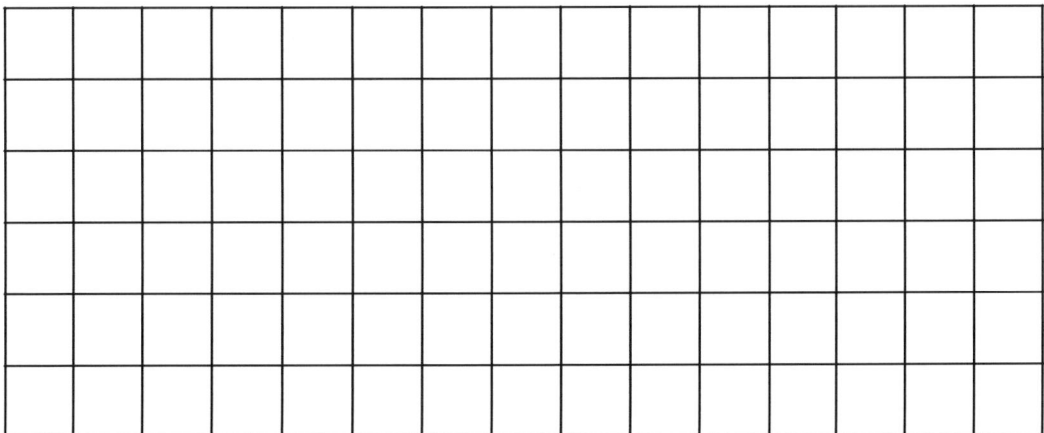

5. Use a ruler to measure the perimeter of these shapes.
   Give your answer in cm.

   a)

   b)

   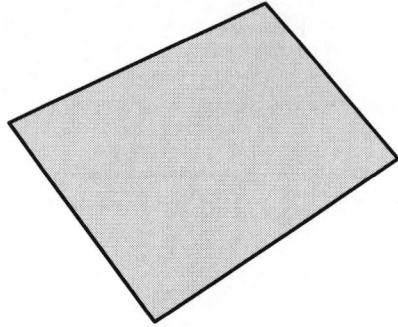

   c)

   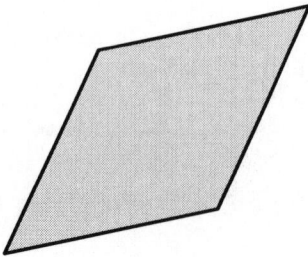

   d)

   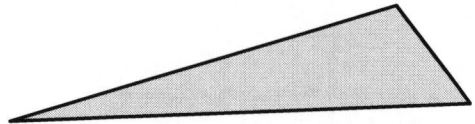

6. In your book, draw a shape with a perimeter of 20cm.

7. How many different shapes can you draw with a perimeter of 20cm?

8. Can you draw a shape with a perimeter of 20cm that also has 20 squares inside?

9. Use the perimeter of each shape to work out the missing side lengths:

   a)

   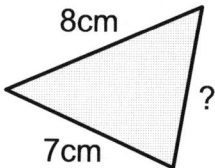

   8cm
   ?
   7cm

   Perimeter = 20cm

   b)

   ?

   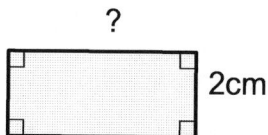

   2cm

   Perimeter = 16cm

   c)

   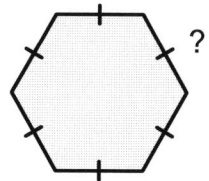

   ?

   Perimeter = 24cm

   d)

   ?

   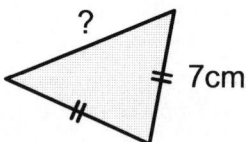

   7cm

   Perimeter = 20cm

   e)

   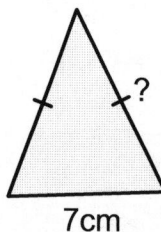

   ?

   7cm

   Perimeter = 23cm

   f)

   ?

   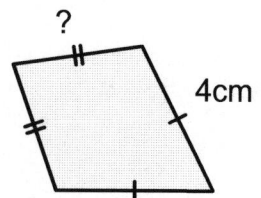

   4cm

   Perimeter = 15cm

10. The side lengths of these shapes are measured in cm.
    Work out their perimeters, giving your answers **as decimals**:

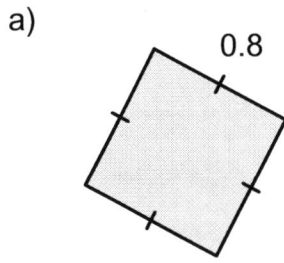

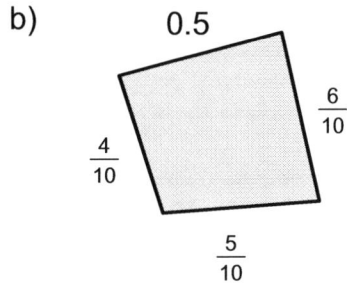

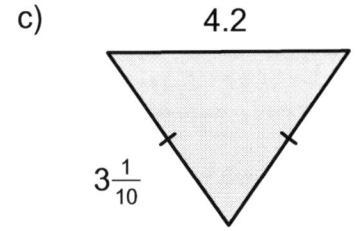

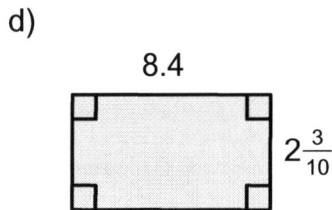

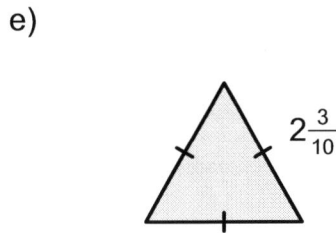

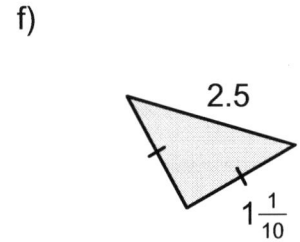

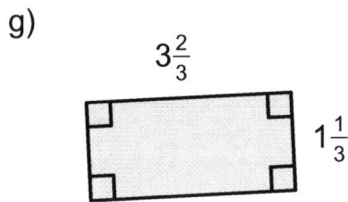

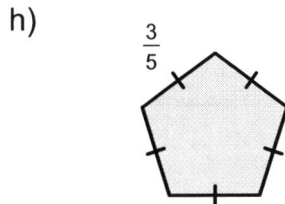

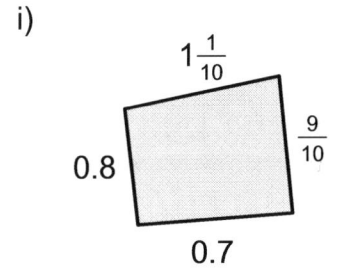

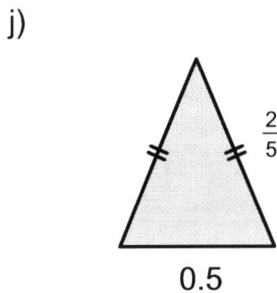

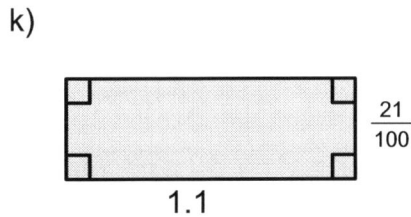

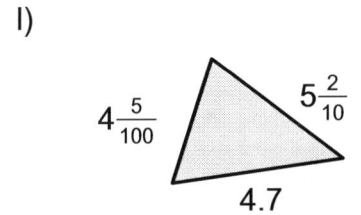

a)

0.8

b)

0.5

$\frac{4}{10}$

$\frac{6}{10}$

$\frac{5}{10}$

c)

4.2

$3\frac{1}{10}$

d)

8.4

$2\frac{3}{10}$

e)

$2\frac{3}{10}$

f)

2.5

$1\frac{1}{10}$

g)

$3\frac{2}{3}$

$1\frac{1}{3}$

h)

$\frac{3}{5}$

i)

$1\frac{1}{10}$

0.8

$\frac{9}{10}$

0.7

j)

$\frac{2}{5}$

0.5

k)

$\frac{21}{100}$

1.1

l)

$4\frac{5}{100}$

$5\frac{2}{10}$

4.7

challenge

11. The perimeter of this rectangle is 18cm.

    Five of these rectangles are put together to make this larger shape.
    Work out the perimeter of this larger shape.

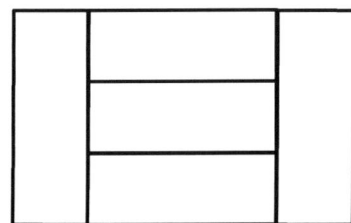

exercise 7j

1. These shapes are all rectilinear (their sides meet at right angles).
    Work out the lengths marked ? in each shape.

a)

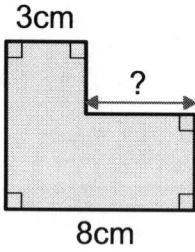

3cm
?
8cm

b)

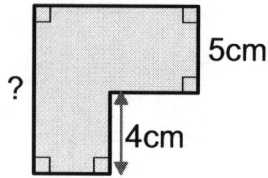

5cm
?
4cm

c)

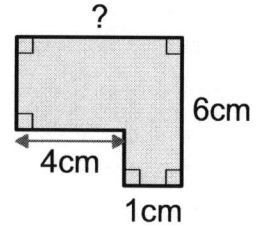

?
6cm
4cm
1cm

d)

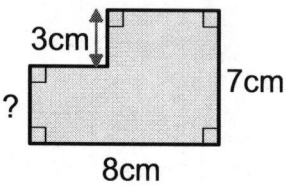

3cm
7cm
?
8cm

e)

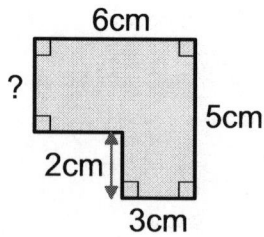

6cm
?
5cm
2cm
3cm

f)

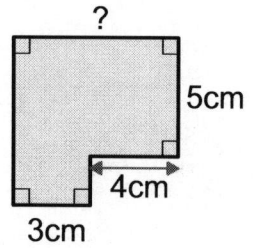

?
5cm
4cm
3cm

g)

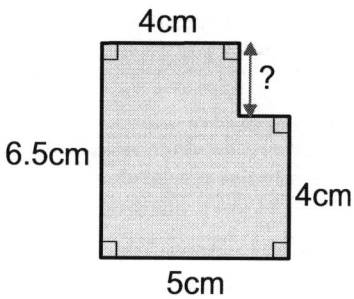

4cm
?
6.5cm
4cm
5cm

h)

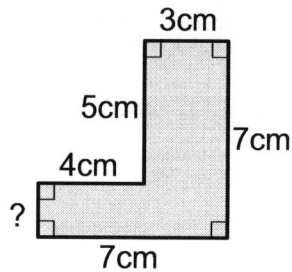

3cm
5cm
7cm
4cm
?
7cm

i)

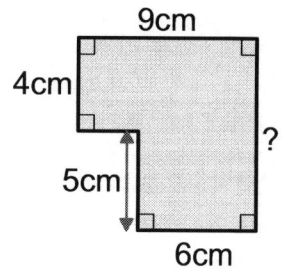

9cm
4cm
?
5cm
6cm

j)

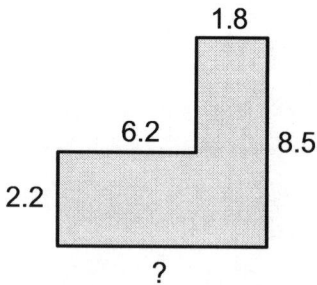

1.8
6.2
8.5
2.2
?

k)

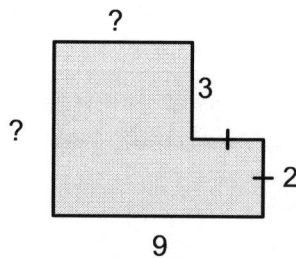

?
3
?
2
9

l)

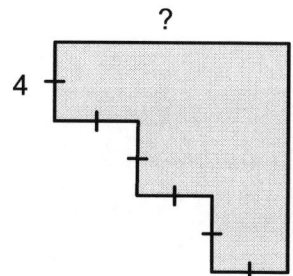

?
4

2. Work out the perimeter of these rectilinear shapes. All lengths are given in centimetres.

a)

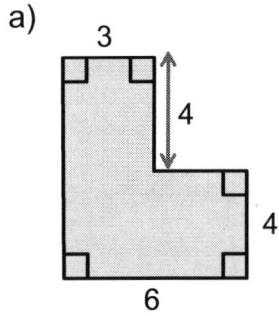

3
4
4
6

b)

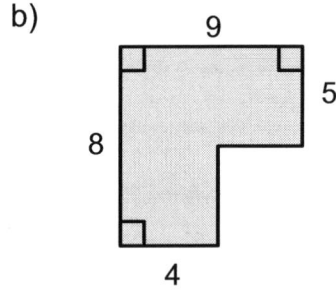

9
5
8
4

c)

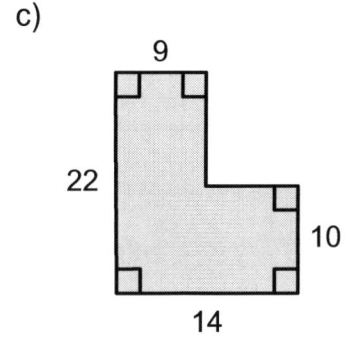

9
22
10
14

d)

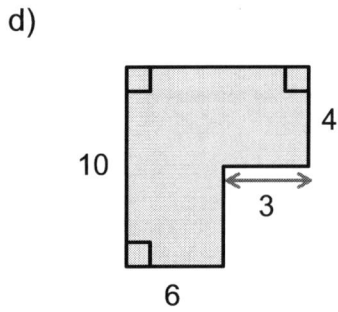

4
10
3
6

e)

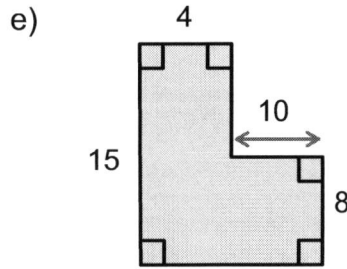

4
10
15
8

f)

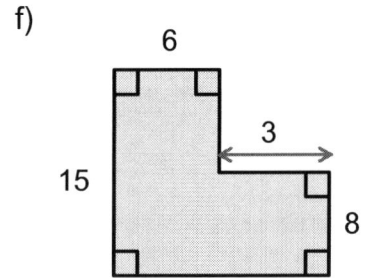

6
3
15
8

g)

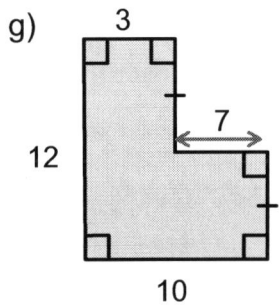

3
7
12
10

h)

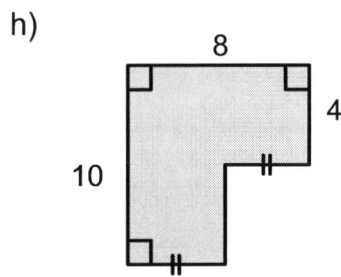

8
4
10

i)

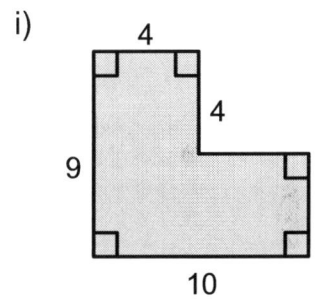

4
4
9
10

2. Work out the missing lengths, given the perimeters shown:

a)

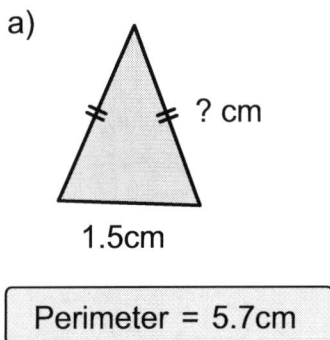

? cm
1.5cm

Perimeter = 5.7cm

b)

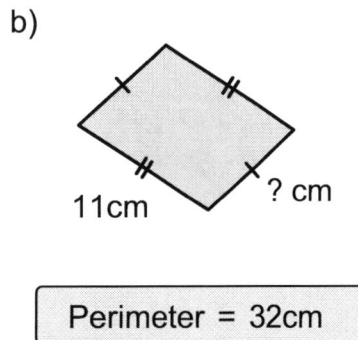

11cm
? cm

Perimeter = 32cm

c)

20 cm

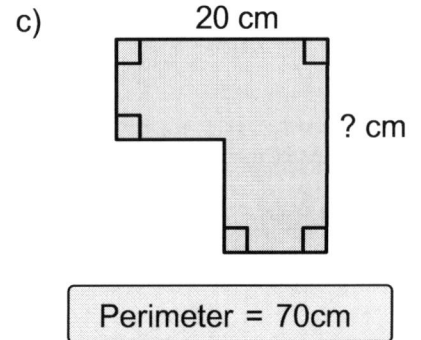

? cm

Perimeter = 70cm

perimeter with unit conversion

example

Calculate the perimeter of this shape:

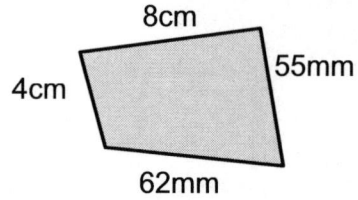

P = 8cm + 5.5cm + 6.2cm + 4cm

= 23.7cm

exercise 7k

1. These shapes are not drawn accurately. Calculate their perimeter.
    Give your answers in cm.

a)

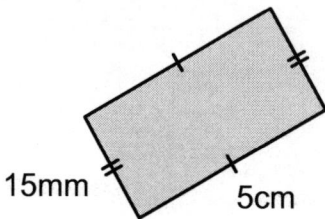

b)

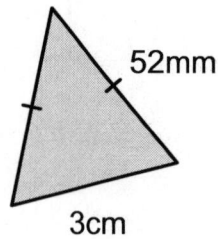

c)

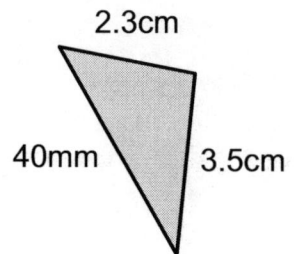

d)

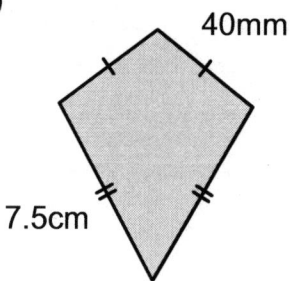

e)

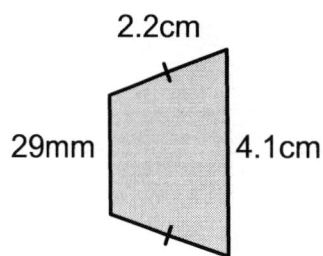

f)

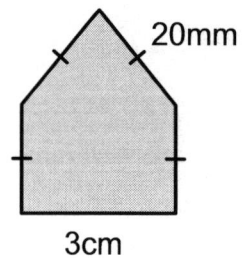

g)

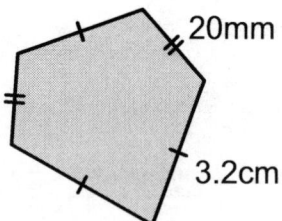

h)

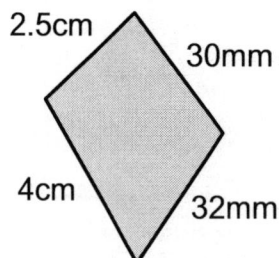

i)

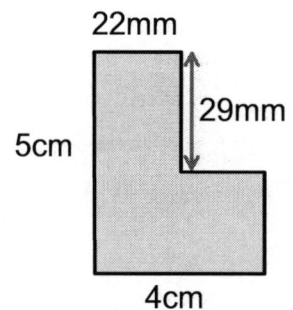

2. Work out the perimeter of these shapes.

a)

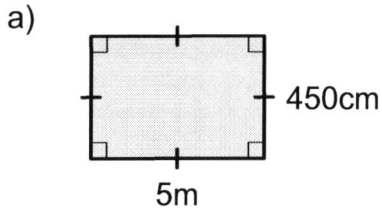

450cm

5m

b)

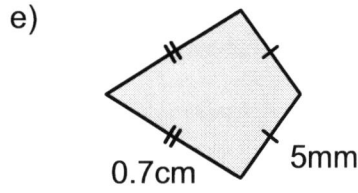

50cm

1.5m

c)

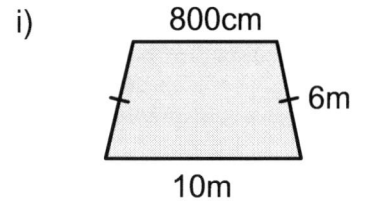

0.3m

50cm

d)

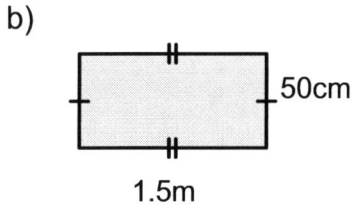

40mm

7cm

e)

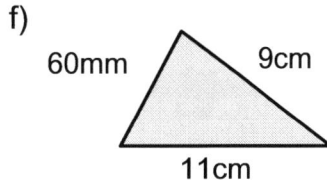

0.7cm

5mm

f)

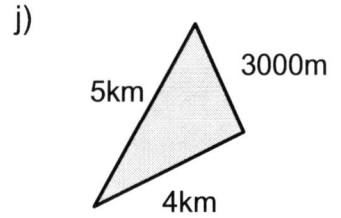

60mm   9cm

11cm

g)

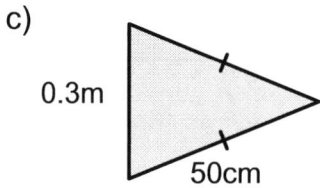

2m

40cm

h)

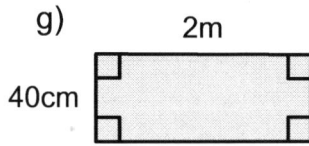

$\frac{1}{2}$ m

1.3m

120cm

i)

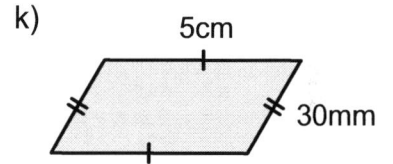

800cm

6m

10m

j)

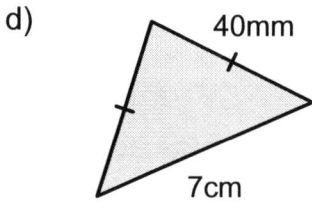

5km   3000m

4km

k)

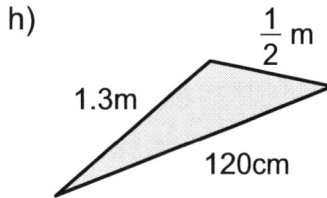

5cm

30mm

l)

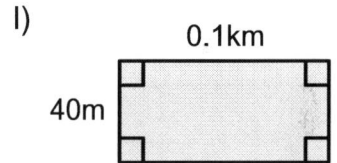

0.1km

40m

3. Work out the missing lengths, given the perimeters shown.

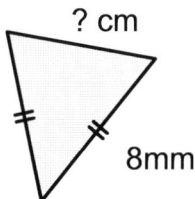

? cm

8mm

Perimeter = 2cm

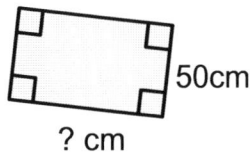

50cm

? cm

Perimeter = 3.4m

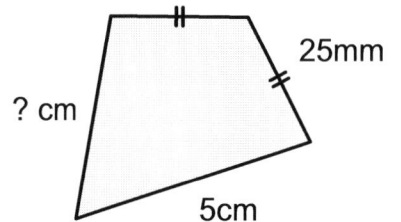

25mm

? cm

5cm

Perimeter = 14.5cm

example

Write an expression for
the perimeter of this shape,
simplifying your answer.

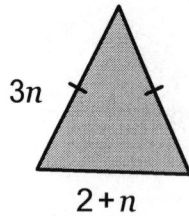

$3n$

$2+n$

$= 3n + 3n + 2 + n$

$= 7n + 2$

exercise 71

1. Write a simplified expression for the perimeter of each of these shapes.

a)

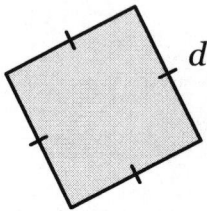

d

b)

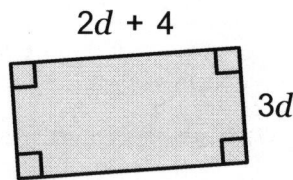

$2d + 4$

$3d$

c)

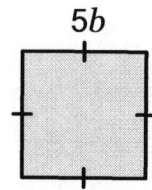

$5b$

d)

$b + 1$

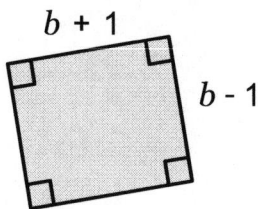

$b - 1$

e)

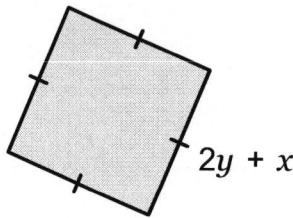

$2y + x$

f)

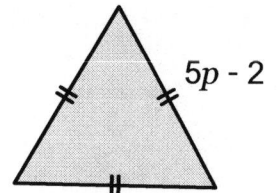

$5p - 2$

g)

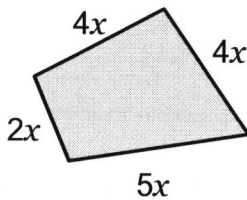

$4x$

$4x$

$2x$

$5x$

h)

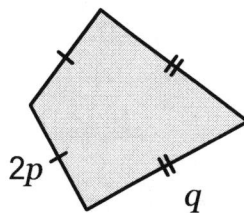

$2p$

q

i)

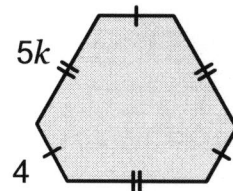

$5k$

4

j)

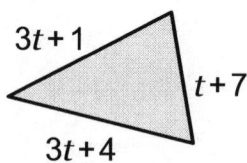

$3t + 1$

$t + 7$

$3t + 4$

k)

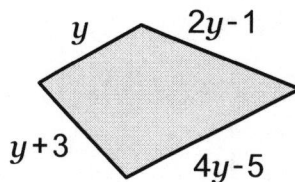

y

$2y - 1$

$y + 3$

$4y - 5$

l)

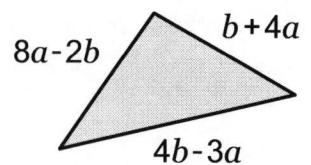

$8a - 2b$

$b + 4a$

$4b - 3a$

measuring time 1 (the first half hour)

learn by heart

The hour hand is the shorter hand

The minute hand is longer

The hour is split into 5 minute intervals.
The 1 represents 1 lot of 5 minutes after the hour

15 minutes past the hour (at 3) is pronounced 'quarter past'

30 minutes past the hour (at 6) is pronounced 'half past'

The minute hand is at 2, this means $2 \times 5 = 10$ minutes past the hour, so 4.10

exercise 7m

1. Write the correct time for each clock.

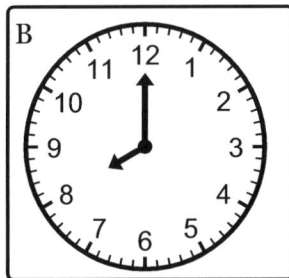

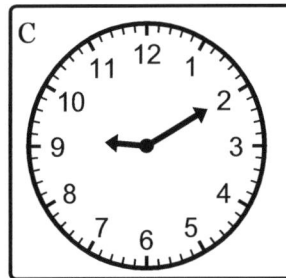

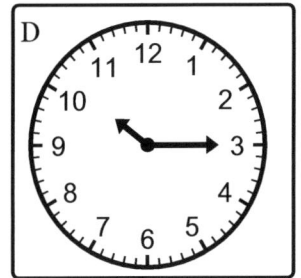

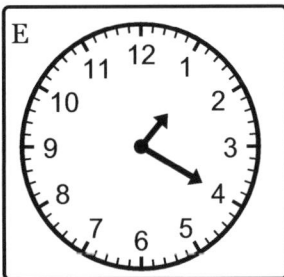

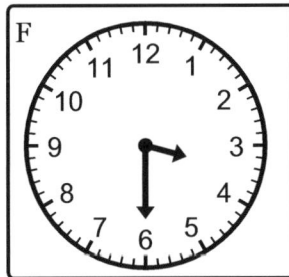

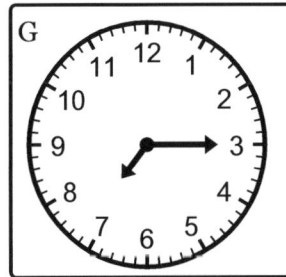

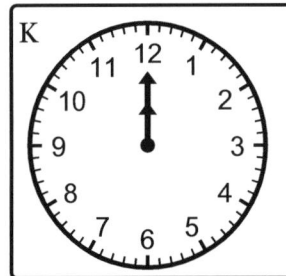

A

B

C

D

E

F

G

H

I

J

K

L

2. On each clock draw the hands in the correct place to show the time given.

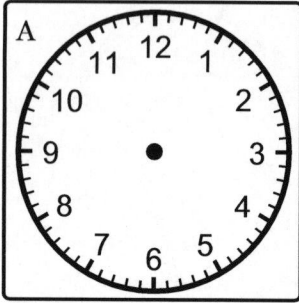

11.05

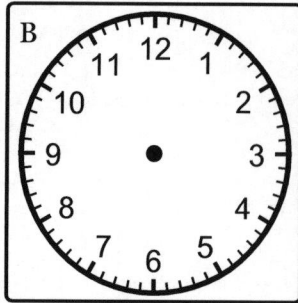

4.15

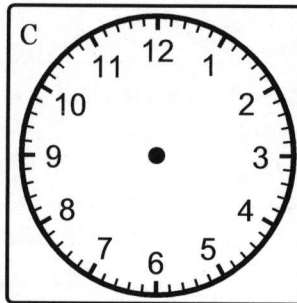

9.20

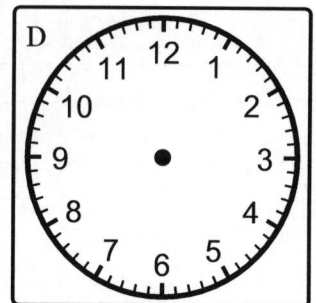

6.30

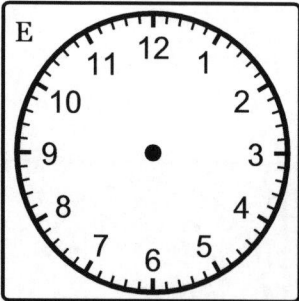

Twenty past eight

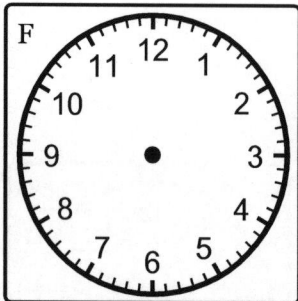

Twenty five past seven

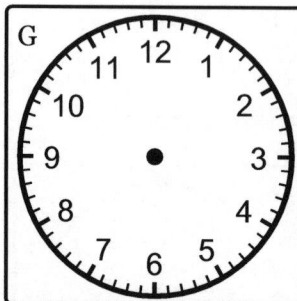

Half past one

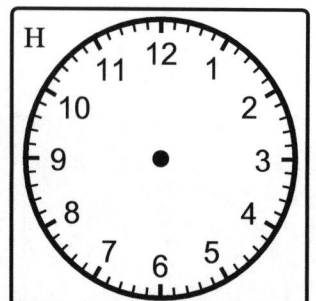

Ten past twelve

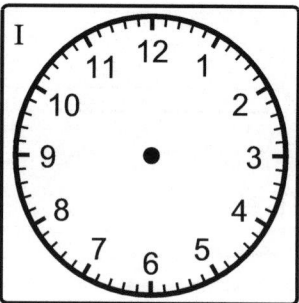

Half past two

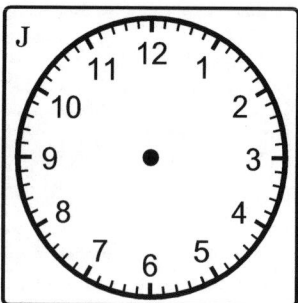

Five o' clock

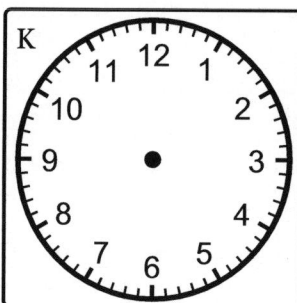

Quarter past six

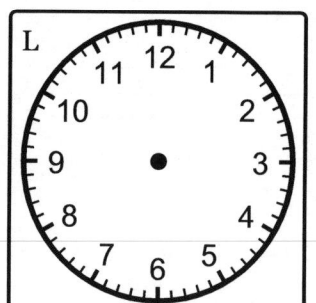

Twenty five past nine

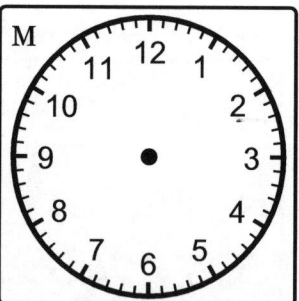

2.06

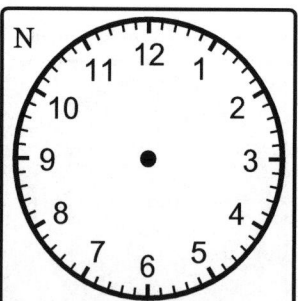

8.29

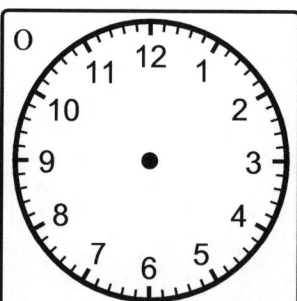

10.01

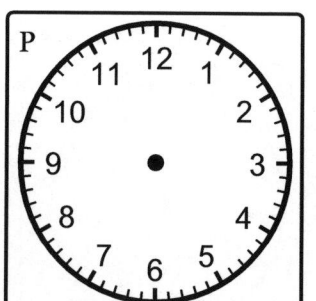

3.16

learn by heart

After half past, we start to say how many minutes it is to the next hour

When the minute hand is at...
7 we can say '25 minutes to'
8 we can say '20 minutes to'
9 we can say 'quarter to'
10 we cn say '10 to'
11 we can say '5 to'

The minute hand is at 9, so we say 'quarter to' and the next hour is 5, so this is 4.45 or 'quarter to 5'

exercise 7n

1. Write the correct time for each clock.

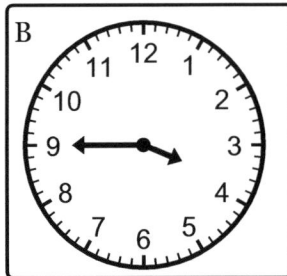

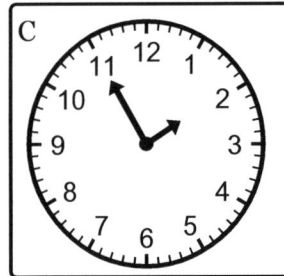

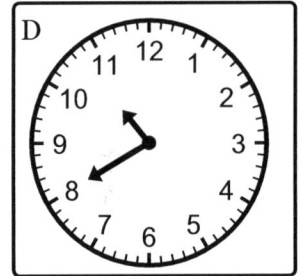

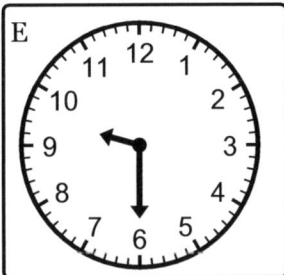

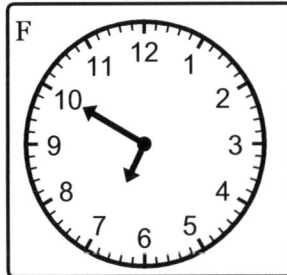

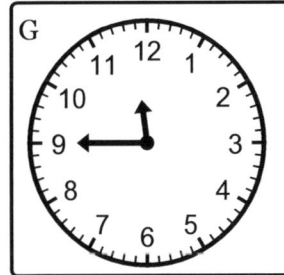

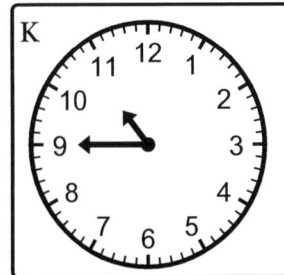

A	B	C	D

E	F	G	H

I	J	K	L

2. On each clock draw the hands in the correct place to show the time given

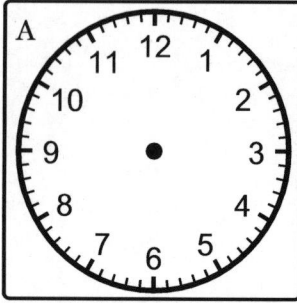

11.40

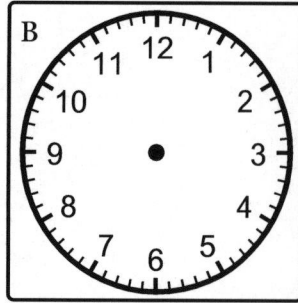

4.35

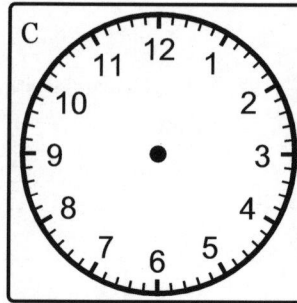

9.55

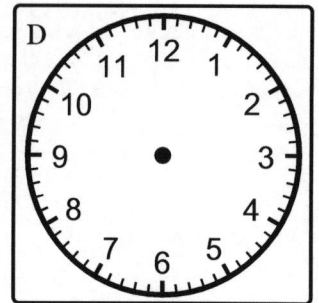

6.45

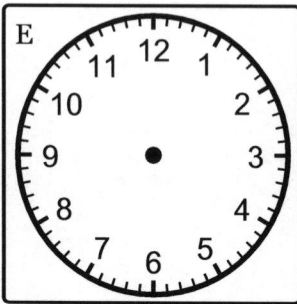

Quarter to four

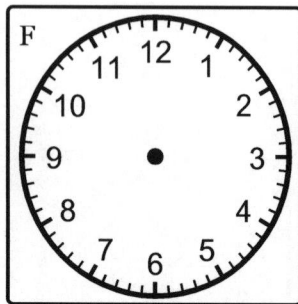

Five to two

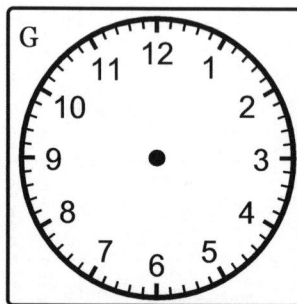

Ten to four

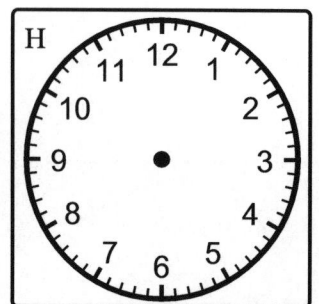

Twenty to one

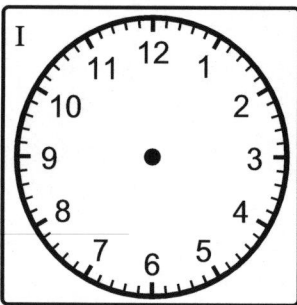

Twenty five to three

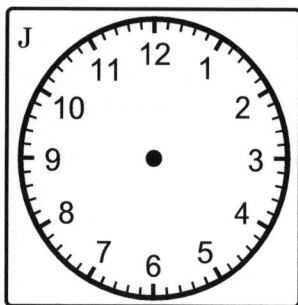

Quarter to six

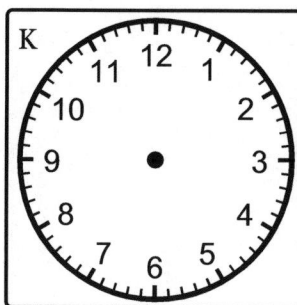

Five to twelve

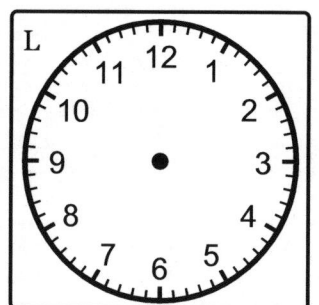

Ten to eight

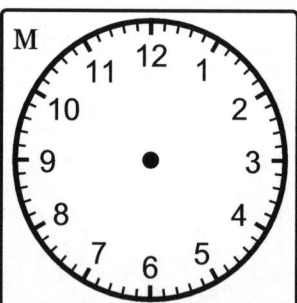

Twenty five to nine

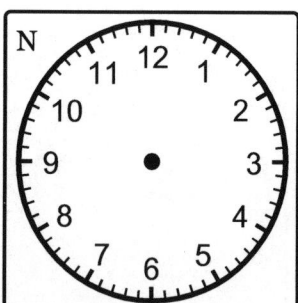

Quarter to nine

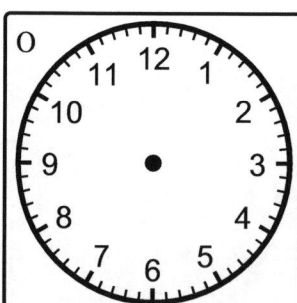

Ten to eleven

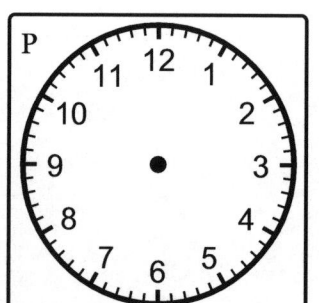

Five to four

fractions of an hour

learn by heart

1 hour = 60 minutes	$\frac{1}{2}$ hour = 30 minutes	$\frac{1}{4}$ hour = 15 minutes	$\frac{1}{3}$ hour = 20 minutes
$\frac{2}{3}$ hour = 40 minutes	$\frac{3}{4}$ hour = 45 minutes	$\frac{1}{10}$ hour = 6 minutes	2 hours = 120 minutes

examples

The time is 3.05pm.
What time will it be in 60 minutes?

*60 minutes = 1 hour,
so add 1 to the hours = 4.05pm*

The time is 10:15am.
What time will it be in $\frac{1}{4}$ of an hour?

*$\frac{1}{4}$ of an hour = 15 minutes,
so add 15 to the minutes = 10.30am*

exercise 70

1. True or false?

    a) $\frac{1}{2}$ of an hour is 50 minutes

    b) 65 minutes is more than 1 hour

    c) 10 hours is 600 minutes

    d) $\frac{1}{4}$ of an hour is 15 minutes

    e) $\frac{1}{10}$ of an hour is 10 minutes

    f) $\frac{1}{2}$ an hour is more than 20 minutes

2. How many minutes is:

    a) 2 hours

    b) 1 hour & 5 minutes

    c) $\frac{3}{4}$ of an hour

    d) $\frac{1}{3}$ of an hour

    e) 3 hours

    f) 1 hour & 10 minutes

3. In each pair, circle the longer time:

    a) $\frac{1}{4}$ of an hour   or   20 minutes

    b) 1 hour   or   55minutes

    c) 25 minutes   or $\frac{1}{3}$ of an hour

    d) 1 hour   or   100 minutes

    e) $\frac{1}{2}$ an hour   or   45 minutes

    f) 2 hours   or   100 minutes

    g) $\frac{3}{4}$ of an hour   or   60 minutes

    h) $\frac{1}{10}$ of an hour   or   10 minutes

4. The time is 9:15 am. What time will it be in $\frac{1}{4}$ of an hour?

5. The time is 7.15 am. What time will it be in $\frac{1}{2}$ an hour?

6. Work out the missing times in these flow diagrams:

7:20 pm	→ 1 hour →	A
4:05 pm	→ 10 minutes →	B
10:00 am	→ $\frac{3}{4}$ of an hour →	C
3.20pm	→ $\frac{1}{2}$ of an hour →	D

2:20pm	→ $\frac{1}{4}$ of an hour →	E
3:00am	→ $\frac{1}{3}$ of an hour →	F
2.15pm	→ G →	2.45pm
H	→ $\frac{1}{2}$ an hour →	5pm
I	→ 7 minutes →	11:06pm

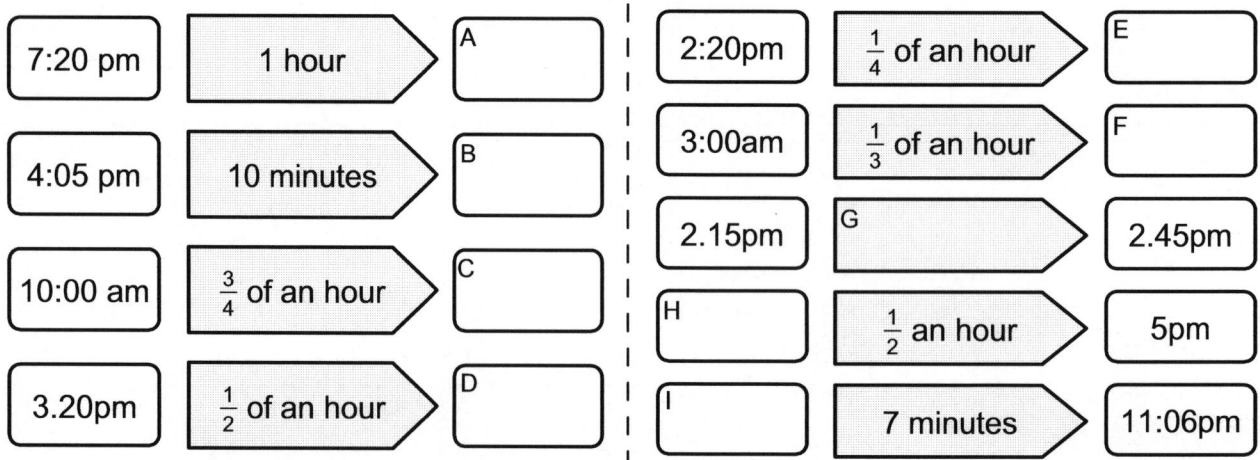

7. Which of these times is longer than $\frac{3}{4}$ of an hour?

a) 40 mins   b) 45 mins   c) 50 mins   d) 5.0 mins

8. Match each time in hours below with a time in minutes from the boxes on the right.

A 2 hours	B 1 hour 5 mins	C $\frac{3}{4}$ of an hour
D $\frac{1}{3}$ of an hour	E 3 hours	F $\frac{1}{2}$ an hour
G $\frac{1}{10}$ of an hour	H $1\frac{1}{4}$ hours	I 1 hour 10 mins
J $1\frac{1}{2}$ hours	K $\frac{2}{3}$ of an hour	L 2 hours 5 mins

180 mins	6 mins
40 mins	65 mins
75 mins	125 mins
45 mins	30 mins
90 mins	120 mins
20 mins	70 mins

A	B	C	D	E	F	G	H	I	J	K	L

9. Put these times in order, starting with the shortest:

a) $1\frac{1}{2}$ hours   b) 65 minutes   c) 70 minutes   d) $1\frac{1}{4}$ hours

24 hour clocks

learn by heart

examples

When we use a 12 hour clock we use 'am' and 'pm' to show whether it is morning or afternoon.

With a 24 hour clock the times after midday continue 13, 14, 15 etc, so 1pm is 13.00

Midday is 12:00 and Midnight is 00:00

Write 5:15pm using a 24 hour clock time.

5pm is 17:00, so this is 17:15

The time is 2:15pm. How many minutes is it until 15:00?

15:00 is 3pm, so it is 45 minutes

exercise 7p

1. Write these times using a 12 hour clock. The first one is done for you:

   a) 14 28   *2:28 pm*   b) 13 15   c) 07 45

   d) 18 30   e) 11 28   f) 21 40

   g) 04 10   h) 00 50   i) 12 33

2. Write these times using a 24 hour clock. The first one is done for you:

   a) 3:27 pm   *15 27*   b) 8:23 am   c) 8:56 pm

   d) 10:20 pm   e) 3:00 am   f) 6:30 pm

   g) 12:08 am   h) 12:38 pm   i) 11:17 pm

3. Which of these times are in the afternoon? Circle all that apply.

   a) 9:04 am   b) 15.01   c) 13.30   d) 4pm

4. The time is 4pm. In one hour it will be:

   a) 14:00   b) 15.00   c) 05:00   d) 17:00

5. The time is 13:00. In one hour it will be:

   a) 2pm   b) 1pm   c) 3pm   d) 4pm

6. Which of these times are before 3pm? Circle all that apply.

   a) 14:00   b) 15.01   c) 1pm   d) 19:00

5. The time is 13.15. What time will it be in $\frac{1}{4}$ of an hour?

6. The time is 14.30. How many minutes is it until 3pm?

7. The time is 7pm. How many hours is it until 21:00?

8. Work out the missing times in these flow diagrams:

15:00	1 hour >	A
21:00	60 minutes >	B
13:10	$\frac{1}{4}$ of an hour >	C
23:00	$\frac{1}{2}$ of an hour >	D

12:00	E >	13:00
14:00	F >	5pm
3.30pm	G >	18:00
21:00	H >	Midnight
12:00	I >	00:00

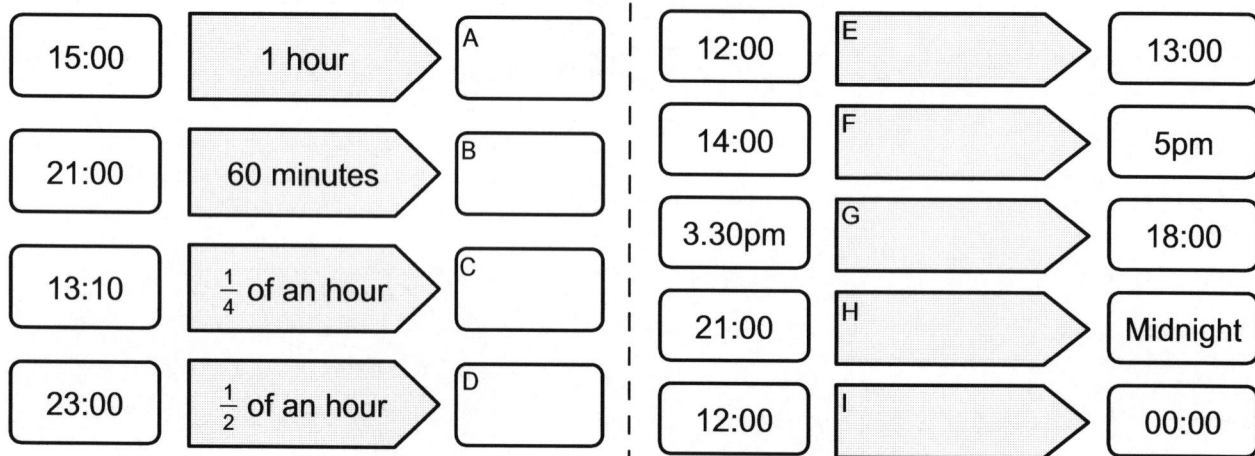

9. The time is 00:30. Which of these are you most likely to be doing?

   a) Eating lunch   b) Sleeping   c) Eating breakfast   d) Coming home from school

10. On the 24 hour clock, midnight is written _____ and midday is written _____ .

matching activity

Match each time on the left with an equivalent time from the right.

A 9pm	B 2am	C 3.15pm
D 5:15pm	E 10am	F 12:15pm
G 1am	H 12:15am	I 1.15pm
J 11.15am	K 11.15pm	L 1:15am

M 11:15	N 17:15	O 02:00
P 15:15	Q 21:00	R 01:00
S 12:15	T 13:15	U 23:15
V 01:15	W 00:15	X 10:00

A	B	C	D	E	F	G	H	I	J	K	L

chapter review

exercise 7g

1. A car could be 4.95_____ long (choose mm / cm / m / km)

2. A kilometre is _____ m.

3. Complete these conversions:

   a) 45cm = _____mm

   b) 2km = _____km

   c) 2.5m = _____cm

   d) 350mm = _____cm

   e) 400cm = _____m

   f) 3000m = _____km

4. Measure the length of this line.
   Give your answer in cm.

5. Work out the perimeter of each of these shapes. All lengths are in cm.
   Give your answer as a decimal.

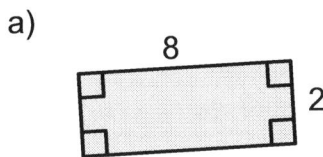

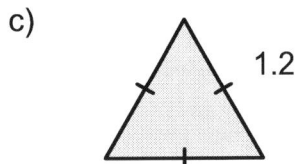

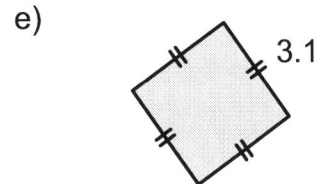

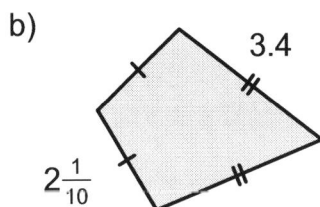

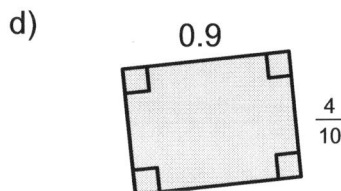

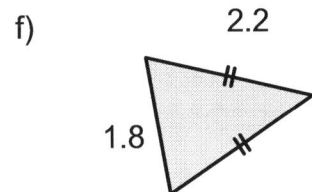

   a)

   8

   2

   c)

   1.2

   e)

   3.1

   b)

   3.4

   $2\frac{1}{10}$

   d)

   0.9

   $\frac{4}{10}$

   f)

   2.2

   1.8

6. Write down the time shown on each of these clocks:

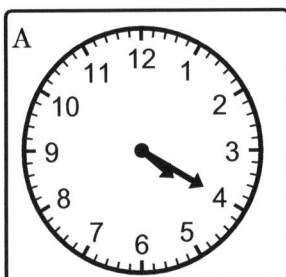

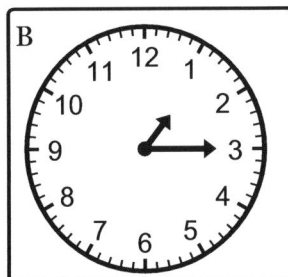

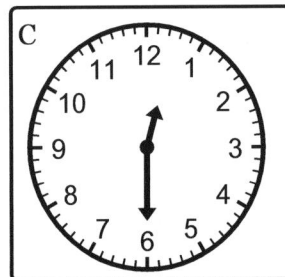

   A

   B

   C

   D

7. Round each number to 1 significant figure:

   a) 274

   c) 4,600

   e) 1.9

   b) 3.8

   d) 250

   f) 3,150

8. The time is 14.25. Which of these are you most likely to be doing?

   a) Eating breakfast   b) Working at school   c) Going to bed   d) Waking up

9. Estimate the height of a lampost.

10. Measure the perimeter of this shape:
    Give your answer in centimetres.

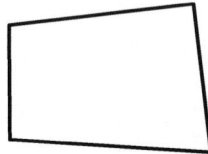

11. Work out the perimeter of each
    of these shapes. Watch out for the units!

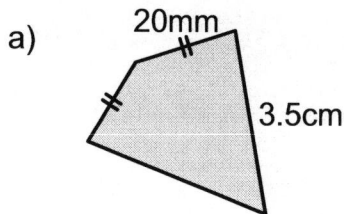

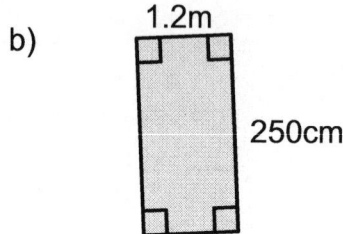

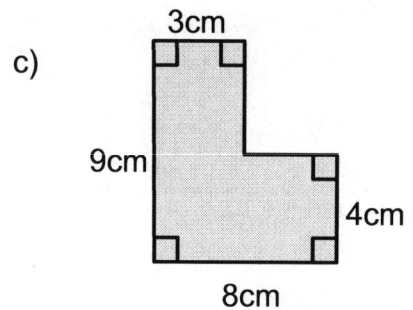

    a) 20mm 3.5cm

    b) 1.2m 250cm

    c) 3cm 9cm 8cm 4cm

12. Estimate the answer to 19.7 × 3.01

13. How many minutes is:

    a) $\frac{1}{2}$ an hour

    c) $\frac{1}{3}$ of an hour

    e) $\frac{1}{10}$ of an hour

    b) 2 hours

    d) $\frac{3}{4}$ of an hour

    f) 1 hour & 10 minutes

14. If it is 4.25pm, a 24 hour clock would show:

    a) 04:25   b) 14:25   c) 16:25   d) 19:25

15. Complete the conversions: *careful!*

    a) 0.7km = _____m   b) 2.8m = _____mm

exercise 7r

1. Write **three thousand and eighteen** in digits

2. Calculate:

   a) -3 + 1   d) -2 × -3   g) 16 ÷ -2

   b) -5 - 2   e) 45 ÷ 2   h) 4.5 × 100

   c) 6 + -4   f) 1.3 × 2   i) 208 ÷ 100

3. Simplify:

   a) $b + b + b + b$ c) $2b + 3b - b$ e) $4b × 2b$

   b) $b × b × b × b$ d) $2b × 6$ f) $b^3 × b^5$

4. Write down the first 12 square numbers

5. *True or false:* 9.3 × 100 = 9.300

6. Write $4\frac{1}{5}$ as an improper fraction

7. On the number line, which whole number is directly below -42?

8. Evaluate:

   a) $\sqrt{49}$ c) $\sqrt{100}$ e) 2^3 g) 0^2

   b) 3^2 d) $\sqrt[3]{27}$ f) 1^4 h) $(-4)^2$

9. If $x = 3$, work out the value of:

   a) $2x$ b) $x - 5$ c) x^2 d) x^3

10. If $a = -2$, work out the value of:

   a) $3a$ b) $a + 10$ c) a^2 d) $4a + 1$

11. Simplify $\frac{15}{30}$

12. Calculate:

   a) $\frac{2}{9} + \frac{1}{9}$

   b) $\frac{1}{4} + \frac{1}{3}$

   c) $\frac{3}{5} - \frac{1}{10}$

13. Write each of these as a decimal:

   a) $\frac{7}{100}$

   d) $\frac{24}{100}$

   g) $\frac{1}{5}$

   j) $\frac{1}{50}$

   b) $\frac{4}{10}$

   e) $\frac{3}{1000}$

   h) $\frac{2}{5}$

   k) $\frac{1}{25}$

   c) $3\frac{1}{10}$

   f) $2\frac{1}{100}$

   i) $\frac{3}{5}$

   l) $\frac{1}{9}$

14. Calculate $3 + 4 \times 2 - 1$

15. Evaluate:

   a) 3^0

   b) 3^1

   c) 3^2

   d) 3^3

16. Calculate:

   a) $\frac{1}{4}$ of 28

   e) $15 \div -5$

   i) $-2 + -5$

   b) 0.7×10

   f) $\frac{2}{3}$ of 21

   j) $300 \div 10$

   c) $473 \div 10$

   g) 0.4×2

   k) 1.5×100

   d) -7×-3

   h) $1.5 + 0.5$

   l) 0.9×3

17. Solve:

   a) $x + 2 = 10$

   c) $2x = 22$

   e) $\frac{x}{3} = 10$

   b) $x - 5 = 1$

   d) $5x = 25$

   f) $\frac{x}{2} = -5$

18. challenge! Calculate $\sqrt{49} + 3 \times 2^2$

chapter 8: shapes & area

[Recommended Time: 9-12 hours]

Contents

The diagrams in this chapter are not drawn to scale

P   For resources marked P, students will need a
photocopy or print out of this activity to work on

learn by heart

Parallel Lines: *straight lines that will never meet. Marked with arrows (one or two)*	Perpendicular: *lines that cross at right angles*	Equal Length Lines : *marked with a dash (or two)*

For lines to be parallel, they must have the same 'up' and 'across' patterns.
E.g. both of these lines go 3 across 1 up, the longer line does it twice

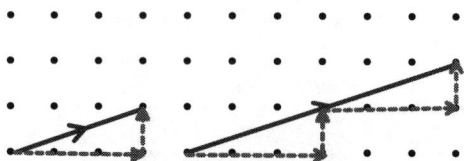

exercise 8a

1. Which of these lines are parallel? Circle all that apply:

a) 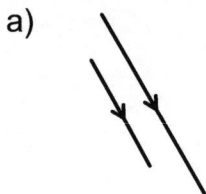   b) 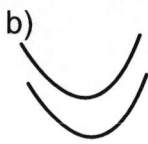   c) 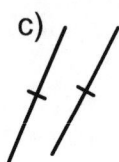   d)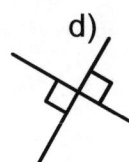

2. For each pair of lines, decide whether they are:

Parallel	Perpendicular	Equal Length	None

a) 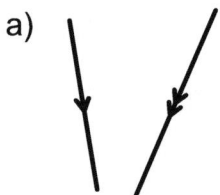   b) 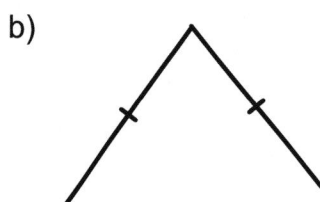   c)

_ _ _ _ _ _ _ _ _ _ _   _ _ _ _ _ _ _ _ _ _   _ _ _ _ _ _ _ _ _

d) 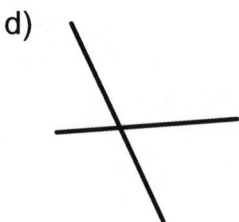   e) 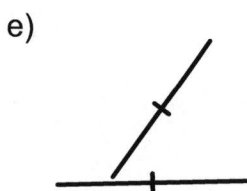   f)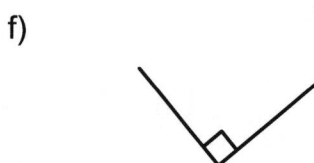

_ _ _ _ _ _ _ _ _ _   _ _ _ _ _ _ _ _ _ _   _ _ _ _ _ _ _ _ _

3. Copy each line and draw another line that is parallel to the one shown and **twice** as long:

a)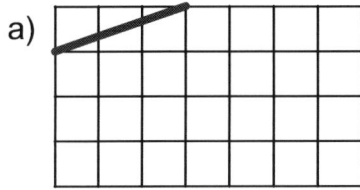

b)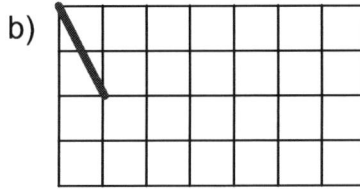

c)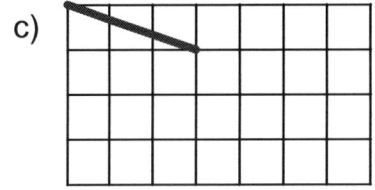

d)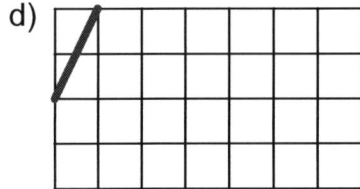

e)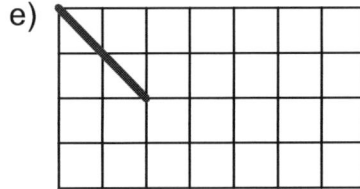

f)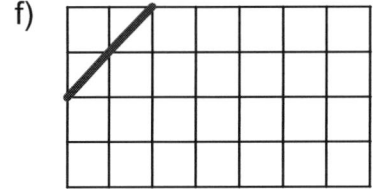

g)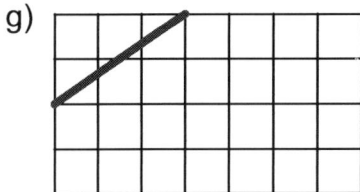

h)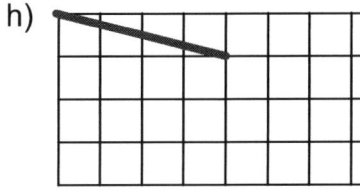

i)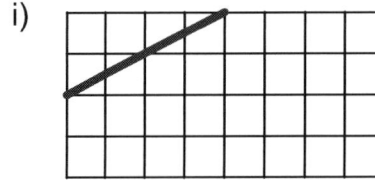

4. Copy each line and draw another one that is parallel and **three times** as long:

a)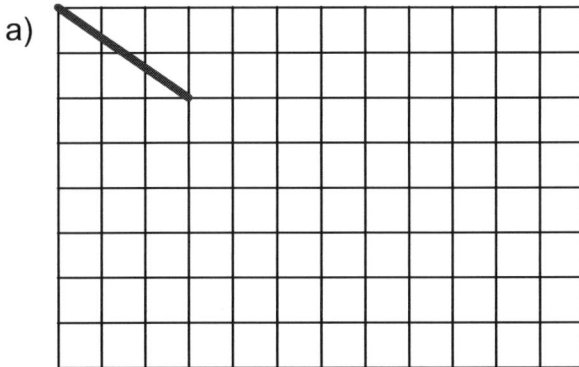

b)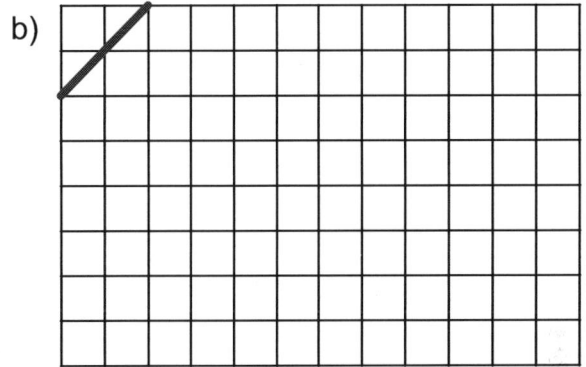

5. Fill in the blanks:

Parallel lines are marked with single or double _____.

Equal length lines are marked with single or double _____.

Perpendicular lines are marked with a _____.

6. a) In the diagram, lines _____

and _____ are equal length.

b) In the diagram, lines _____

and _____ are parallel.

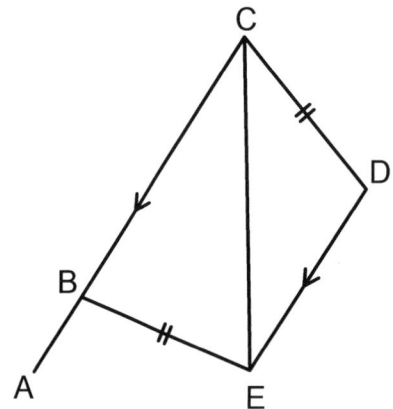

7. One of the boxes below contains perpendicular lines. Which one?

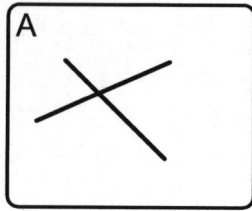 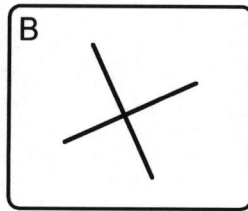 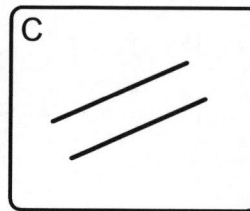 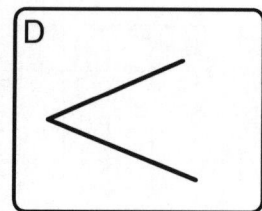

8. True or False?

a) Parallel lines will never cross.

b) Parallel lines can curve, so long as they never meet.

c) All straight lines are parallel.

d) If lines are the same length, they must be parallel.

e) Perpendicular lines meet or cross each other at right angles.

f) A triangle can never contain parallel lines.

9. Complete the statements about the lines in the diagram.

AI is perpendicular to _____

BH is perpendicular to _____

CG is perpendicular to _____

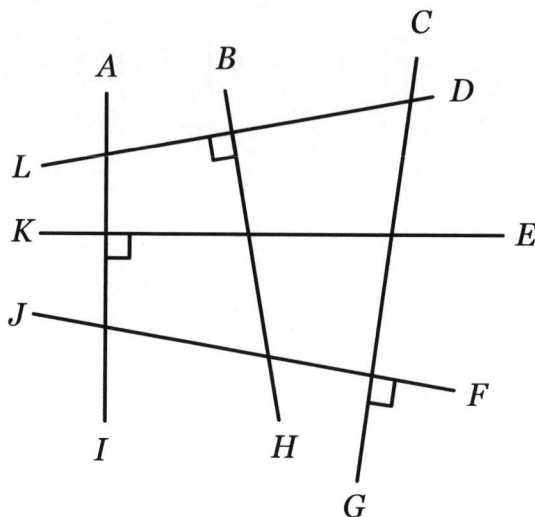

10. Add arrows, dashes and squares to the diagrams below to show that:

a) AB is equal in length to AD

b) EF is perpendicular to FG

c) EH is parallel to FG

d) BC is equal length to CD

e) EF is parallel to GH

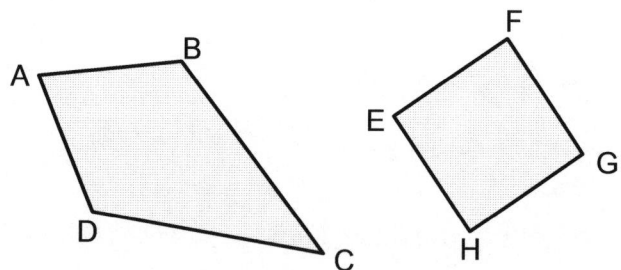

types of quadrilaterals: parallelograms

learn by heart

Quadrilateral: *4 sided shape*	Parallelogram : *Opposite sides are parallel*
Rectangle : *parallelogram with 4 right angles*	Square : *4 right angles & all sides equal*

Rectangles & Squares are special parallelograms

exercise 8b

1. Which of the shapes below are parallelograms? Circle 2 answers.

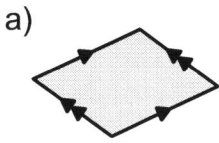

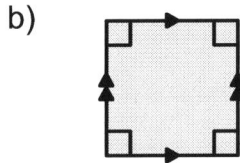

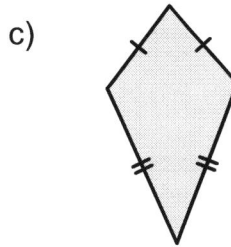

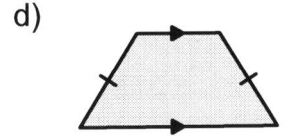

   a)   b)   c)   d)

2. Which of the shapes below are rectangles? Circle 2 answers.

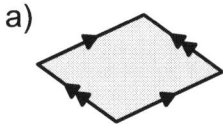

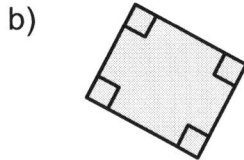

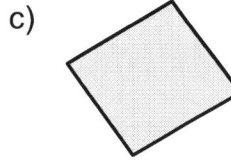

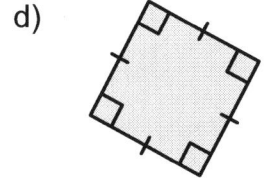

   a)   b)   c)   d)

3. Which of these shapes are squares?

   a)   b)   c)   d)

4. Draw arrows on the parallel sides of these parallelograms:

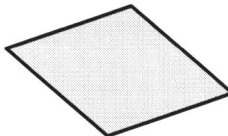

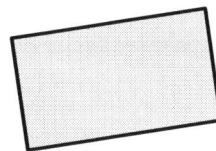

5. Which of these shapes are squares? Circle 2 answers.

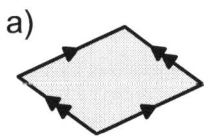

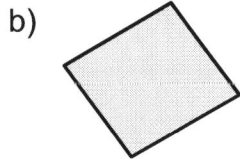

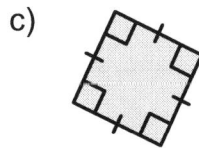

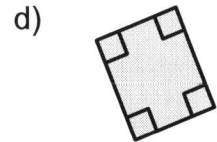

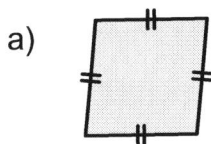

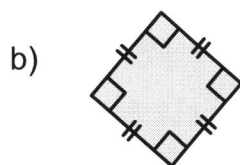

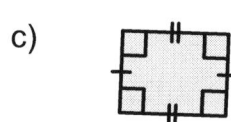

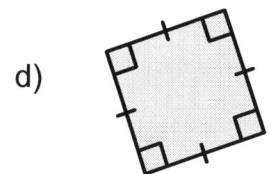

   a)   b)   c)   d)

6. Copy and draw in extra lines to make 3 parallelograms:

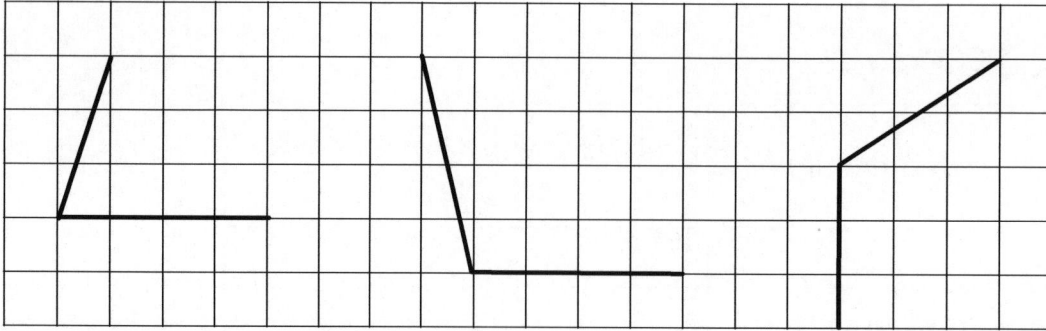

7. True or False?

a) A square has four equal sides.

b) The sides of a square are perpendicular to each other.

c) A square is a type of parallelogram.

d) A rectangle always has four equal sides.

e) The opposite sides of a rectangle are parallel.

f) A parallelogram can have four equal sides.

g) You can cut a parallelogram in half to make two triangles.

8. How many parallelograms are in the picture?

9. Copy and complete the lines drawn to make each shape:

a) Square   b) Rectangle   c) Parallelogram

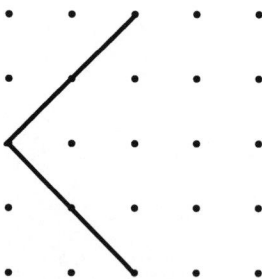   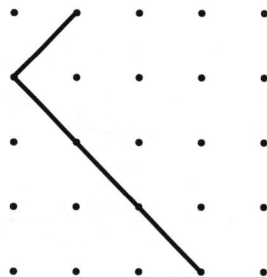   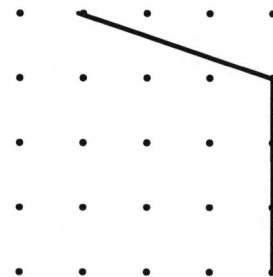

learn by heart

Rhombus	Trapezium	Kite
Four equal sides. Opposite sides parallel.	One pair of parallel sides.	Two pairs of adjacent sides equal.

Right-angled Trapezium	Isosceles Trapezium

exercise 8c

1. Match each shape to its name:

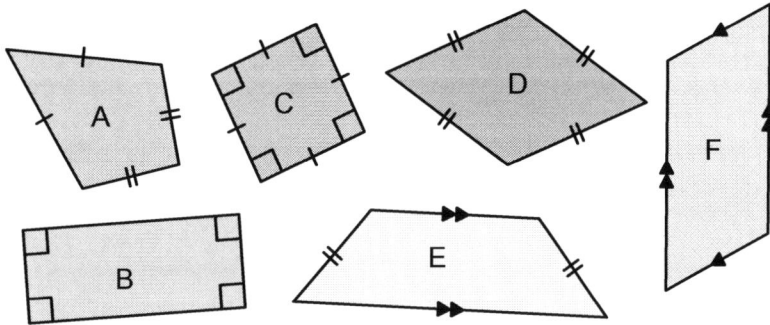

A   C   D   F

B   E

Rectangle	
Square	
Kite	
Parallelogram	
Isosceles Trapezium	
Rhombus	

2. Decide if each shape is a rhombus, kite or trapezium:

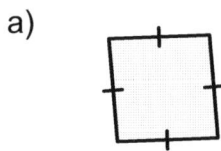

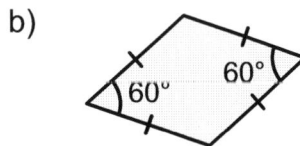

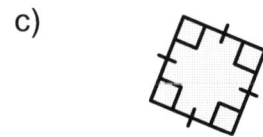

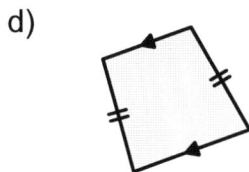

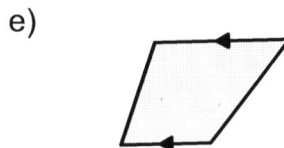

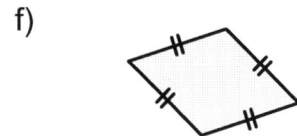

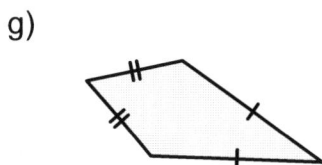

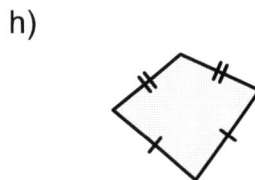

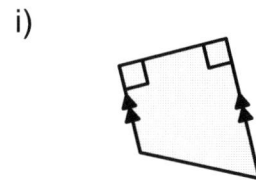

a)

b) 60° 60°

c)

d)

e)

f)

g)

h)

i)

3. Match each shape to its name:

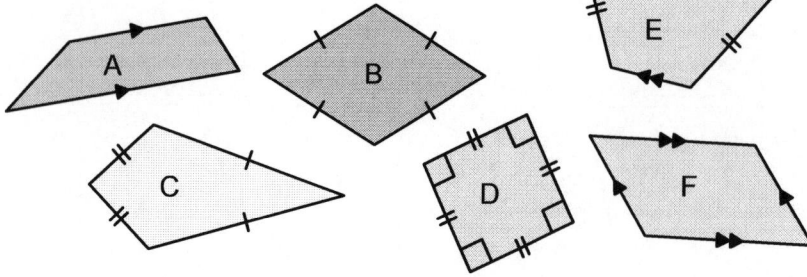

Rhombus	
Parallelogram	
Kite	
Square	
Trapezium	
Isosceles Trapezium	

4. Which shape below is a trapezium?

a)
b)
c)
d)

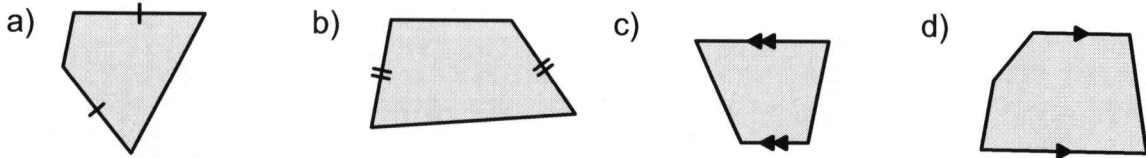

5. Sketch a parallelogram and a trapezium.
   Explain the difference between these two shapes.

6. From the shapes below, decide if these statements are true or false:

   a) Shape A is a square

   b) Shape D is a parallelogram

   c) Shape F is a rhombus

   d) Shapes B and E are trapeziums

   e) Shape A is a rhombus

   f) Shape E is a right angled trapezium

   g) Shape B is an isosceles trapezium

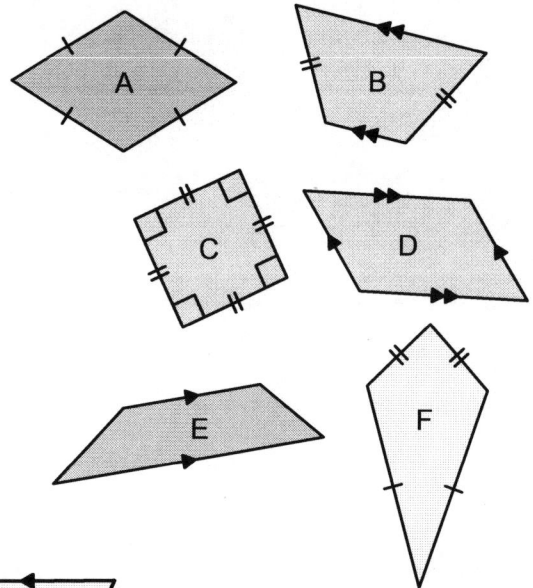

7. Explain why this shape is not a trapezium:

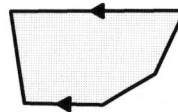

8. Decide if each shape is a trapezium or a parallelogram:

a)
b)
c)
d)

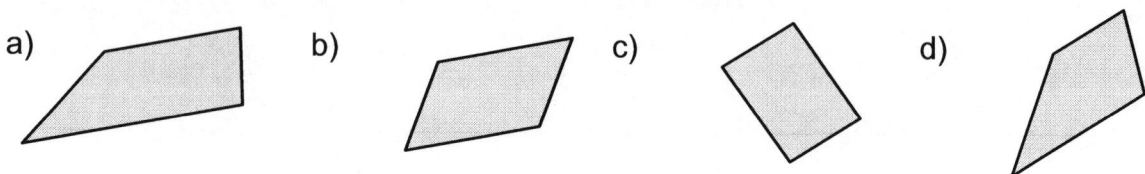

252

Connect the Dots P

In each box, connect four dots to make the required shape

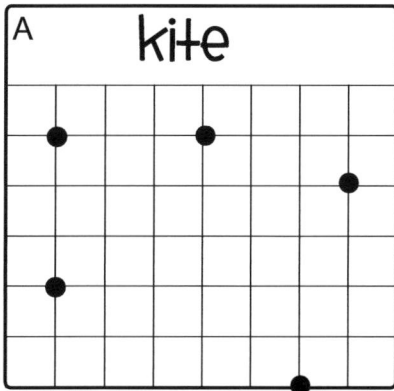

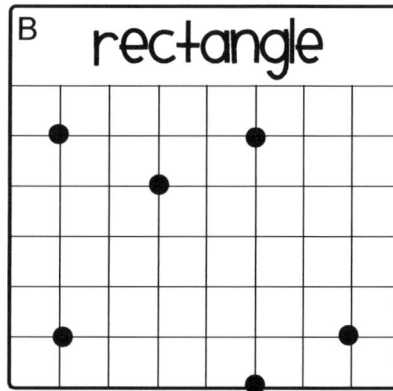

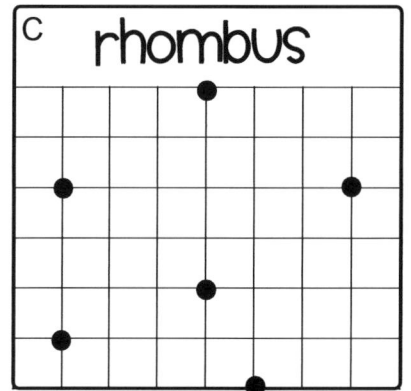

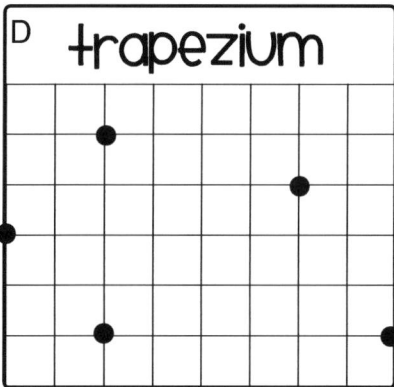

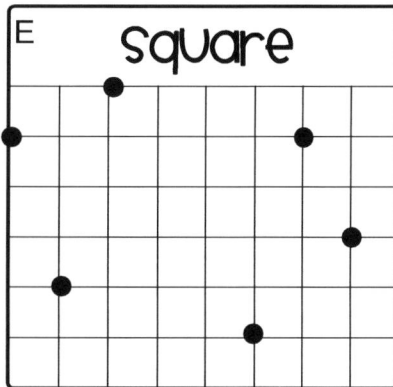

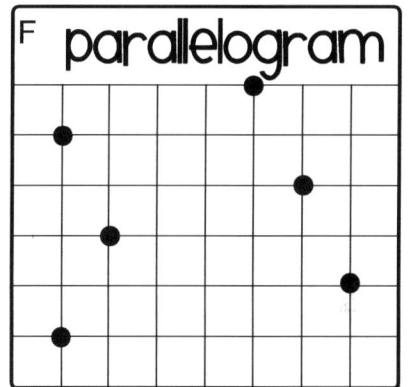

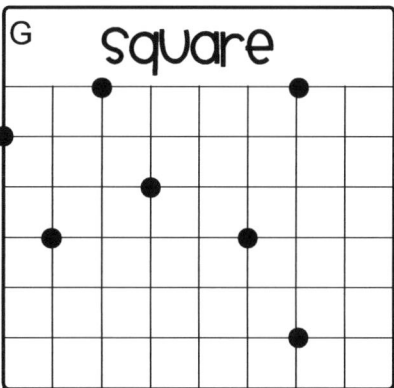

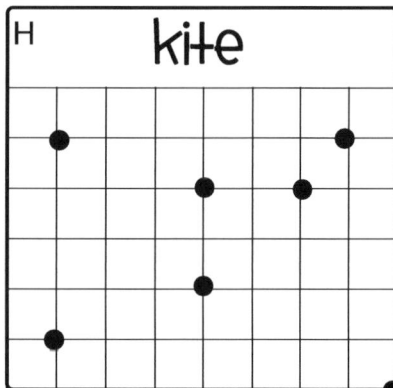

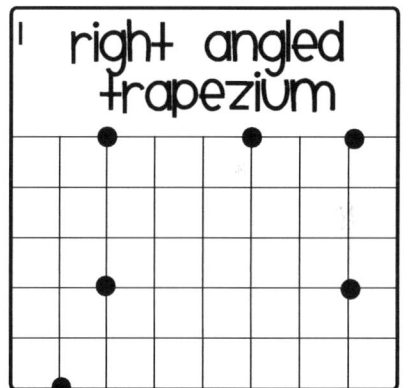

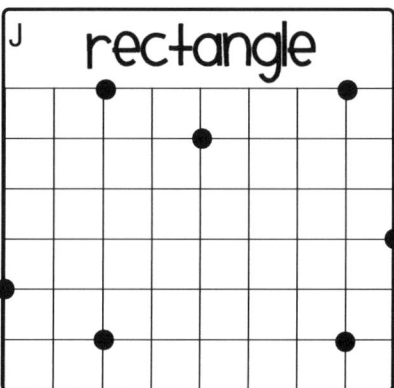

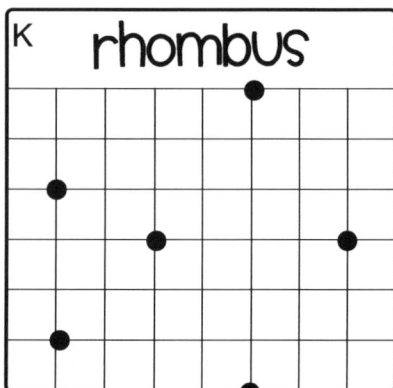

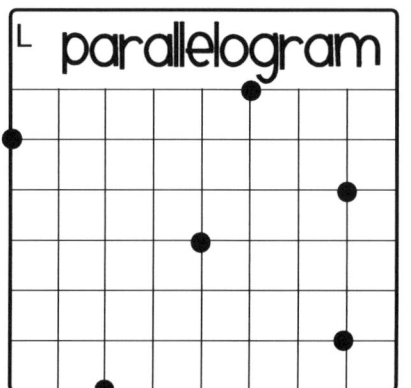

A kite	B rectangle	C rhombus

D trapezium	E square	F parallelogram

G square	H kite	I right angled trapezium

J rectangle	K rhombus	L parallelogram

253

Sort it Out!

Copy the table below and sort these shapes into the correct place:

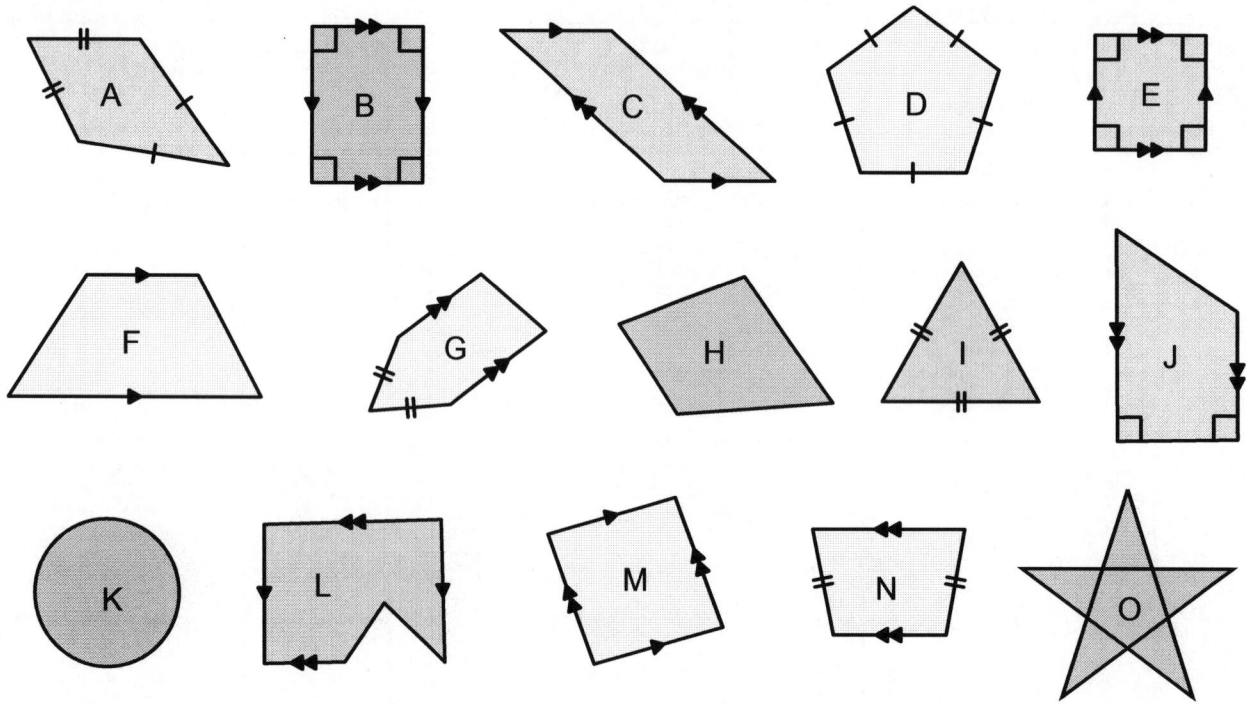

	Quadrilateral	Not a Quadrilateral
Has no parallel sides		
Has 1 pair of parallel sides		
Has 2 pairs of parallel sides		

learn by heart

Area *is the amount of 2d space a shape takes up. It is measured in square units.*

'1 square centimeter' is written $1cm^2$

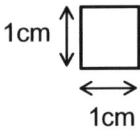

1cm $\updownarrow$ ☐
$\longleftrightarrow$
1cm

'1 square metre', is written $1m^2$

1m $\updownarrow$ ☐
$\longleftrightarrow$
1m

example

We can calculate the area of a shape by counting the number of whole squares inside it:

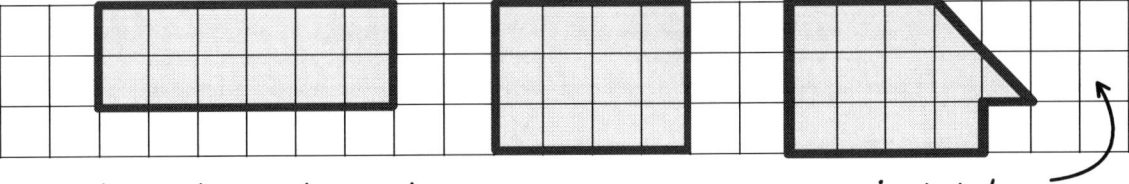

These shapes have the same area – 12 squares in total

exercise 8d

1. Write down the area of each shape:

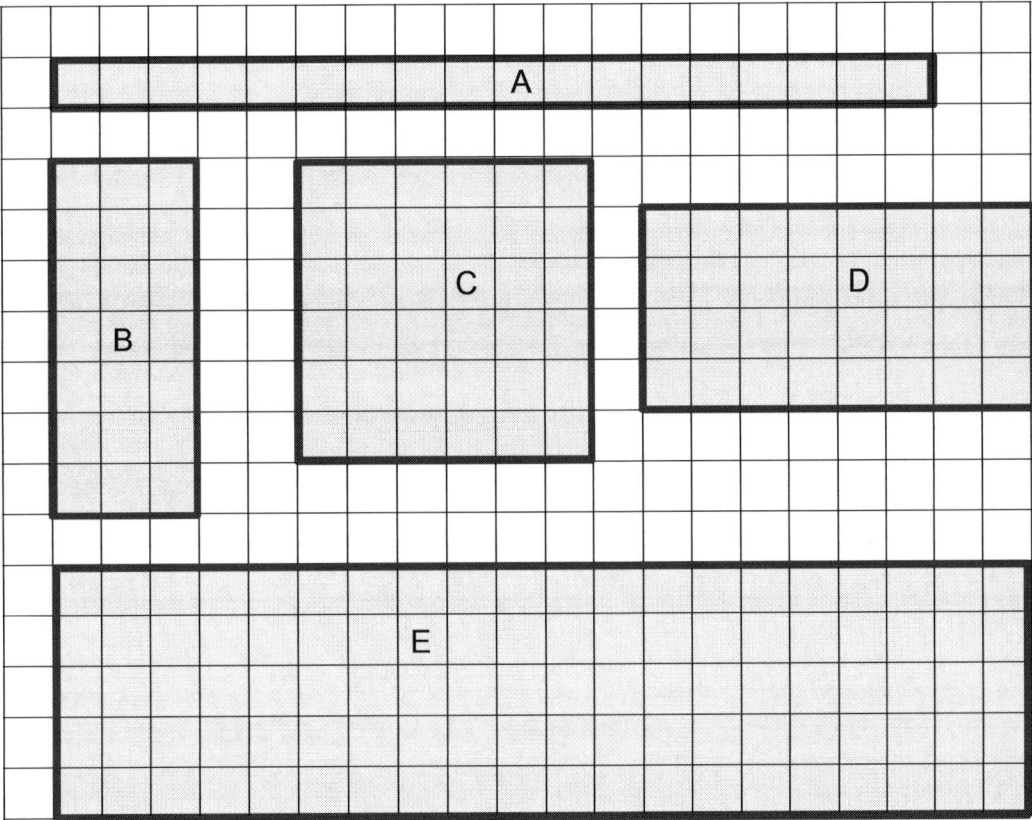

A

B

C

D

E

2. For shape E, is there a way to find the total number of squares without counting all of them?

3. In your book or on squared paper, draw a rectangle with an area of 12 squares. How many different rectangles can you find with an area of 12 squares?

4. Work out the area of these shapes:

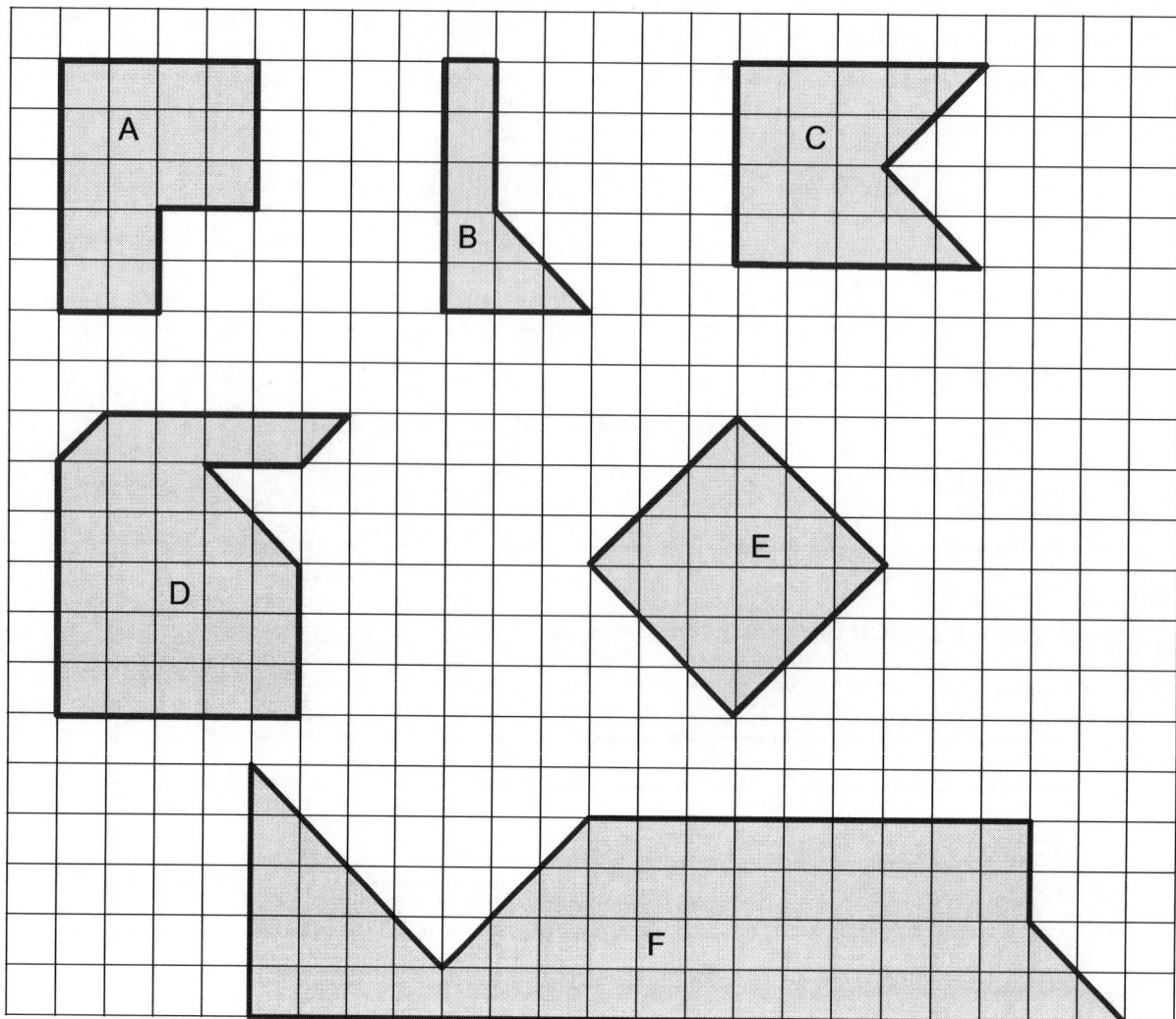

5. Sara says the area of this shape is 6 squares. Explain why she is wrong.

6. Ken says the area of this shape is 4 squares. Explain why he is wrong.

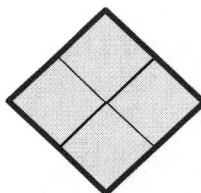

7. Aisha says these two shapes both have the same area. Explain why she is wrong.

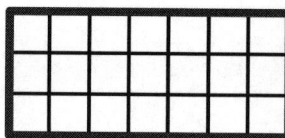

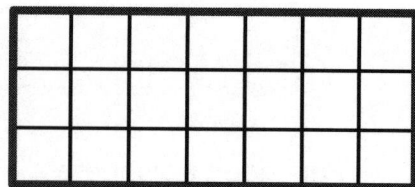

8. Choose the correct answer:

a) The area of a floor could be:

| 20m² | 20m | 20cm |

b) The area of a stamp could be:

| 6cm | 6km² | 6cm² |

c) The area of a hand could be:

| 100cm | 120cm² | 1m² |

d) The area of a door could be:

| 2m | 2m² | 2km² |

e) The area of a ruler could be:

| 60cm² | 60m² | 60km² |

f) The floor area of a house could be:

| 5cm² | 1km² | 100m² |

9. Match each object to its area:

| Area of the UK |
| Area of a piece of A4 paper |
| Area of a 10p coin |
| Area of the top of a table |

| 1.8m² |
| 240,000km² |
| 2km² |
| 600cm² |
| 5mm² |
| 5cm² |

investigate perfect squares

10. A perfect square is a square made of whole squares.

A perfect square can be made with 9 squares, like this:

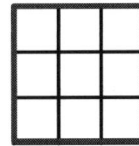

On squared paper, try to draw a perfect square with an area of:

a) 1   b) 3   c) 4   d) 5   e) 6   f) 8

g) 9   h) 12   i) 15   j) 16   k) 25   l) 36

11. Can you predict which numbers will make perfect squares?
Will 100 be a perfect square? How do you know?

area of parallelograms (including squares & rectangles)

learn by heart

Area of Squares, Rectangles & Parallelograms: *base × perpendicular height*

examples

Calculate the area

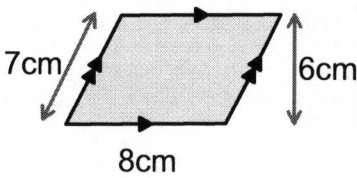

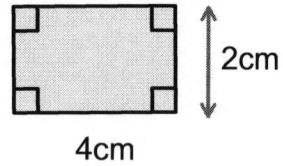

7cm, 8cm, 6cm

= 8 × 6
= 48cm²

Calculate the area

2cm, 4cm

= 2 × 4
= 8cm²

exercise 8e

1. Work out the area of each shape.

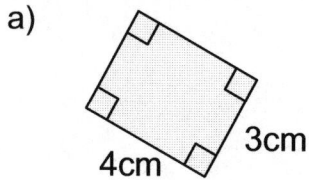

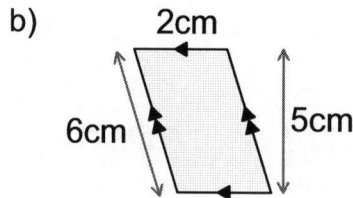

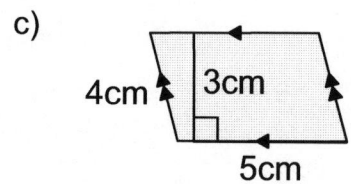

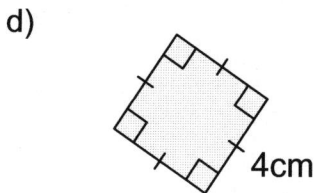

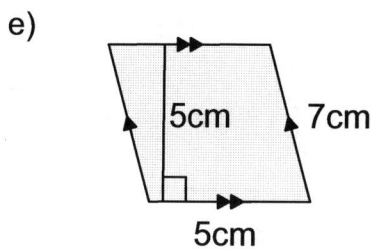

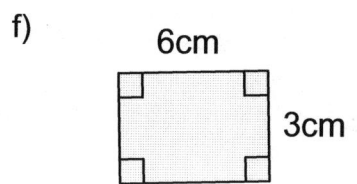

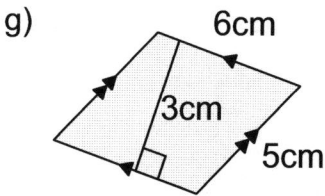

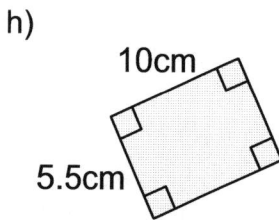

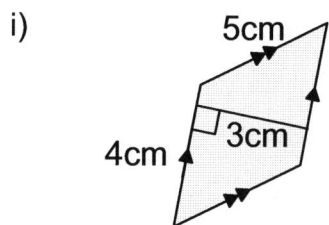

a)
4cm, 3cm

b)
2cm, 6cm, 5cm

c)
4cm, 3cm, 5cm

d)
4cm

e)
5cm, 7cm, 5cm

f)
6cm, 3cm

g)
6cm, 3cm, 5cm

h)
10cm, 5.5cm

i)
5cm, 4cm, 3cm

2. Given the area, work out the side length of each of these squares:

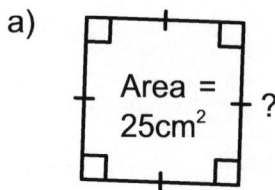

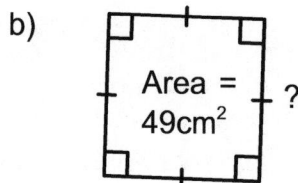

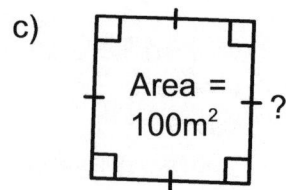

a)
Area = 25cm² ?

b)
Area = 49cm² ?

c)
Area = 100m² ?

3. Explain why we can't work out
    the area of this shape:

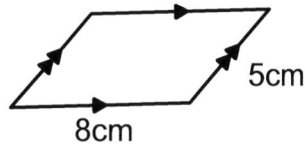

5cm

8cm

4. These shapes are made of rectangles and parallelograms.
    Work out the total area of each shape:

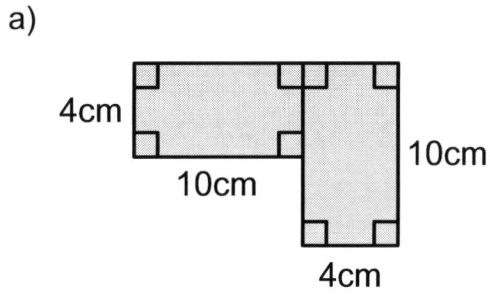

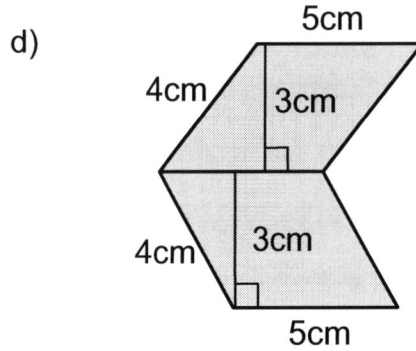

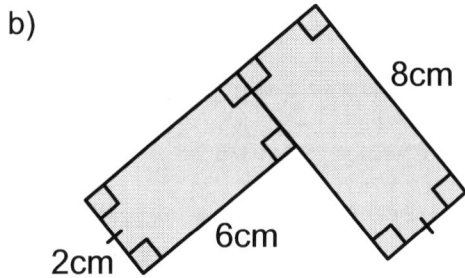

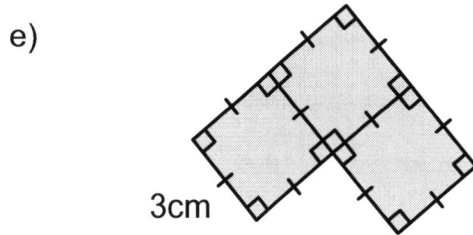

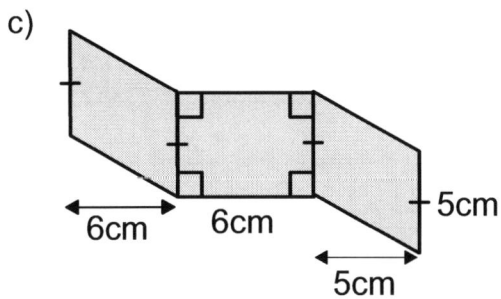

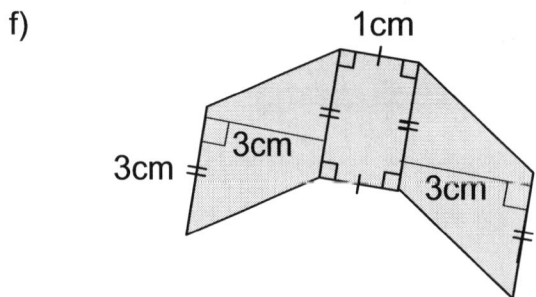

a)

4cm

10cm

10cm

4cm

d)

5cm

4cm   3cm

4cm   3cm

5cm

b)

8cm

6cm

2cm

e)

3cm

c)

6cm   6cm

5cm

5cm

f)

1cm

3cm   3cm

3cm

3cm

problem

This rectangle and parallelogram
have the same area.

Can you work out the missing
length of the rectangle?

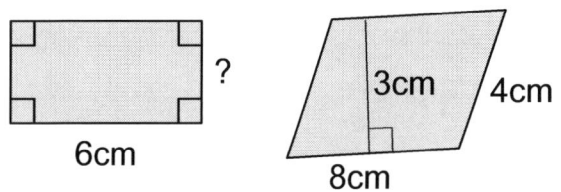

?

6cm

3cm   4cm

8cm

L shape areas

example

Calculate the area:

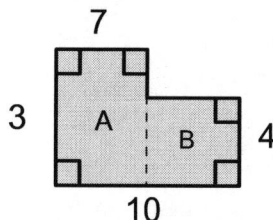

Rectangle A = 7 × 3 = 21cm²
Rectangle B = 3 × 4 = 12cm²
Total Area = 21 + 12 = 33cm²

exercise 8f

1. Work out the area of each shape:

a)

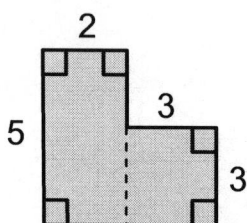

b)

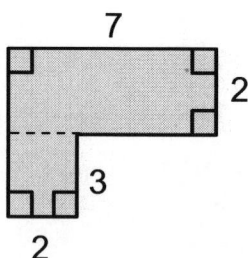

c)

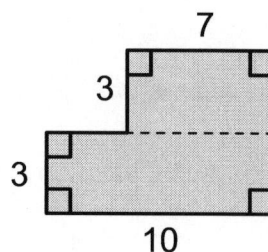

d)

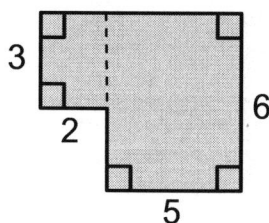

e)

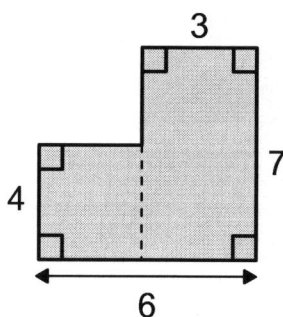

f)

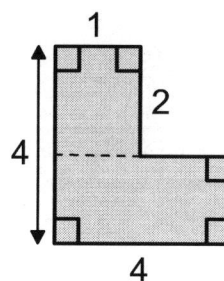

2. Work out the missing length in each shape:

a)

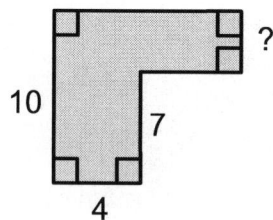

b)

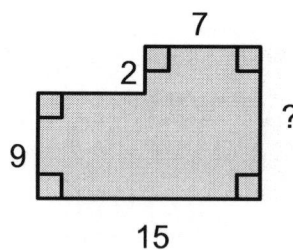

3. Work out the area of each shape.

a)

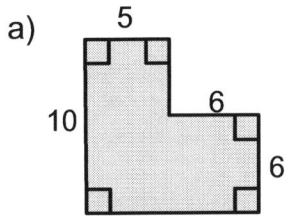

5
10
6
6

b)

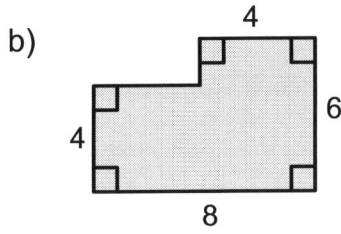

4
4
6
8

c)

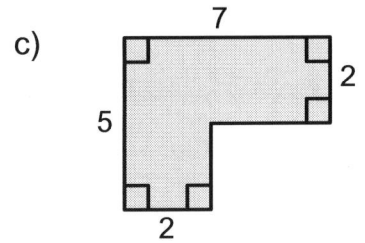

7
5
2
2

d)

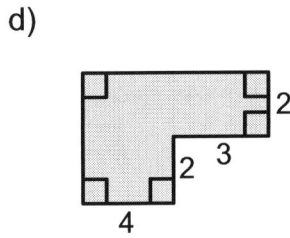

2
2   3
4

e)

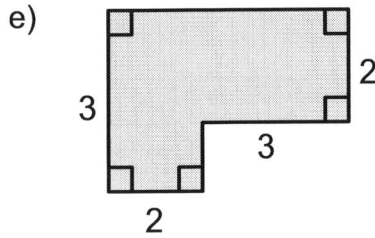

3
3
2
2

f)

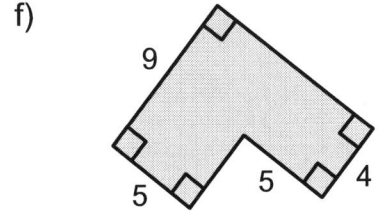

9
5   5   4

g)

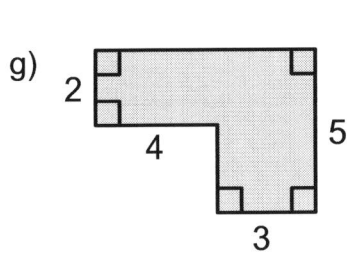

2
4
5
3

h)

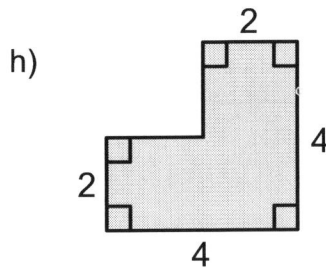

2
2
4
4

i)

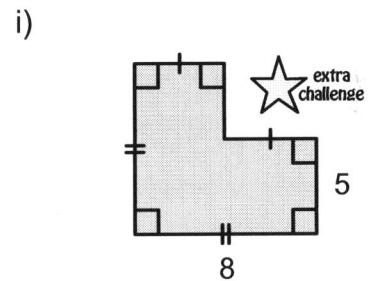

⭐ extra challenge

5
8

mixed practice

4. Work out the area of each shape:

a)

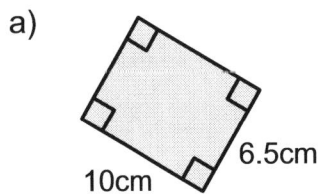

6.5cm
10cm

b)

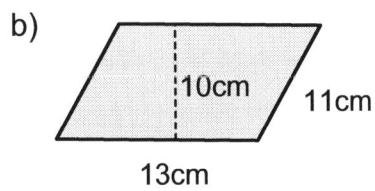

10cm   11cm
13cm

c)

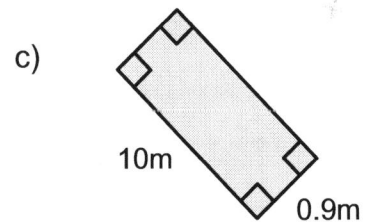

10m
0.9m

d)

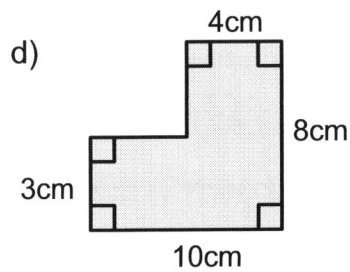

4cm
8cm
3cm
10cm

e)

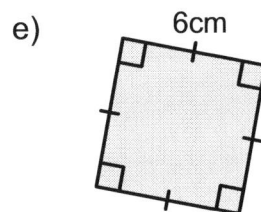

6cm

f)

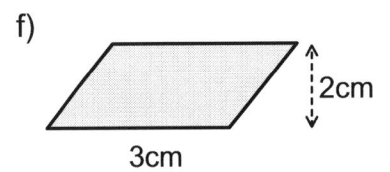

2cm
3cm

261

area of triangles

learn by heart

Area of a Triangle:
(base × perpendicular height) ÷ 2

example

Calculate the area:

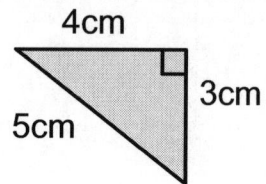

= (4 × 3) ÷ 2
= 6cm²

exercise 8g

1. In this triangle, the base is _____ long and
   the perpendicular height is _____ long.

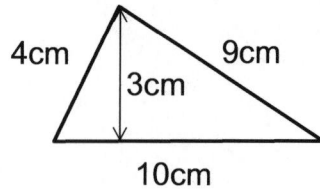

2. On each triangle the **base** is shown.
   Copy the triangle and draw on the perpendicular height.

a)

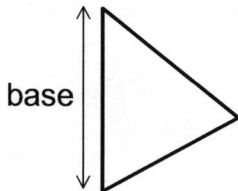

b)

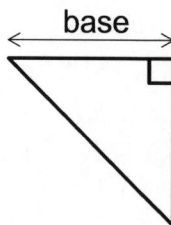

c)

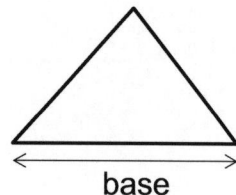

d)

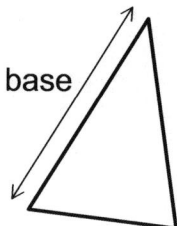

e)

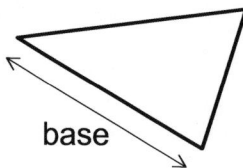

f)

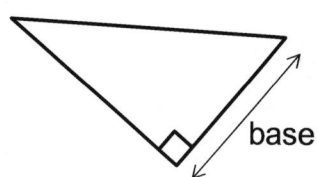

3. Which calculation works out the area of this triangle?

   a) $\frac{10 \times 6}{2}$

   b) $\frac{6 + 8}{2}$

   c) $\frac{6 \times 8}{2}$

   d) $\frac{10 \times 8}{2}$

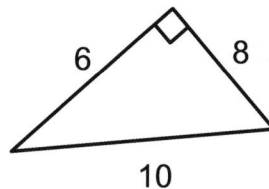

4. Which calculation can be used to work out the area of this triangle?

   a) $\frac{15 \times 9}{2}$

   b) $\frac{15 \times 12}{2}$

   c) $\frac{9 \times 12}{2}$

   d) $\frac{9 \times 12 \times 15}{2}$

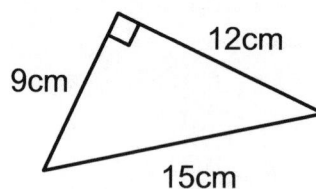

5. Calculate the area of each triangle. Lengths are all measured in cm.

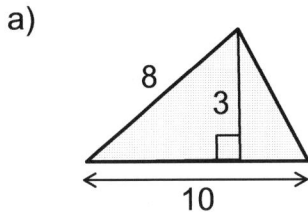

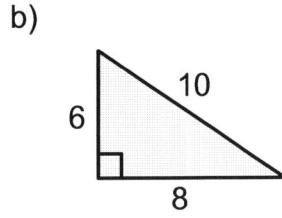

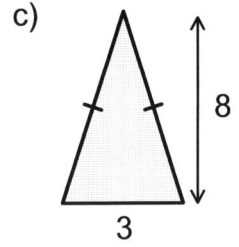

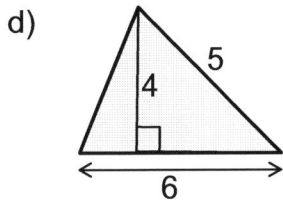

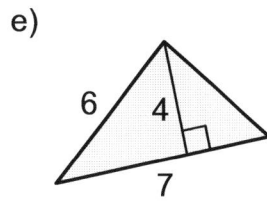

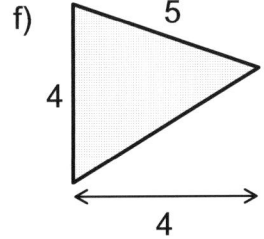

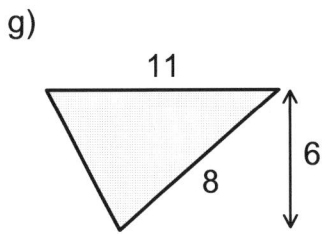

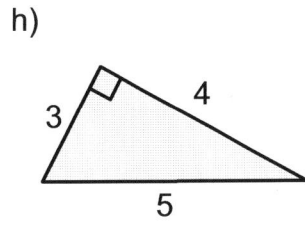

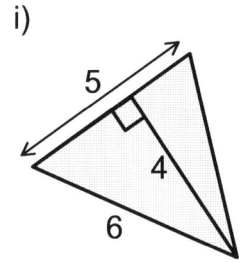

a)

8

3

10

b)

6

10

8

c)

8

3

d)

4

5

6

e)

6

4

7

f)

5

4

4

g)

11

6

8

h)

3

4

5

i)

5

4

6

6. Why can't we work out the area of this triangle?

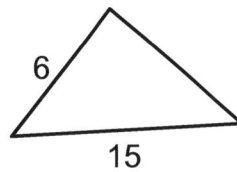

6

15

7. Draw two more triangles with the same area as the one given:

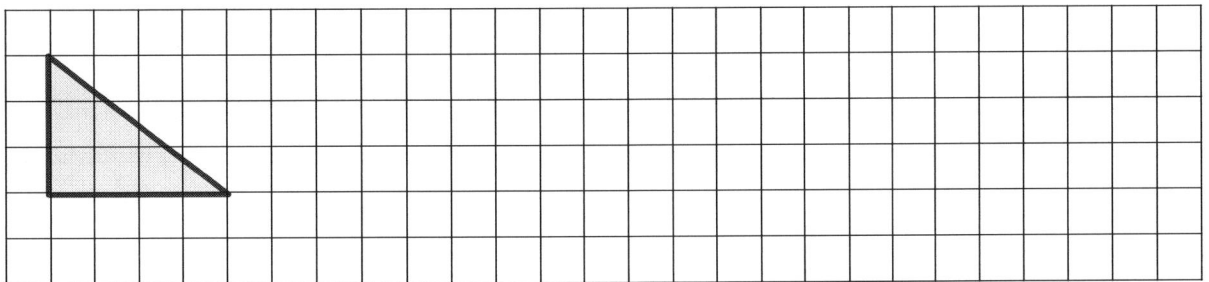

8. The triangle and the parallelogram have the same area. Work out x.

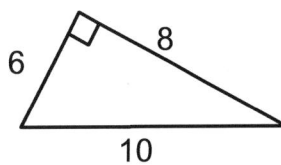

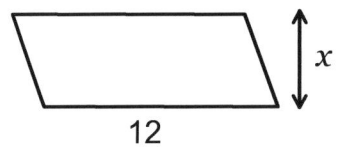

6

8

10

12

x

263

learn by heart

Area of a Trapezium: $\dfrac{a + b}{2} \times h$

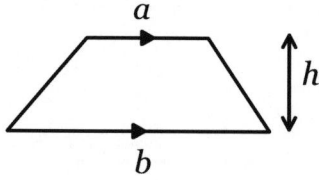

a and b are the parallel sides of a trapezium

example

Calculate the area:

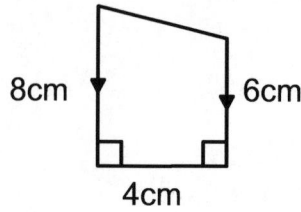

$$Area = \dfrac{8 + 6}{2} \times 4$$
$$= \dfrac{14}{2} \times 4$$
$$= 7 \times 4$$
$$= 28cm^2$$

exercise 8h

1. Calculate the area of each trapezium:

a)

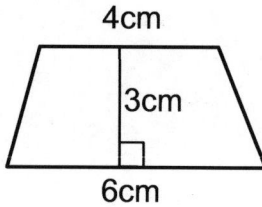

4cm
3cm
6cm

b)

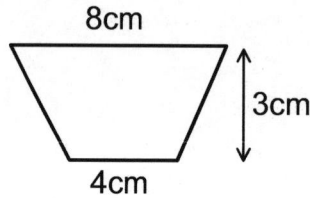

8cm
3cm
4cm

c)

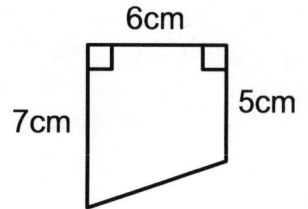

6cm
7cm
5cm

d)

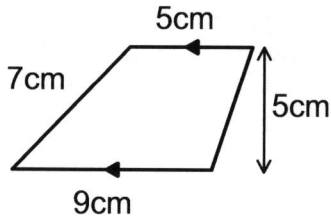

5cm
7cm
5cm
9cm

e)

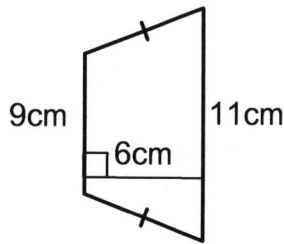

9cm
11cm
6cm

f)

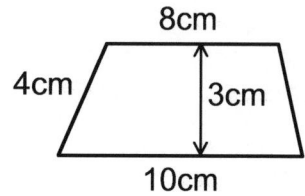

8cm
4cm
3cm
10cm

g)

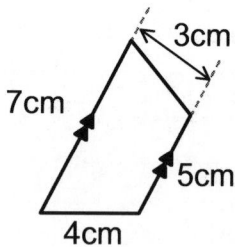

3cm
7cm
5cm
4cm

h)

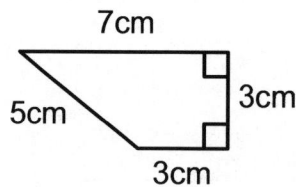

7cm
3cm
5cm
3cm

i)

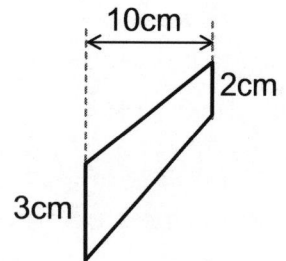

10cm
2cm
3cm

exercise 8i : mixed area practice

1.   Calculate the area of each shape.

a)

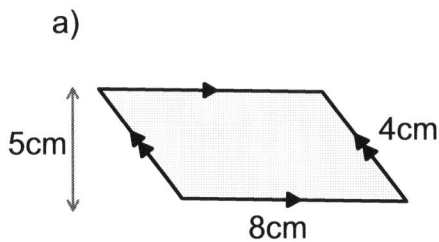
5cm
4cm
8cm

b)

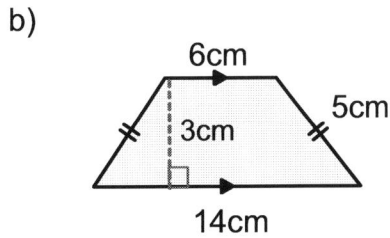
6cm
5cm
3cm
14cm

c)

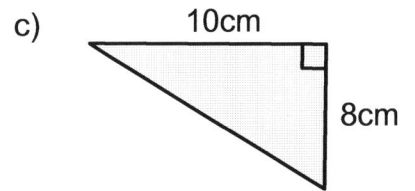
10cm
8cm

d)

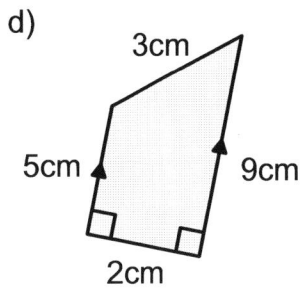
3cm
5cm
9cm
2cm

e)

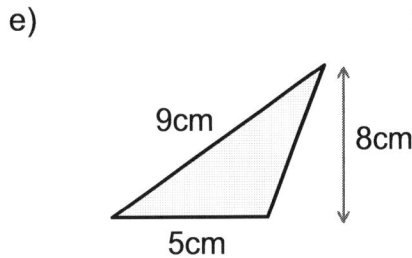
9cm
8cm
5cm

f)

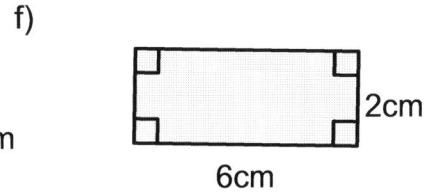
2cm
6cm

g)

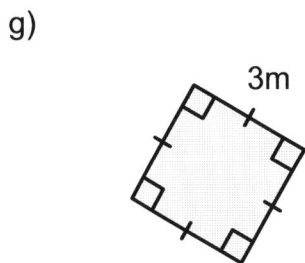
3m

h)

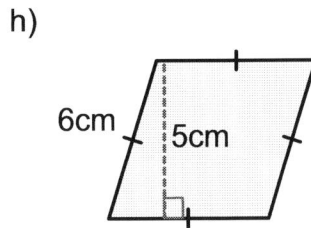
6cm
5cm

i)

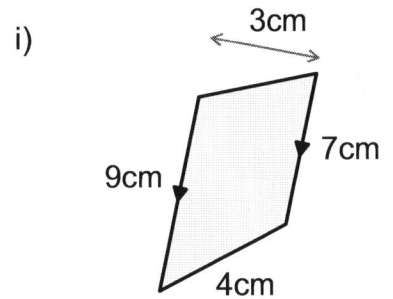
3cm
9cm
7cm
4cm

j)

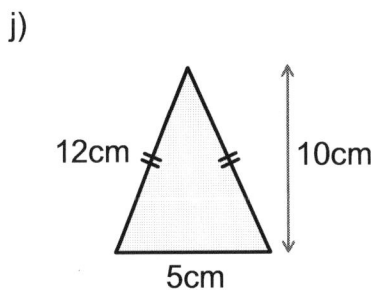
12cm
10cm
5cm

k)

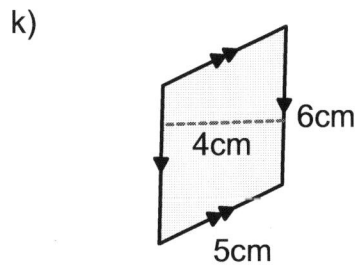
6cm
4cm
5cm

l)

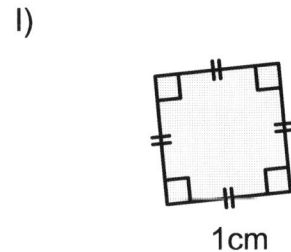
1cm

2.   Draw a rectangle, square and a parallelogram that all have the same area:

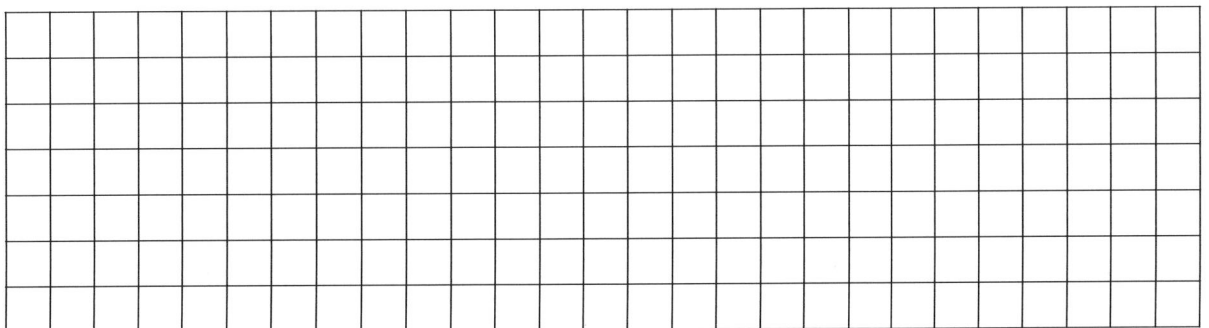

area and perimeter mixed problems

recall

Perimeter is the distance around the edge of a shape. It is measured in mm, cm, m or km.	Area is the space inside a 2D shape. It is measured in mm^2, cm^2, m^2 or km^2

exercise 8j

1. The grid is made of 1cm by 1cm squares.
   Work out the area and perimeter of each shape.
   Record your answers in the table:

Shape	Area	Perimeter
A		
B		
C		
D		
E		
F		
G		
H		
I		

2. Draw a shape that has an area of 20cm² and a perimeter of 18cm:

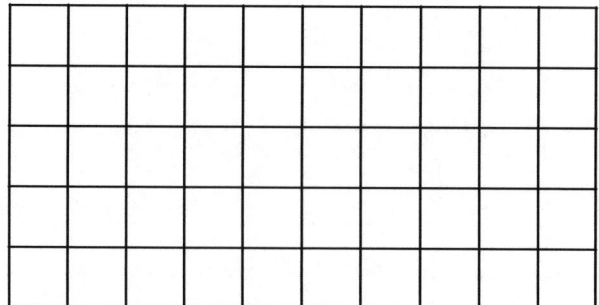

2. Work out the area and perimeter of each shape.

A

Area = ...

Perimeter = ...

B

Area = ...

Perimeter = ...

C

Area = ...

Perimeter = ...

D

Area = ...

Perimeter = ...

E

Area = ...

Perimeter = ...

F

Area = ...

Perimeter = ...

G

Area = ...

Perimeter = ...

H

Area = ...

Perimeter = ...

I

Area = ...

Perimeter = ...

J

Area = ...

Perimeter = ...

K

Area = ...

Perimeter = ...

L

Area = ...

Perimeter = ...

3. Copy and complete each drawing to make a parallelogram and then work out the area. The grids are 1cm by 1cm grids.

a)

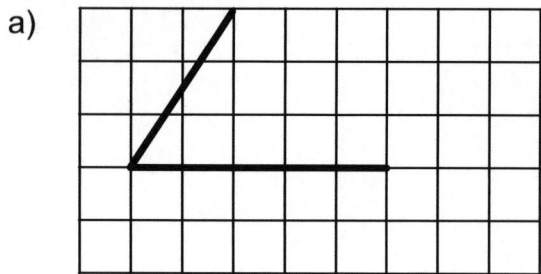

Area = ...

c)

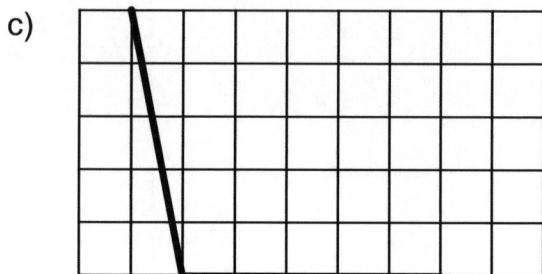

Area = ...

b)

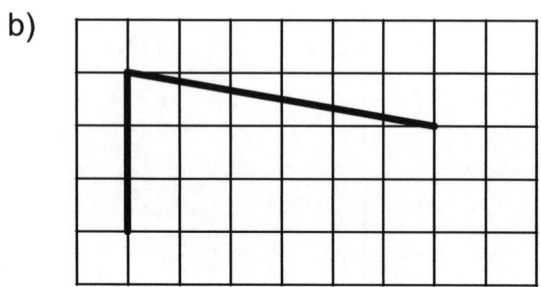

Area = ...

d)

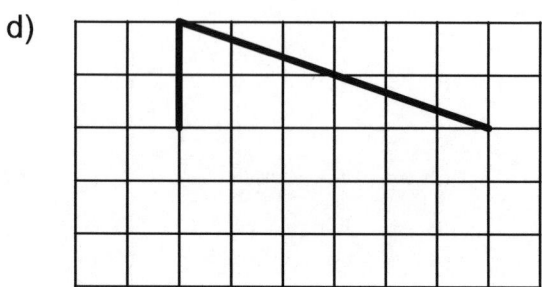

Area = ...

4. The area of this square is 49cm^2. What is its perimeter?

5. The area of this square is 100cm^2. What is its perimeter?

6. The perimeter of this square is 24cm. What is its area?

7. On square or dotty paper, draw three squares with areas of 4cm^2 , 9cm^2 and 16cm^2:

area and perimeter with mixed units

recall

| 1cm = 10mm | 1m = 100cm | 1km = 1000m |

example

Work out the area of this shape.
Give your answer in cm².

Area = base × height
70mm = 7cm
Area = 7cm × 5cm = 35cm²

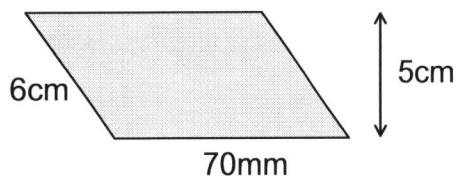

6cm

5cm

70mm

exercise 8k

1. Work out the **area** of each shape. Give your answer in cm²

a)

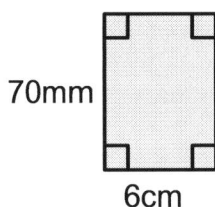

70mm

6cm

b)

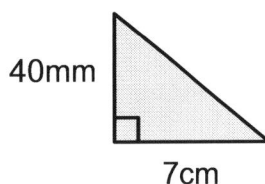

40mm

7cm

c)

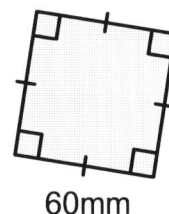

60mm

d)

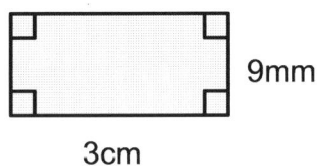

9mm

3cm

e)

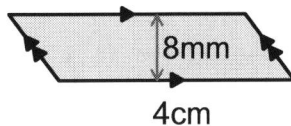

8mm

4cm

f)

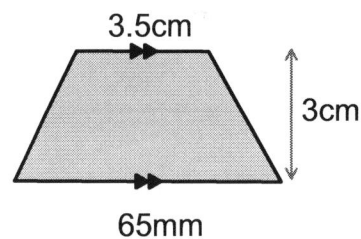

3.5cm

3cm

65mm

g)

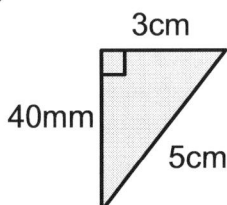

3cm

40mm

5cm

h)

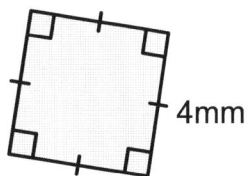

4mm

i)

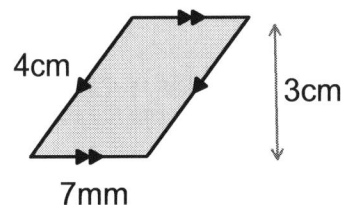

4cm

3cm

7mm

2. Work out the **perimeter** of each shape. Give your answer in metres.

a)
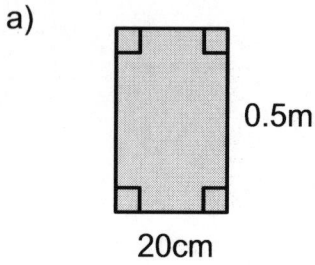
0.5m
20cm

b)
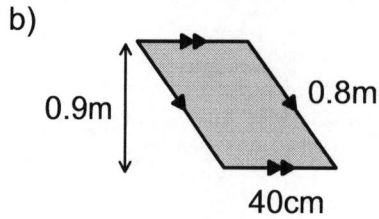
0.9m
0.8m
40cm

c)
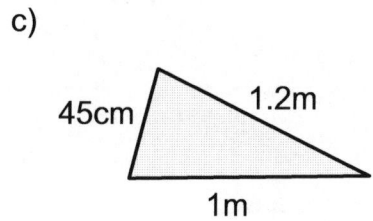
45cm
1.2m
1m

d)
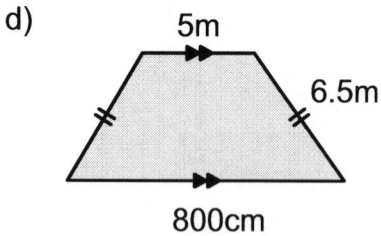
5m
6.5m
800cm

e)
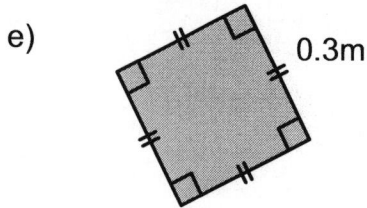
0.3m

f)
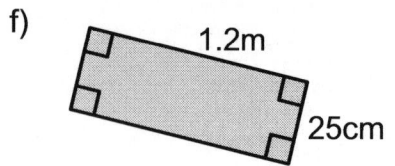
1.2m
25cm

3. Work out the **area** of each shape. Give your answer in cm²

a)
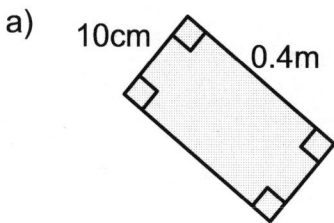
10cm
0.4m

b)
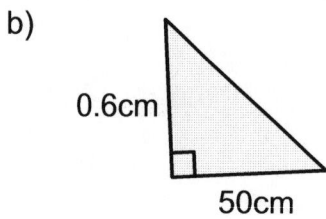
0.6cm
50cm

c)
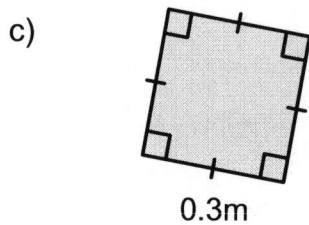
0.3m

d)
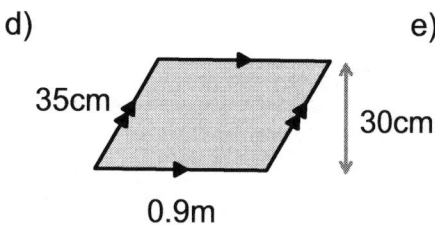
35cm
30cm
0.9m

e)
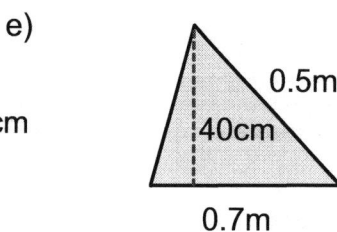
0.5m
40cm
0.7m

f)
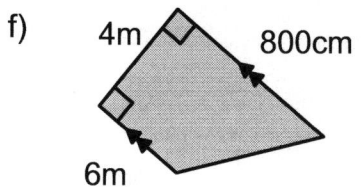
4m
800cm
6m

4. Looking at the shapes A, B and C on the right, fill in the gaps:

a) Shape _____ has the smallest perimeter

b) Shape _____ is a trapezium

c) Shape _____ is a parallelogram

d) Shape _____ has the largest area

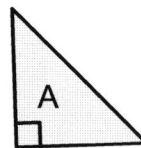
A

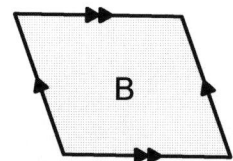
B

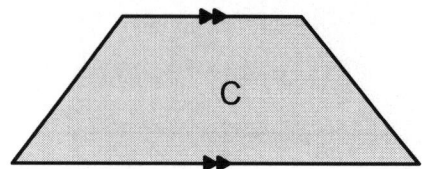
C

chapter review

exercise 8|

1. Work out the area of each shape:

a)

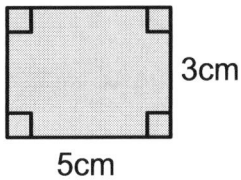

b)

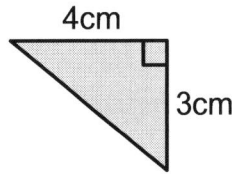

c)

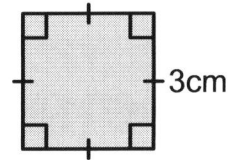

d)

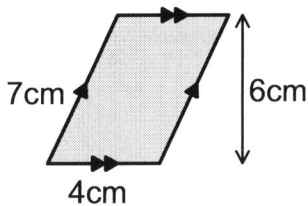

e)

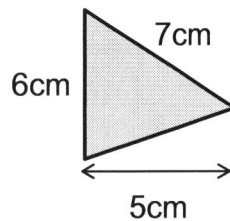

f)

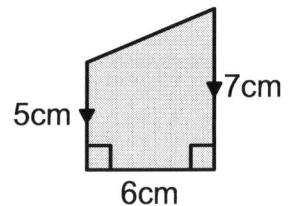

g)

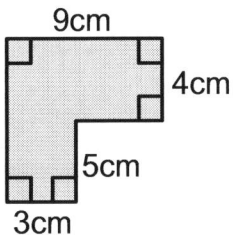

h)

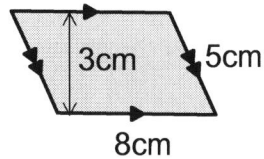

i)

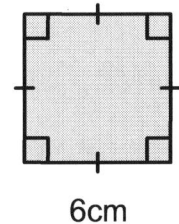

j)

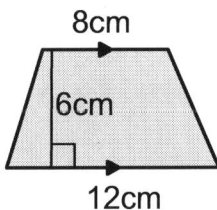

k)

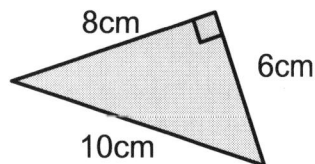

l)

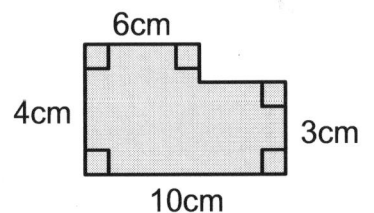

2. Given the area shown, can you work out the missing dimensions of these shapes, labelled with a ?

a)

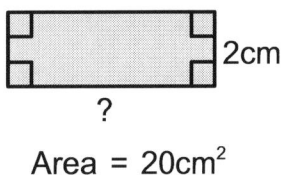

Area = 20cm^2

b)

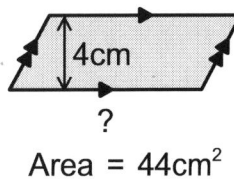

Area = 44cm^2

c)

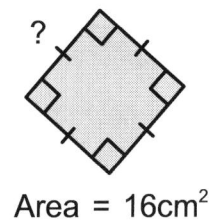

Area = 16cm^2

3. Sketch a kite, a rhombus, a paralleogram and a trapezium and explain the differences between them.

4. Which of these is most likely the area of a postage stamp?

   a) $4mm^2$ b) $6cm^2$ c) $2m^2$ d) $1km^2$

5. A shape with 4 equal sides is called a _____.

6. Copy and complete each shape:

   a)

   Square

   b)

   Parallelogram

   c)

   Kite

7. a) In the diagram, lines _____ and _____ are equal length.

   b) In the diagram, lines _____ and _____ are parallel.

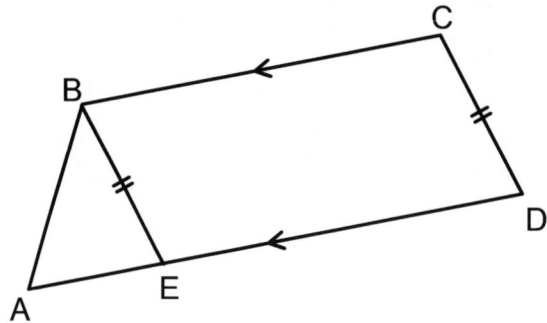

8. On square or dotty paper, draw three different parallelograms with an area of $10cm^2$

exercise 8m

1. Calculate

   a) $\frac{3}{5} + \frac{1}{5}$

   b) $1 - \frac{1}{10}$

   c) -6 - 3

   d) -4 + 2

   e) 3 × -4

   f) 5^2

   g) 156 ÷ 4

   h) 0.5 × 3

   i) $\frac{2}{3} - \frac{2}{3}$

2. Solve these equations:

   a) $4x = 20$

   b) $x + 4 = 20$

   c) $\frac{x}{4} = 20$

3. Fill in the blanks:

   a) 45 ÷ 10 = _____

   b) 3.6 × _____ = 360

   c) 8.6 ÷ _____ = 0.86

   d) 0.065 × 10 = _____

   e) 1cm = _____mm

   f) 1m = _____cm

   g) 1km = _____m

   h) 65cm = _____m

   i) 405mm = _____cm

4. Simplify:

   a) $b + b + b$

   b) $b × b × b$

   c) $b × 3 × 2$

5. Write down the first six cube numbers.

6. Work out:

   a) $\sqrt{49}$

   b) $\sqrt{1}$

   c) $\sqrt[3]{27}$

   d) 4^2

   e) 0^3

   f) 1^5

   g) $(-2)^3$

   h) $(-2)^4$

7. Simplify:

   a) $4b + b + b$

   b) $3b - b$

   c) $5b + 2 + 3b$

   d) $10b - b$

   e) $10b - 3 + b$

   f) $6b + 4 - 10b$

8. Which two numbers below have the same value? Circle them.

   a) 2.1   b) 21   c) 2.0   d) 20   e) 2

9. Explain what is wrong with this subtraction:

$$\begin{array}{r} 9735 \\ 451 - \\ \hline 5220 \end{array}$$

10. In each number, write down the value of the digit in bold:

    a) **4**3,060   b) **2**08,931   c) **84**,156,209

11. Write as decimals:

    a) 4 tenths   d) $\frac{7}{10}$ g) $1\frac{9}{10}$

    b) 9 hundredths   e) $\frac{6}{1000}$ h) $2\frac{3}{100}$

    c) 1 thousandth   f) $\frac{1}{100}$ i) $5\frac{1}{10}$

12. Which number has 5 tens and 7 hundredths?

    a) 50.07   b) 50.7   c) 0.57   d) 750   e) 5.7

13. Calculate:

    a) 3^2 d) 2^3 g) $(-3)^2$

    b) 5^2 e) 3^3 h) 1^4

    c) 1^3 f) $(-2)^2$ i) 10^2

14. Write as a fraction:

    a) 0.3   b) 0.07   c) 0.001

15. Which of these numbers has a 3 in the tenths column?

    a) 0.03   b) 0.3   c) 3.0   d) 30   e) 300

16. Which two of these are the same?

    a) 3^{-1} b) 3^0 c) 3   d) 3^1 e) 3^2

17. If we multiply 3 negative numbers, will the answer be positive or negative?

chapter 9: fractions, decimals & percentages

[Recommended Time : 11-13 hours]

Contents

P For resources marked P, students will need a photocopy or print out of this activity to work on

review: mixed numbers and improper fractions

recall

Mixed numbers and improper fractions are more than 1 whole

examples

Write $\frac{10}{3}$ as a mixed number

$10 \div 3 = 3$ remainder 1

so $\frac{10}{3} = 3\frac{1}{3}$

Write $4\frac{2}{3}$ as an improper fraction

$4 \times 3 + 2 = 14$

so $4\frac{2}{3} = \frac{14}{3}$

exercise 9a

1. Which of these are MORE than 1 whole? Circle three answers.

   a) $\frac{2}{7}$
   b) $1\frac{1}{3}$
   c) $\frac{7}{2}$
   d) $\frac{5}{5}$
   e) $2\frac{3}{4}$

2. Fill in the blanks:

   a) One whole is _____ tenths
   b) One whole is _____ sixths

3. Fill in the blanks with >, < or =

   a) $\frac{3}{5}$ _____ 1
   c) $\frac{10}{2}$ _____ 1
   e) $\frac{7}{3}$ _____ 1

   b) $\frac{6}{6}$ _____ 1
   d) $\frac{1}{9}$ _____ 1
   f) $\frac{9}{9}$ _____ 1

4. What number does each arrow point to? Write your answer as a mixed number.

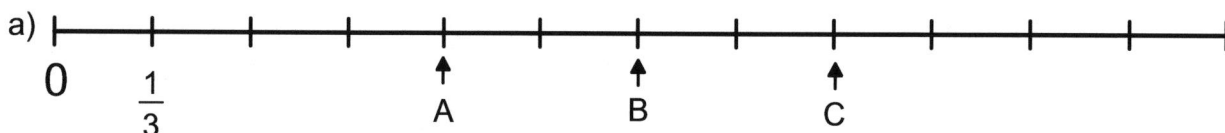

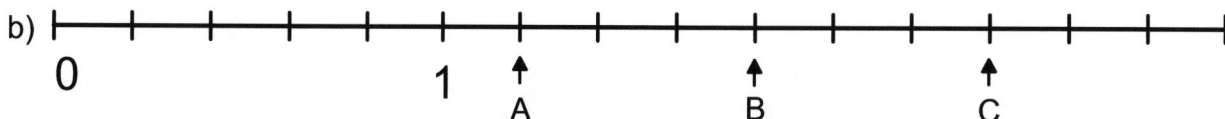

   a)

   0     $\frac{1}{3}$ A   B   C

   b)

   0   1   A   B   C

5. Which of these is an improper fraction?

   a) $\frac{2}{3}$
   b) 2
   c) $1\frac{1}{5}$
   d) $\frac{7}{3}$
   e) $\frac{3}{7}$

6. Match the following:

A	Unit Fraction
B	Improper Fraction
C	Equals One Whole
D	Mixed Number

E	$\frac{8}{8}$
F	$\frac{1}{9}$
G	$3\frac{2}{5}$
H	$\frac{12}{5}$

A	
B	
C	
D	

7. Write these as improper fractions:

a) $3\frac{1}{4}$ b) $5\frac{1}{3}$ c) $2\frac{3}{5}$ d) $2\frac{3}{4}$

8. Write these as mixed numbers:

a) $\frac{5}{4}$ c) $\frac{10}{3}$ e) $\frac{9}{2}$

b) $\frac{7}{4}$ d) $\frac{7}{5}$ f) $\frac{12}{5}$

9. Which of these is the same as $4\frac{1}{5}$?

a) $\frac{9}{5}$ b) $\frac{10}{5}$ c) $\frac{20}{5}$ d) $\frac{21}{5}$

10. What number does each arrow point to?
Write your answer as a mixed number if it is more than 1 whole.

a)

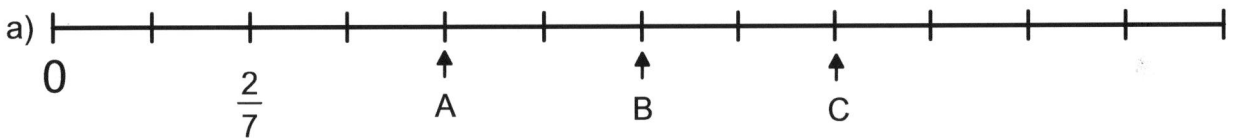

b)

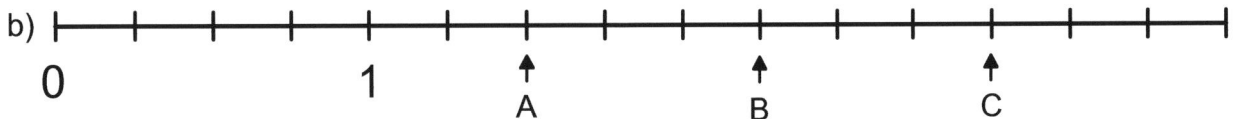

c)

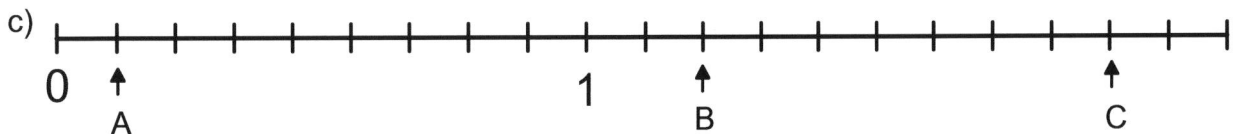

comparing & ordering fractions 1

learn by heart

> Unit fraction: a fraction like $\frac{1}{8}$ or $\frac{1}{10}$ where the numerator is 1
>
> Unit fractions get smaller as their denominator increases, so $\frac{1}{8} > \frac{1}{10}$

examples

Which is bigger, $\frac{1}{3}$ or $\frac{2}{3}$? $\frac{2}{3}$ is bigger because it has 2 parts and the denominators are the same.	Which is bigger, $\frac{3}{3}$ or $1\frac{1}{3}$? $\frac{3}{3}$ equals 1, so $1\frac{1}{3}$ is more.	Which is bigger, $\frac{8}{3}$ or $1\frac{2}{3}$? $1\frac{2}{3}$ is $\frac{5}{3}$, so $\frac{8}{3}$ is bigger

convert mixed numbers to improper fractions in order to compare them

exercise 9b

1. Which of these fractions are **more** than $\frac{4}{7}$? Circle all that apply.

   a) $\frac{1}{7}$ b) $\frac{3}{7}$ c) $\frac{4}{7}$ d) $\frac{5}{7}$ e) $1\frac{2}{7}$

2. In each pair, which fraction is **larger?**

   a) $\frac{1}{5}$ or $\frac{3}{5}$ b) $1\frac{1}{9}$ or $\frac{2}{9}$ c) $\frac{3}{4}$ or $1\frac{1}{4}$

3. Which of these fractions is **largest?** $\boxed{\frac{1}{3}}$ $\boxed{\frac{1}{4}}$ $\boxed{\frac{1}{5}}$ $\boxed{\frac{1}{6}}$ $\boxed{\frac{1}{7}}$

4. True or False?

   a) $\frac{1}{8}$ is less than $\frac{3}{8}$ d) $\frac{1}{5} > \frac{3}{5}$ g) $\frac{5}{10} > 1$

   b) $\frac{4}{10}$ is more than $\frac{3}{10}$ e) $\frac{5}{3} > \frac{2}{3}$ h) $\frac{9}{9} > \frac{1}{9}$

   c) $1\frac{1}{5}$ is more than 1 whole   f) $\frac{3}{3} = 1$ i) $\frac{5}{5} > 1\frac{1}{5}$

5. In each pair, which fraction is **larger?**

   a) $\frac{1}{5}$ or $\frac{1}{3}$ b) $\frac{1}{8}$ or $\frac{1}{10}$ c) $\frac{1}{100}$ or $\frac{1}{101}$

6. Write the biggest & smallest number in each row:

	Smallest	Biggest

a) A $\frac{1}{5}$ B $\frac{1}{3}$ C $\frac{1}{4}$ D $\frac{1}{2}$

b) A $\frac{2}{5}$ B $\frac{1}{5}$ C $\frac{3}{5}$ D $\frac{6}{5}$

c) A $\frac{3}{7}$ B $\frac{9}{7}$ C 1 D $\frac{1}{7}$

d) A $\frac{2}{3}$ B $1\frac{1}{3}$ C $\frac{1}{3}$ D $\frac{5}{3}$

e) A $2\frac{1}{6}$ B $2\frac{5}{6}$ C $\frac{10}{6}$ D $\frac{18}{6}$

7. True or False?

a) $\frac{1}{5}$ is less than $\frac{1}{4}$.

b) $\frac{1}{5}$ is less than $\frac{1}{6}$

c) $\frac{2}{3}$ is greater than $\frac{1}{3}$.

d) $\frac{3}{10}$ is smaller than $\frac{7}{10}$.

e) $\frac{10}{10}$ equals 1 whole.

f) $1\frac{3}{5} > 1\frac{2}{5}$

g) $\frac{12}{5}$ is smaller than 3

h) $\frac{1}{4} > \frac{1}{5}$

8. Complete these statements with the symbols >, < or =

a) $\frac{1}{2}$ ◯ $\frac{1}{4}$

b) $\frac{1}{3}$ ◯ $\frac{1}{5}$

c) $\frac{6}{6}$ ◯ 1

d) $\frac{2}{10}$ ◯ $\frac{7}{10}$

e) $\frac{3}{5}$ ◯ $\frac{2}{5}$

f) $\frac{1}{9}$ ◯ $\frac{1}{8}$

g) $\frac{3}{10}$ ◯ $\frac{6}{20}$

h) $\frac{9}{5}$ ◯ 1

i) $2\frac{1}{2}$ ◯ $\frac{5}{2}$

j) 3 ◯ $\frac{16}{5}$

9. Put these in order of size, from smallest to largest:

$\frac{4}{5}$ $\frac{1}{5}$ $1\frac{3}{5}$ $\frac{1}{10}$ $\frac{6}{5}$

10. Put these fractions in order, from smallest to largest:

$1\frac{2}{7}$ $\frac{1}{7}$ $1\frac{5}{7}$ $\frac{7}{7}$ $\frac{3}{7}$ __ __ __ __ __

11. In each pair, circle the **larger** number, or say if they are equal:

a) $\frac{1}{5}$ or $\frac{4}{5}$ d) $\frac{15}{10}$ or $1\frac{3}{10}$ g) $\frac{5}{4}$ or 1

b) $\frac{2}{7}$ or $1\frac{1}{7}$ e) $3\frac{2}{5}$ or $\frac{18}{5}$ h) $\frac{15}{10}$ or 2

c) $3\frac{5}{10}$ or $2\frac{7}{10}$ f) $7\frac{3}{4}$ or $\frac{19}{4}$ i) $\frac{3}{3}$ or 1

12. Put these fractions in order, from smallest to largest:

$\frac{10}{4}$ $1\frac{1}{4}$ $\frac{12}{4}$ $2\frac{1}{4}$ $\frac{3}{4}$ __ __ __ __ __

13. True or False?

a) $\frac{1}{5}$ is more than $\frac{1}{10}$ b) $\frac{1}{8}$ is smaller than $1\frac{1}{7}$

14. Which of these fractions **equal** 1 whole? Circle three answers.

a) $\frac{4}{4}$ b) $\frac{3}{5}$ c) $\frac{2}{2}$ d) $\frac{100}{100}$ e) $1\frac{5}{10}$

15. Which fractions are **more** than 1 whole? Circle two answers.

a) $\frac{3}{5}$ b) $1\frac{1}{5}$ c) $\frac{7}{7}$ d) $\frac{2}{7}$ e) $\frac{9}{7}$

16. Put these fractions in order, from smallest to largest:

1    $\frac{1}{5}$ $1\frac{1}{4}$ $\frac{1}{8}$ $1\frac{1}{5}$ __ __ __ __ __

17. Which of these fractions are **smaller** than 1? Circle 2 answers.

a) $\frac{9}{5}$ b) $\frac{5}{5}$ c) $\frac{4}{5}$ d) $\frac{0}{5}$ e) $1\frac{1}{5}$

comparing & ordering fractions 2

example

Which is more, $\frac{2}{3}$ or $\frac{4}{5}$?

$\frac{2}{3} = \frac{10}{15}$ and $\frac{4}{5} = \frac{8}{10}$

so $\frac{2}{3}$ is more

If the denominators are different, first make equivalent fractions to compare

exercise 9c

1. Work out which fraction is largest in each pair.

   a) $\frac{5}{8}$ or $\frac{3}{4}$

   b) $\frac{3}{7}$ or $\frac{7}{21}$

   c) $\frac{14}{18}$ or $\frac{5}{6}$

   d) $\frac{1}{4}$ or $\frac{3}{8}$

   e) $\frac{7}{10}$ or $\frac{2}{3}$

   f) $\frac{7}{10}$ or $\frac{11}{20}$

2. Which of these is largest? $\boxed{\frac{3}{10}}$ $\boxed{\frac{2}{5}}$ $\boxed{\frac{7}{20}}$ $\boxed{\frac{9}{10}}$

3. Which of these is largest? $\boxed{\frac{1}{4}}$ $\boxed{\frac{1}{3}}$ $\boxed{\frac{5}{12}}$ $\boxed{\frac{3}{4}}$

4. Put these fractions in order, from smallest to largest:

   $\boxed{\frac{2}{3}}$ $\boxed{\frac{1}{3}}$ $\boxed{\frac{3}{5}}$ $\boxed{\frac{6}{15}}$ ____ ____ ____ ____

5. Put these fractions in order, from smallest to largest:

   $\boxed{\frac{1}{2}}$ $\boxed{\frac{2}{7}}$ $\boxed{\frac{5}{14}}$ $\boxed{\frac{7}{7}}$ ____ ____ ____ ____

6. Circle all the numbers that are **more** than $\frac{5}{9}$:

   a) $\frac{1}{9}$ b) $\frac{7}{9}$ c) $\frac{9}{9}$ d) 1   e) $\frac{3}{9}$ f) $1\frac{1}{9}$ g) $\frac{1}{10}$

7. Find **three** fractions in this list that are equivalent to $\frac{4}{6}$.

$\frac{40}{60}$ $\frac{2}{5}$ $\frac{24}{26}$ $\frac{2}{3}$ $\frac{6}{8}$ $\frac{6}{4}$ $\frac{8}{12}$ $\frac{9}{15}$

8. Which of these fractions are more than $\frac{8}{5}$?

$\frac{11}{10}$ $\frac{15}{10}$ $\frac{18}{10}$ $\frac{24}{10}$

9. Insert one of the symbols $<$ $=$ $>$ to make a true statement.

a) $\frac{4}{5}$ ◯ $\frac{1}{2}$

b) $\frac{3}{7}$ ◯ $\frac{1}{2}$

c) $\frac{5}{10}$ ◯ $\frac{1}{2}$

d) $\frac{9}{20}$ ◯ $\frac{1}{2}$

e) $\frac{6}{9}$ ◯ $\frac{1}{2}$

f) $\frac{7}{13}$ ◯ $\frac{1}{2}$

10. Shade all the fractions that are **more** than $\frac{1}{3}$. There are six correct answers.

A $\frac{1}{2}$	B $\frac{1}{6}$	C $\frac{2}{6}$	D $\frac{2}{5}$	E $\frac{2}{3}$	F $\frac{2}{20}$	G $\frac{4}{10}$
H $\frac{1}{4}$	I $\frac{4}{5}$	J $\frac{1}{10}$	K $\frac{4}{9}$	L $\frac{1}{100}$	M $\frac{3}{9}$	N $\frac{1}{3}$

11. Complete each statement using >, < or =

a) $\frac{1}{3}$ ____ $\frac{2}{5}$

b) $\frac{7}{8}$ ____ $\frac{3}{4}$

c) $\frac{3}{10}$ ____ $\frac{4}{5}$

12. True or false?

a) $\frac{3}{3}$ = 1

c) $\frac{12}{15}$ = $\frac{4}{5}$

e) $\frac{1}{9}$ > $\frac{1}{10}$

b) $\frac{1}{5}$ > $\frac{1}{4}$

d) $\frac{2}{5}$ > $\frac{4}{10}$

f) $\frac{1}{5}$ > $\frac{2}{3}$

challenge ☆ extra challenge

13. Choose 4 of these fractions to make the puzzle below true:

$2\frac{1}{4}$ $\frac{5}{3}$ $\frac{9}{4}$ $1\frac{1}{3}$ $1\frac{2}{3}$ $1\frac{3}{4}$ $\frac{15}{9}$

◻ = ◻ = ◻ > ◻

recall

tens	units	●	tenths	hundredths	thousandths
10	1		$\frac{1}{10} = 0.1$	$\frac{1}{100} = 0.01$	$\frac{1}{1000} = 0.001$

The decimal point: *is to the right* of the units column

examples

Tenths	Hundredths	Thousandths
$\frac{3}{10} = 0.3$	$\frac{3}{100} = 0.03$	$\frac{3}{1000} = 0.003$
$\frac{2}{5} = \frac{4}{10} = 0.4$	$\frac{24}{100} = 0.24$	$\frac{37}{1000} = 0.037$
$\frac{14}{10} = 1.4$	$\frac{206}{100} = 2.06$	$\frac{409}{1000} = 0.409$

We can read this decimal as '37 thousandths'.

It ends in the thousandths column.

exercise 9d

1. Write as a decimal:

   watch out!

   a) 3 tenths

   b) 7 hundredths

   c) 9 thousandths

   d) 3 tens

   e) $\frac{5}{10}$

   f) $\frac{8}{100}$

   g) $\frac{1}{10}$

   h) $\frac{3}{1000}$

   i) $\frac{9}{100}$

2. Write as a fraction:

   a) 0.9   b) 0.02   c) 0.005   d) 0.0007

3. Which of these is 4 tens + 4 hundredths?

   a) 0.44   b) 0.404   c) 4.4   d) 40.4   e) 40.04   f) 40.44

4. Which of these is 7 hundreds + 3 tenths?

   a) 0.37   b) 0.73   c) 7.3   d) 70.3   e) 700.3

5. Write as a decimal number:

a) 5 tens + 3 tenths

b) 2 units + 6 hundredths

c) 8 tens + 1 tenth

d) 5 hundreds + 3 hundredths

e) 9 units + 3 tenths

f) 1 thousand + 4 thousandths

6. Write these fractions as decimals:

a) $\frac{71}{100}$

b) $\frac{901}{1000}$

c) $\frac{1}{1000}$

d) $\frac{37}{100}$

e) $\frac{9}{10}$

f) $\frac{409}{1000}$

g) $\frac{2}{10}$

h) $\frac{28}{1000}$

i) $\frac{8}{100}$

7. What is 0.45 as a fraction? Circle your answer.

a) $4\frac{5}{100}$

b) $\frac{45}{10}$

c) $\frac{45}{100}$

d) $\frac{45}{1000}$

e) $\frac{4.5}{100}$

8. True or False?

a) $0.3 = \frac{1}{3}$

b) 4 tens = 0.4

c) $6.6 = 6 + \frac{6}{10}$

9. Write as a decimal:

a) $4\frac{1}{10}$

c) $3\frac{4}{100}$

e) $100\frac{2}{100}$

g) $1\frac{7}{100}$

b) $20\frac{1}{100}$

d) $\frac{7}{1000}$

f) $5\frac{1}{10}$

h) $17\frac{6}{10}$

10. The value of the digit 9 in the number 4.0**9** is:

a) 9 tens

b) 9 tenths

c) 9 hundredths

d) 9 thousandths

11. Write down the value of the digits in bold. Give your answer as a fraction or integer:

a) 3.**5**

c) 1.00**9**

e) 50.0**9**

b) 2.0**7**

d) **4**5.63

f) **2**00.314

12. Which of these is largest?

   a) 4 tens   b) 4 tenths   c) 4 hundreds   d) 4 thousandths

13. Which of these is 3.06?

   a) $3\frac{6}{10}$ b) $3\frac{6}{100}$ c) $3\frac{6}{1000}$ d) $30\frac{6}{10}$ e) $30\frac{6}{100}$

14. In each pair, circle the **larger** number:

   a) 3 tens or 3 hundreds   c) $\frac{7}{10}$ or 7 tens

   b) 5 tenths or 5 tens   d) $\frac{3}{100}$ or 3 thousandths

15. Fill in the blanks:

   a) 4.62 is _____ units, _____ tenths and 2 _____.

   b) 10.03 is 1 _____ and 3 _____.

   c) 90.9 is 9 _____ and 9 _____.

   d) 8.032 is 8 _____, 3 _____ and 2 _____.

16. Write these decimals as fractions:

   a) 0.27 = $\frac{}{100}$ b) 0.009 = $\frac{}{1000}$ c) 0.4 = $\frac{}{10}$

   d) 0.047 = $\frac{}{1000}$ e) 0.1   f) 1.15

   g) 0.06   h) 0.909   i) 0.099

17. True or false?

   a) $\frac{309}{1000}$ = 0.39   b) $\frac{2}{100}$ = 0.2   c) $\frac{48}{1000}$ = 0.048

18. Which calculation equals zero?

   a) 0.7 - $\frac{7}{10}$ b) 0.7 - $\frac{7}{100}$ c) 0.7 - $\frac{7}{1000}$ d) 0.7 - 7

19. Which of these equal 0.6? Circle all that apply.

   a) $\frac{6}{10}$ b) $\frac{60}{100}$ c) $\frac{600}{1000}$ d) $\frac{6000}{10,000}$

review: converting fractions and decimals (all types)

learn by heart

To convert a fraction to a decimal....

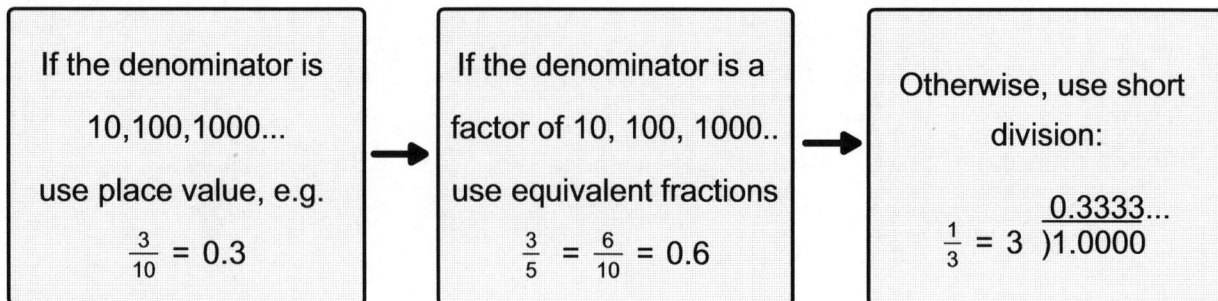

| If the denominator is 10,100,1000... use place value, e.g. $\frac{3}{10} = 0.3$ | → | If the denominator is a factor of 10, 100, 1000.. use equivalent fractions $\frac{3}{5} = \frac{6}{10} = 0.6$ | → | Otherwise, use short division: $\frac{1}{3} = 3\overline{)1.0000}^{\;0.3333...}$ |

exercise 9e

1. Write these fractions as decimals:

   a) $\frac{4}{5}$

   b) $\frac{14}{50}$

   c) $\frac{1}{25}$

   d) $\frac{3}{50}$

   e) $\frac{1}{50}$

   f) $\frac{2}{25}$

   g) $\frac{3}{20}$

   h) $\frac{2}{5}$

2. Use short division to write these fractions as decimals:

   a) $\frac{1}{3}$

   b) $\frac{1}{9}$

   c) $\frac{1}{8}$

3. Convert to decimals:

   a) $\frac{9}{100}$

   b) $\frac{3}{50}$

   c) $4\frac{1}{10}$

   d) $\frac{1}{1000}$

   e) $\frac{2}{3}$

   f) $\frac{8}{10}$

   g) $\frac{1}{5}$

   h) $\frac{34}{100}$

   i) $\frac{3}{4}$

4. True or False?

   a) $\frac{1}{3} = 0.3$

   b) $\frac{3}{5} = 0.3$

   c) $\frac{1}{100} = 0.01$

5. Which of these are equal to $\frac{1}{5}$? Circle two answers.

   a) 0.5

   b) $\frac{5}{10}$

   c) $\frac{2}{10}$

   d) 0.2

286

6. Write as decimals:

a) $\frac{7}{10}$

d) $\frac{7}{50}$

g) $\frac{2}{5}$

j) $\frac{1}{25}$

b) $2\frac{3}{100}$

e) $\frac{1}{3}$

h) $\frac{6}{1000}$

k) $\frac{1}{2}$

c) $\frac{1}{5}$

f) $\frac{1}{4}$

i) $\frac{24}{100}$

l) $\frac{2}{3}$

7. Which of these is the same as $\frac{1}{25}$? Circle two answers.

a) $\frac{4}{100}$

b) 0.4

c) 0.04

d) 0.25

8. True or false?

a) $3\frac{1}{5}$ = 3.5

b) $4\frac{2}{3}$ = 4.66666...

c) $\frac{1}{50}$ = 0.50

d) $\frac{1}{6}$ = 0.6

e) 0.5 = $\frac{1}{2}$

f) $5\frac{1}{50}$ = 5.02

matching activity

Match pairs of equivalent fractions and decimals.
Record your answers in the table below.

A $\frac{3}{100}$	B $\frac{11}{50}$	C $\frac{3}{1000}$	D $\frac{44}{1000}$		M 0.6	N 0.$\dot{3}$	O 0.044	P 0.3
E $\frac{22}{50}$	F $\frac{3}{5}$	G $\frac{1}{5}$	H $\frac{3}{50}$		Q 0.2	R 0.202	S 0.03	T 0.22
I $\frac{22}{1000}$	J $\frac{3}{10}$	K $\frac{1}{3}$	L $\frac{202}{1000}$		U 0.003	V 0.44	W 0.022	X 0.06

A	B	C	D	E	F	G	H	I	J	K	L

comparing & ordering fractions and decimals

example

Which is more, 0.3 or $\frac{4}{100}$?	Which is more, 0.35 or $\frac{4}{10}$?
$\frac{4}{100} = 0.04$, so 0.3 is more	$\frac{4}{10} = 0.4$, so $\frac{4}{10}$ is more

exercise 9f

1. In each pair, circle the **larger** number:

    a) 0.1 or $\frac{3}{10}$

    b) 0.9 or $\frac{8}{10}$

    c) 0.4 or $\frac{6}{100}$

    d) $\frac{8}{1000}$ or 0.8

    e) $\frac{3}{100}$ or 0.1

    f) 0.5 or $\frac{6}{100}$

2. Which of these is largest?

    a) $\frac{2}{10}$ b) $\frac{2}{100}$ c) 0.4   d) $\frac{25}{100}$ e) $\frac{3}{10}$

3. True or false?

    a) 0.4 is more than $\frac{4}{100}$

    b) $\frac{31}{100}$ is more than 0.31

    c) 0.9 is more than $\frac{9}{100}$

    d) $\frac{3}{100}$ is more than 0.02

    e) 0.6 is equal to $\frac{6}{100}$

    f) 0.4 > $\frac{2}{10}$

4. Which of these is largest?

    a) 0.1   b) $\frac{1}{100}$ c) $\frac{1}{1000}$ d) $\frac{3}{10}$ e) $\frac{3}{1000}$

5. Put these numbers in order of size, starting with the smallest:

    | 0.007 | $\frac{7}{10}$ | $\frac{7}{100}$ | $1\frac{7}{10}$ |

    ____   ____   ____   ____

6. Which of these are more than $\frac{1}{3}$? Circle two answers.

    a) 0.3   b) 0.34   c) 0.03   d) 0.3333   e) $\frac{34}{100}$

7. In each pair, decide which is bigger, or say if they are equal:

    a) 0.3 or $\frac{4}{10}$ c) 0.1 or $\frac{1}{100}$ e) $\frac{2}{100}$ or 0.1

    b) 0.07 or $\frac{3}{10}$ d) $\frac{3}{100}$ or 0.05   f) $1\frac{3}{100}$ or 1.2

8. Fill in the gaps with >, < or =

    a) 0.4 _____ $\frac{32}{100}$ d) 0.605 _____ $\frac{6}{10}$ g) $\frac{3}{5}$ _____ 0.4

    b) $\frac{1}{10}$ _____ 0.15   e) 0.08 _____ $\frac{8}{100}$ h) $\frac{6}{50}$ _____ 0.1

    c) $\frac{12}{100}$ _____ 0.3   f) $1\frac{3}{10}$ _____ 1.6   i) $\frac{1}{25}$ _____ 0.02

9. Put these numbers in order, starting with the smallest:

A	B	C	D
0.49	$\frac{4}{100}$	0.05	4.9

10. Put these numbers in order, starting with the smallest:

A	B	C	D
$\frac{1}{4}$	$\frac{4}{10}$	0.3	$\frac{29}{100}$

11. Give an example of a decimal that is between $\frac{7}{10}$ and $\frac{8}{10}$

With Your Partner: 3 in a Line

Copy the number line below.
Take it in turns with your partner to choose a number from the list below.
Estimate where you think the number you have chosen goes on the number line and place a cross. Make sure your partner agrees the position!
The first person to get three numbers in a line, wins!

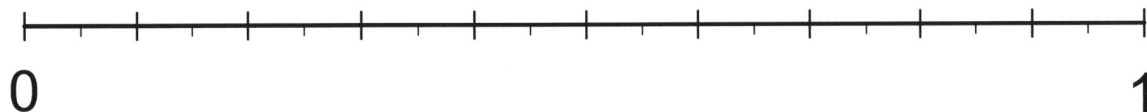

$\vdash$————————————————————————————————$\dashv$
0   1

$\frac{2}{3}$	0.1	$\frac{3}{10}$	0.42	0.01	$\frac{1}{4}$	0.6	$\frac{3}{8}$	0.18
0.9	$0.\dot{2}$	$\frac{1}{5}$	$\frac{1}{6}$	$\frac{6}{5}$	0.203	$\frac{19}{100}$	$\frac{3}{100}$	$\frac{4}{5}$

fractions to percentages

examples

Convert $\frac{4}{50}$ to a percentage

$$\frac{4}{50} = \frac{8}{100} = 8\%$$

Convert $\frac{3}{5}$ to a percentage

$$\frac{3}{5} = \frac{6}{10} = \frac{60}{100} = 60\%$$

Convert $\frac{14}{200}$ to a percentage

$$\frac{14}{200} = \frac{7}{100} = 7\%$$

exercise 9g

1. Convert these fractions to percentages:

   a) $\frac{3}{10}$

   b) $\frac{1}{50}$

   c) $\frac{4}{20}$

   d) $\frac{7}{20}$

   e) $\frac{1}{25}$

   f) $\frac{8}{25}$

   g) $\frac{18}{100}$

   h) $\frac{5}{100}$

   i) $\frac{5}{10}$

   j) $\frac{3}{5}$

   k) $\frac{1}{2}$

   l) $\frac{4}{5}$

2. On a test Julie scored $\frac{10}{25}$. Andrew scored 85%. Who did better?

3. Write down the percentage of each shape that is shaded.

   a)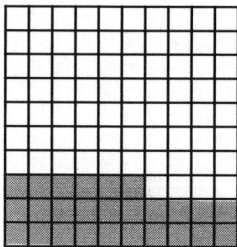

   b)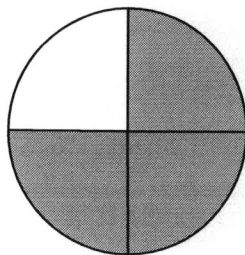

   c)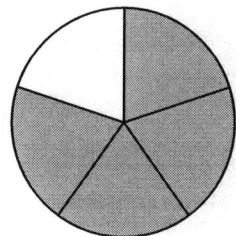

   d)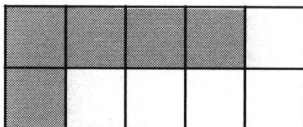

   e)

   f)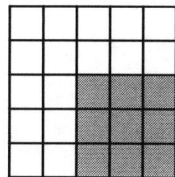

4. Which of these is largest?

   a) $\frac{3}{5}$

   b) 40%

   c) $\frac{1}{10}$

   d) 35%

5. In each pair, circle the larger number:

   a) $\frac{3}{10}$ or 40%

   b) $\frac{3}{5}$ or 50%

   c) $\frac{8}{50}$ or 8%

6. Write these numbers as percentages and put them in order of size, staring smallest.

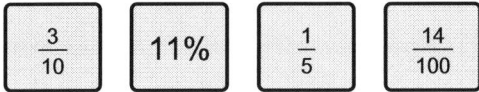

| $\frac{3}{10}$ | 11% | $\frac{1}{5}$ | $\frac{14}{100}$ |

_____ _____ _____ _____

7. Convert these fractions to percentages. You will need to simplify them first.

a) $\frac{80}{200}$ d) $\frac{15}{30}$ g) $\frac{12}{400}$ j) $\frac{49}{70}$

b) $\frac{16}{200}$ e) $\frac{500}{1000}$ h) $\frac{6}{200}$ k) $\frac{250}{1000}$

c) $\frac{9}{300}$ f) $\frac{4}{40}$ i) $\frac{90}{1000}$ l) $\frac{400}{1000}$

8. In which diagram is 50% shaded?

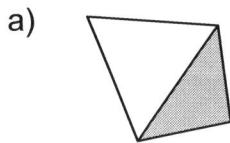

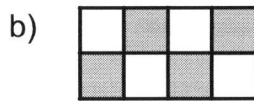

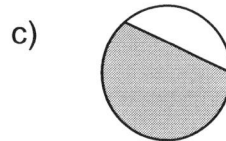

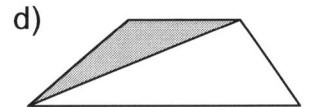

a)   b)   c)   d)

9. Put these in order of size, from smallest to largest:

| 25% | $\frac{1}{5}$ | $\frac{1}{2}$ | 35% |

_____ _____ _____ _____

10. Fill in each blank with >, < or =

a) $\frac{3}{5}$ _____ 60%   c) $\frac{8}{10}$ _____ 9%   e) $\frac{14}{70}$ _____ 20%

b) $\frac{2}{50}$ _____ 2%   d) $\frac{9}{25}$ _____ 40%   f) $\frac{6}{15}$ _____ 50%

11. Which of these numbers is more than 70%?

a) $\frac{3}{5}$ b) $\frac{7}{10}$ c) $\frac{4}{5}$ d) $\frac{1}{2}$

12. Which of these equal 100%? Circle 2 correct answers.

a) $\frac{50}{50}$ b) $\frac{100}{1}$ c) $\frac{1}{100}$ d) $\frac{20}{20}$ e) $\frac{15}{20}$ f) $\frac{100}{0}$

fractions, decimals and percentages

examples

Convert 18% to a decimal.	Convert 0.45 to a percentage.
$\frac{18}{100} = 0.18$	$0.45 = \frac{45}{100} = 45\%$

exercise 9g

1. Write as a decimal:

   a) 15%   c) 25%   e) 99%   g) 10%

   b) 1%   d) 3%   f) 9%   h) 100%

2. Write as a percentage:

   a) 0.21   c) 0.06   e) 0.91   g) 0.05

   b) 0.3   d) 0.1   f) 0.5   h) 1

3. True or false?

   a) 5% = 0.5   b) 5% = 0.05   c) 5% = 5.0

4. In each pair, decide which number is BIGGER:

   a) 15% or 0.1   c) 0.9 or 9%   e) 20% or 0.02

   b) 40% or 0.04   d) 0.3 or 31%   f) 8% or 0.8

5. Which is largest?

   a) 8%   b) 0.8   c) 9.5%   .   d) 0.09

6. Which is largest?   a) 0.5   b) 8%   c) $\frac{1}{2}$ d) $\frac{3}{4}$

7. Put these numbers in order of size, starting with the smallest:

   | 4% | | 0.4 | | 35% | | 0.03 |

   ____   ____   ____   ____

8. Complete the table of equivalent fractions, decimals and percentages.
Give your fractions in their simplest form. Find your answers below.

F	D	P
$\frac{1}{2}$		
$\frac{2}{10}$		
	0.9	
	0.09	
		2%
		25%
$\frac{3}{5}$		
$\frac{3}{20}$		
	0.4	
	0.8	
		8%
$\frac{3}{25}$		
		6%
$\frac{9}{20}$		
	2	

0.45

60%

0.12

0.2

$\frac{2}{25}$

90%

$\frac{9}{100}$

40%

0.15

45%

$\frac{2}{5}$

80%

0.06

$\frac{1}{4}$

20%

200%

0.6

$\frac{4}{5}$

$\frac{1}{50}$

$\frac{3}{50}$

0.08

0.02

$\frac{2}{1}$

0.25

$\frac{9}{10}$

12%

9%

15%

0.5

50%

Fractions, Decimals and Percentages - Odd One Out

In each box, cover up pairs of number that are **equivalent** to each other.
Find the number that is left over.

A

0.1	$\frac{6}{100}$	0.6
1%	60%	10%
6%	$\frac{1}{100}$	100%

B

70%	7%	30%
14%	$\frac{3}{10}$	$\frac{30}{50}$
$\frac{7}{50}$	60%	0.7

C

0.8	$\frac{2}{10}$	0.08
$\frac{8}{100}$	20%	80%
0.02	$\frac{2}{50}$	4%

D

0.4	50%	13%
4%	$\frac{1}{4}$	40%
0.25	$\frac{13}{100}$	$\frac{1}{2}$

E

$\frac{3}{10}$	0.02	$\frac{1}{10}$
$\frac{3}{4}$	10%	0.2
2%	0.3	75%

F

$\frac{1}{5}$	0.15	$\frac{1}{2}$
0.25	15%	20%
0.5	5%	$\frac{5}{20}$

G

$\frac{3}{5}$	80%	$\frac{9}{10}$
70%	0.6	40%
$\frac{4}{5}$	0.9	$\frac{7}{10}$

H

5%	$\frac{1}{25}$	6%
0.06	0.4	$\frac{1}{20}$
$\frac{1}{50}$	2%	0.04

I

$\frac{13}{50}$	16%	0.13
20%	$\frac{3}{20}$	15%
$\frac{4}{25}$	0.2	0.26

J

$1\frac{1}{10}$	$\frac{45}{100}$	$\frac{45}{50}$
100%	90%	1.1
9%	0.45	1

K

25%	$\frac{300}{400}$	0.15
0.08	$\frac{25}{100}$	$\frac{1}{8}$
0.125	15%	75%

L

$\frac{1}{3}$	0.03	$\frac{3}{10}$
$\frac{3}{5}$	$0.\dot{3}$	$\frac{2}{9}$
$0.\dot{2}$	3%	60%

percentage of an amount (1%, 10%, 50%)

learn by heart

$10\% = \frac{1}{10}$	To find 10%, divide by 10

$50\% = \frac{1}{2}$	To find 50%, divide by 2

$1\% = \frac{1}{100}$	To find 1%, divide by 100

examples

Work out 10% of 53
$$10\% = 5.3$$

Work out 1% of 80
$$1\% = 0.8$$

exercise 9h

1. Work out 10% of:

   a) 500   c) 40   e) 182   g) 12

   b) 89   d) 35   f) 1004   h) 0.8

2. Work out 1% of:

   a) 900   b) 400   c) 126   d) 34

3. Fill in the grid:

Number	10%	50%	1%
80			
120			
300			
350			
82			

4. Fill in the blanks:

   a) 50% of _____ = 30   d) 10% of _____ = 18

   b) 50% of _____ = 35   e) 10% of _____ = 7.2

   c) 10% of _____ = 6   f) 1% of _____ = 9

6. Fill in the blanks:

   a) To find 50% we should divde the number by _____

   b) To find 1% we should divide the number by _____

   c) To find 10% we should divide the number by _____

7. Which is more, 10% of 90 or 50% of 40? Explain your answer.

8. True or false?

   a) 50% of 18 = 9

   b) $\frac{1}{10}$ of 25 = 10% of 25

   c) 10% of 99 = 0.99

   d) 1% of 80 = 8

   e) $\frac{1}{2}$ of 80 = 50% of 80

   f) $\frac{1}{2}$ of 60 = 10% of 600

   g) $\frac{1}{10}$ of 55 = 5

   h) 1% of 450 = 10% of 45

9. Fill in the blanks:

   a) 50% of 60 = _____

   b) 50% of _____ = 8

   c) 50% of _____ = 1.2

   d) 10% of 35 = _____

   e) 10% of _____ = 2.6

   f) 10% of _____ = 140

   g) 1% of 831 = _____

   h) 1% of _____ = 4.6

   i) 1% of _____ = 0.3

10. If we work out 1% of _____, the answer will be a decimal.

11. If we work out 1% of _____, the answer will be a whole number.

12. Calculate 10% of 50% of 600.

13. 50% × _____ = 100%

14. 10% × _____ = 100%

15. 1% × _____ = 100%

percentage of an amount (5%, 30% etc)

learn by heart

| 5% = Half of 10% | 25% = Half of 50% = $\frac{1}{4}$ | 20% = 2 × 10% |

examples

Work out 30% of 80

      10% of 80 = 8

      30% of 80 = 24

Work out 25% of 60

      50% of 60 = 30

      25% of 60 = 15

exercise 9i

1. Work out:

   a) 20% of 50

   b) 30% of 90

   c) 70% of 60

   d) 5% of 80

   e) 5% of 60

   f) 25% of 80

   g) 20% of 32

   h) 40% of 120

   i) 25% of 120

2. Fill in the table:

Number	10%	20%	5%	25%
140				
60				
300				
84				
450				

3. Carly is thinking of a number.
   10% of her number is 12. What is 20% of her number?

4. Paul is thinking of a number.
   10% of his number is 6.
   What is 5% of his number?

5. True or false?

    a) 5% of 50 = 5

    b) 30% is more than 20%

    c) 5% is double 10%

    d) 10% × 5 = 50%

    e) To find 5% of a number,
       divide it by 10 and then by 2

    f) To find 25% of a number,
       divide it by 4

6. Work out:

    a) 30% of 50

    b) 25% of 48

    c) 5% of 30

    d) 5% of 40

    e) 70% of 110

    f) 20% of 80

    g) 40% of 60

    h) 60% of 40

    i) 30% of 320

7. Use the cards (once each) to complete these statements.

    a) 50% of £9 = _____

    b) 50% of £1 = _____

    c) 10% of £450 = _____

    d) 50% of _____ = £35

    e) 10% of _____ = 7p

    f) 10% of _____ = 2p

| 50p | £70 | £45 | 20p | £4.50 | 70p |

- -

Percentage of an Amount Puzzle

Use nine of the numbers on the left to make 3 true statements:

10%	20
20	18
50	30%
5.5	60
40%	2

☐ of ☐ = ☐

☐ of ☐ = ☐

☐ of ☐ = ☐

percentage of an amount (15, 35% etc)

learn by heart

15% = 10% + 5%	11% = 10% + 1%

examples

Work out 15% of 80 10% of 80 = 8 5% of 80 = 4 15% of 80 = 12	Work out 31% of 60 10% of 60 = 6 1% of 60 = 0.6 31% of 60 = 18.6

exercise 9j

1. Work out:

    a) 15% of 60   d) 55% of 120   g) 2% of 600

    b) 55% of 80   e) 15% of 30   h) 6% of 500

    c) 11% of 200   f) 21% of 700   i) 51% of 300

2. Given the information below, work out the percentages:

10% of 900 = 90	1% of 900 = 9	5% of 900 = 45	50% of 900 = 450

    a) 12% of 900 = _____   c) 6% of 900 = _____

    b) 56% of 900 = _____   d) 9% of 900 = _____

3. Gemma is thinking of a number.
    10% of her number is 54.
    What is her number?

4. Paula is thinking of a number.
    10% of her number is 80.
    1% of her number is 8.
    Work out 11% of her number.

5. Stephanie is thinking of a number. 5% of her number is 12. What is a her number?

Percentage of an Amount Jumbled Answers P

Complete the missing numbers.
The answers are below, jumbled up. Tick them off as you find them.

100%	10%	1%	5%	15%	30%	11%
90						
60						
	8					
		6				
			12			
			2			
					9	

mixed up answers

9	13.5	18	4	0.9	4.5	30
36	26.4	24	0.4	1.5	72	9
0.6	66	2.4	9.9	4	12	600
12	3.3	60	40	240	4.5	30
0.8	180	6.6	4.4	6	80	8.8
24	6	0.3	27	3	3	90

Sarah's Homework 🖩

Below is Sarah's completed homework.
Mark her work. If she has made a mistake,
give her some feedback. At the end, give her a score.

1

Calculate
30% of 70

10% = 7
3 × 7 = 21

2

Calculate
50% of
250

250 ÷ 50 =
50

3

Calculate
20% of 25

10% = 2.5
20% = 2 × 2.5
= 5

4

Calculate
1% of 960

960 ÷ 100
= 9.6

5

Calculate
5% of 60

10% is 6
5% is 2 × 6 =
12

6

Calculate
11% of 80

10% is 8
1% is 0.8
11% = 8 + 0.8
= 8.8

7

Calculate
90% of 20

10% = 2
9 × 2 = 18

8

Calculate
2% of 230

1% = 2.3
2% = 2 × 2.3
= 4.6

9

Calculate
50% of
130

130 ÷ 2 =
60

10

Calculate
25% of
2000

2000 ÷ 4 =
500

11

Calculate
11% of
700

10% = 70
1% = 7
11% = 77

12

Calculate
3% of 510

1% = 51
3% = 51 × 3 =
153

301

exercise 9k

1. Fill in the table to show equivalent fractions (simplest form), decimals and percentages:

F			$\frac{3}{5}$				
D		0.2		0.1			
P	9%				1%	8%	2%

2. Write as a decimal:

   a) $\frac{1}{2}$

   b) $\frac{23}{100}$

   c) $1\frac{3}{100}$

3. Which of these is $3\frac{1}{10}$?

   a) 0.3
   b) 310
   c) 3.01
   d) 3.1

4. Put these fractions in order, from smallest to largest:

   $1\frac{3}{5}$ $\frac{1}{5}$ $1\frac{1}{5}$ $\frac{5}{5}$ $\frac{4}{5}$ ____ ____ ____ ____ ____

5. Which of the following is 5%? Circle two answers:

   a) 0.5
   b) $\frac{5}{100}$
   c) 0.05
   d) $\frac{0.5}{100}$
   e) $\frac{5}{1000}$

6. To find 10% of a number, we can divide it by _____ and to find 1% of a number, we can divide it by _____.

7. Which is larger, $\frac{2}{5}$ or 0.44?

8. Write the following as decimals:

   a) $\frac{1}{3}$
   b) $2\frac{7}{100}$
   c) $\frac{1}{9}$
   d) $\frac{5}{1000}$

9. Write 0.7 as a fraction.

10. Put these in order, from smallest to largest:

    a) 0.7
    b) $\frac{7}{100}$
    c) 7.1
    d) $\frac{71}{100}$

11. Calculate:

    a) 20% of 300   c) 1% of 900   e) 15% of 20

    b) 5% of 40   d) 3% of 900   f) 30% of 220

12. Which of these are more than 0.4? Circle two answers.

    a) $\frac{4}{10}$ b) $\frac{4}{100}$ c) 0.40   d) $\frac{3}{5}$ e) $\frac{2}{3}$

13. Write as a decimal:

    a) $\frac{9}{10}$ c) $\frac{3}{100}$ e) 65%   g) 2%

    b) 40%   d) $\frac{4}{5}$ f) $\frac{4}{50}$ h) $\frac{24}{100}$

14. True or false: 0.5 = 5%

15. In each pair, circle the bigger number:

    a) 0.41 or 0.401   c) $\frac{4}{10}$ or 0.05   e) $\frac{1}{4}$ or $\frac{1}{3}$

    b) 3.5 or 3.35   d) 50% or $\frac{3}{5}$ f) $\frac{4}{5}$ or 60%

16. Write as a fraction, in its simplest form:

    a) 0.1   c) 50%   e) 0.02   g) 20%

    b) 0.01   d) 30%   f) 4%   h) 150%

17. Fill in the gaps with > , < or =

    a) 50% _____ $\frac{1}{2}$ c) 0.1 _____ 0.10   e) 12% _____ 0.12

    b) $\frac{1}{4}$ _____ $\frac{1}{3}$ d) $\frac{2}{3}$ _____ 0.6   f) $\frac{4}{5}$ _____ 0.7

18. To work out 25% of a number, we can divide it by _____

19. Which of these numbers are more than 1 whole? Circle two answers.

    a) $\frac{12}{13}$ b) $1\frac{2}{3}$ c) $\frac{17}{18}$ d) $\frac{1}{15}$ e) $\frac{3}{2}$

20. True or false: All decimal numbers are less than 1 whole.

Find the Greatest Integer ⭐ extra challenge

For each statement, work out the biggest whole number that could go in the empty box to make the statement true

A
$$\frac{\square}{45} < 1$$

B
$$\frac{\square}{100} < 24\%$$

C
$$0.8 > \frac{\square}{10}$$

D
$$\square\% < \frac{19}{100}$$

E
$$\square\% < 0.9$$

F
$$\frac{\square}{29} < 100\%$$

G
$$\frac{\square}{10} < 75\%$$

H
$$0.5 > \frac{\square}{100}$$

I
$$\square\% < \frac{3}{4}$$

J
$$0.7 > \frac{\square}{5}$$

K
$$\frac{1}{2} > \frac{\square}{12}$$

L
$$\frac{\square}{15} < 100\%$$

M
$$\frac{2}{5} > \square\%$$

N
$$\frac{\square}{10} < 50\%$$

O
$$\frac{\square}{16} < 25\%$$

P
$$\frac{\square}{15} < \frac{2}{3}$$

Q
$$\frac{\square}{3} < 0.5$$

R
$$\frac{\square}{4} < 101\%$$

S
$$\frac{\square}{8} \leq 0.5$$

T
$$82\% > \frac{\square}{50}$$

U
$$\frac{\square}{20} \leq \frac{3}{5}$$

V
$$2 > \square\%$$

W
$$\frac{\square}{10} < 0.1$$

X
$$\frac{1}{\square} > 20\%$$

exercise 9l

1. Calculate

   a) -4 - 3

   b) -4 × -3

   c) -4 + 3

   d) 4 + -3

   e) -4 + -3

   f) -4 × 3

   g) 4 - - 3

   h) -4 - - 3

2. Evaluate:

   a) $\sqrt{49}$

   b) 6^2

   c) 2^3

   d) 1^4

   e) 0^2

   f) $\sqrt[3]{8}$

   g) 9^2

   h) $\sqrt{64}$

3. Which of these are **more** than 0.5? Circle all that apply.

   a) 0.6   b) 0.50   c) 0.45   d) 0.450   e) 0.501

4. Simplify:

   a) $4b - 3b$

   b) $a + a + 3a$

   c) $a \times a$

   d) $4y + 2 + 3y$

   e) $y + y$

   f) $4 \times a \times 2 \times b$

   g) $3a \times 2b$

   h) $b \times b \times b$

   i) $a^5 \times a^3$

5. True or False?

   a) 4 + 3 × 2 = 14

   b) 10 - 3 + 4 = 3

   c) 20 ÷ 2 + 3 = 4

   d) 6 - 2 × 3 + 1 = 1

6. Which number has 5 tens and 7 hundredths?

   a) 50.07   b) 50.7   c) 0.57   d) 750   e) 5.7

7. Round these numbers as shown:

   a) 41 (nearest ten)

   b) 163 (nearest ten)

   c) 2465 (nearest ten)

   d) 1.8 (nearest whole number)

   e) 2.47 (nearest whole number)

   f) 201.3 (nearest whole number)

8. Which calculation helps us work out $\sqrt{25}$?

    a) 25 ÷ 2   b) 25 + 2   c) 25 - 2   d) None of these

9. Circle the square numbers:

    a) 1   b) 2   c) 3   d) 4   e) 10

10. True or false?

    a) $3^4 \times 3^5 = 3^9$ c) $4^5 \times 4^3 = 16^8$

    b) $2^4 \times 3^5 = 6^9$ d) $2^5 \times 2^5 = 2^{25}$

11. Simplify: $4^5 \times 4^2 \times 4^{-1}$

12. Solve: $5x = 30$

13. Calculate $4 + 3 \times 2^2 - \sqrt{25}$

- -

Percentage of an Amount Puzzle 2

Use all of the numbers on the left to make 4 true statements:

2	45
20%	20
10	30%
10	150
5%	50
200	10%

⬜ of ⬜ = ⬜

⬜ of ⬜ = ⬜

⬜ of ⬜ = ⬜

⬜ of ⬜ = ⬜

Printed in Great Britain
by Amazon